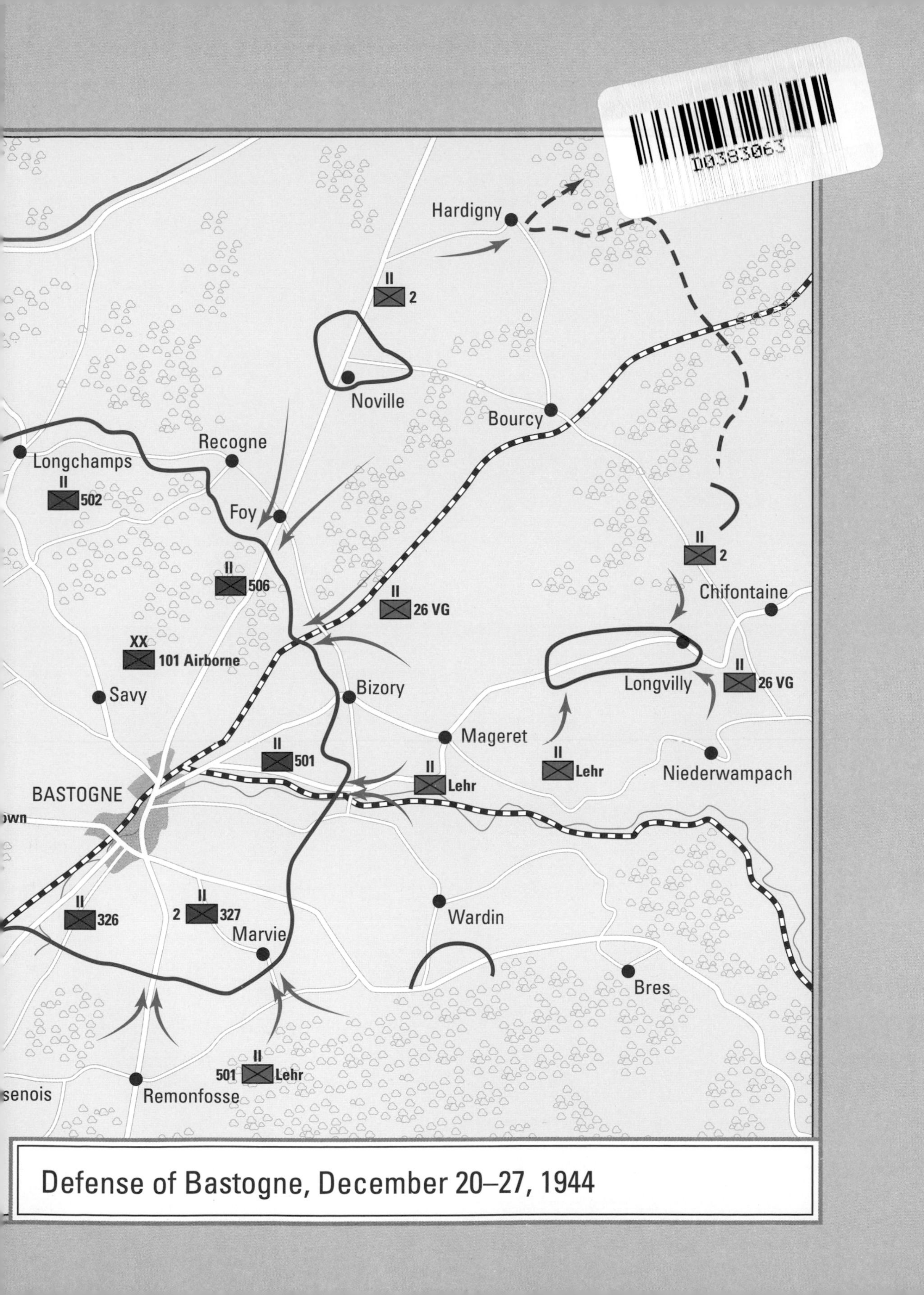

Defense of Bastogne, December 20–27, 1944

THE AIRBORNE IN WORLD WAR II

THE AIRBORNE IN WORLD WAR II

MICHAEL E. HASKEW

THOMAS DUNNE BOOKS
ST. MARTIN'S PRESS NEW YORK

THOMAS DUNNE BOOKS
An imprint of St. Martin's Press

The Marines in World War II.

For information, address St. Martin's Press, 175 Fifth Avenue,
New York, N.Y. 10010.

www.thomasdunnebooks.com
www.stmartins.com

Library of Congress Cataloging-in-Publication Data
on file at the Library of Congress

ISBN: 978-1-250-12446-3 (hardcover)
ISBN: 978-1-250-124470 (e-book)

Editorial and design by
Amber Books Ltd
74–77 White Lion Street
London N1 9PF
United Kingdom
www.amberbooks.co.uk

Project editor: Michael Spilling
Designer: Jerry Williams
Cover design: Nikolaas Eickelbeck
Picture research: Terry Forshaw

Printed in China

First U.S. Edition: published August 2017
10 9 8 7 6 5 4 3 2 1

Picture Credits

Alamy: 44 (Jason O. Watson/historicalmarkers.org), 54/55 (Granger Historical Picture Archive), 73 (Everett Collection), 78/79 (Photo12), 99 (A.F. Archive), 108 (Pictorial Press), 133 (Maurice Savage), 139 (Photo12), 149 (Granger Historical Picture Archive), 196 (Photo12), 205 (Photo12)

Art-Tech: 11, 34/35, 37, 46, 48, 51, 64, 77, 80, 81, 86, 89, 97, 113, 127, 136/137, 152–155 all, 157, 166, 178, 179, 182, 184/185, 186, 190, 200, 201, 208

Cody Images: 5, 47, 56, 58, 60, 62, 63, 67, 70, 76, 82, 92, 95, 100/101, 103, 107, 119, 122, 126, 132, 135, 138, 148, 156, 158, 160, 168–172 all, 174/175, 183, 188, 191, 197, 198, 202/203, 212, 215–221 all

Dreamstime: 102 (Enrico Della Pietra)

Mary Evans Picture Library: 145 (Illustrated London News)

Getty Images: 6 (Frank S. Errigo Archive), 15 (Bettmann), 18/19 (Photo Quest), 20 (Frank S. Errigo Archive), 21 (Photo Quest), 22 (Frank S. Errigo Archive), 28 (Photo Quest), 30 (Photo Quest), 33 (Bettmann), 39 (Gamma-Keystone), 57 (Hulton), 65 (Bettmann), 75 (Hulton), 90 (Ullstein Bild), 104/105 (Bettmann), 111 (Keystone), 112 (Time Life), 116 (Hulton), 120 (Time Life), 131 (Photo12), 140 (Imperial War Museum), 146 (Hulton), 151 (Hulton), 164 (Photo12), 173 (Hulton), 192/193 (Gamma-Keystone), 195 (Iconic Archive), 199 (Hulton), 207 (Hulton), 210 (Hulton), 211 (Bettmann), 213 (Time Life)

Thomas McHale: 32/33

NARA: 14 both, 16, 26, 27, 36, 40, 41, 45, 50, 52, 114/115

Public domain: 10, 12, 13, 17, 24, 31, 84/85, 96, 98, 123, 161, 163

U. S. Department of Defense: 8, 9, 61, 69, 91, 124/125, 128, 142/143, 165, 180, 181

Contents

CHAPTER 1

TRAINING

In a matter of months, the U.S. Army's airborne forces grew from theoretical to a practical weapon of warfare, and their fighting prowess was soon proven during World War II.

First Lieutenant William T. Ryder was a pioneer. On August 16, 1940, after the heavy cargo door of the Douglas C-33 transport aircraft was wrested open and a blast of turbulent wind filled the plane's fuselage, Ryder leaped from the safety of the hold above Lawson Army Airfield near Fort Benning, Georgia, and became the first man to officially parachute from an aircraft while a soldier of the United States' Army.

Ryder, the commander of the Army's Parachute Test Platoon, authorized just six weeks earlier, was followed by 10 members of his command, including the first enlisted man to jump, Private William N. "Red" King. A sense of urgency accompanied Ryder's historic jump, a necessary step in the evolution of an American airborne force that was destined to write a uniquely heroic chapter during World War II, a conflict that was already raging in Europe while it seemed inevitable that the United States would eventually become a belligerent.

Opposite: Fully loaded for a practice jump, a paratrooper stands near the door of a Douglas C-47 transport at Fort Benning, Georgia, in 1943. His reserve parachute pack and M-1 carbine are prominently visible.

The Airborne Idea

Among the Army's senior officers, the notion that soldiers might descend from the sky in great numbers and assault objectives behind enemy lines in a "vertical envelopment" was nothing new. In fact, the idea had been put forth by the controversial Brigadier General William "Billy" Mitchell, who became famous between the world wars as an advocate of airpower. Mitchell was aware that the parachute was already in use during World War I. Balloons were prime targets for fighter planes, and when these menacing aircraft came into sight the observers quickly exited their baskets and floated to the ground. The French and Italians had also used parachutes to insert demolition teams behind German lines.

In the fall of 1918, Mitchell proposed an airborne operation to utilize British Handley Page and Italian Caproni bombers to transport troops of the 1st Infantry Division across the trenchlines of No-Man's Land, parachuting the soldiers in the vicinity of the fortress city of Metz, France, which was heavily defended by the Germans. Fighter planes would strafe enemy positions, suppressing their response as the parachutists descended, assembled, and then opened fire, paving the way for a ground offensive that would capture the city. The armistice that ended the Great War preempted Mitchell's operation; however, the idea had received more than passing consideration.

After World War I ended, Mitchell maintained his interest in airborne operations. He wrote of a meeting with General of the Armies John J. Pershing: "I proposed to him that in the spring of 1919, when I would have a great force of bombardment planes, he should assign one of the infantry divisions permanently to the air force, preferably the 1st Division; that we would arm the men with a great number of machine guns and train them to go over the front in our large airplanes, which would carry 10 or 15 soldiers. We could equip each man with a parachute, so when we desired to make a rear attack on the enemy, we could carry these men over the lines and drop them off...."

Interwar Malaise

During the interwar years, enthusiasm for the development of airborne forces, including parachute and glider formations, waned substantially within the U.S. Army. Although some research and experimentation took place during the late 1920s, airborne concepts lay dormant for another decade. In 1938, officers at

Left: Pictured in full jump gear, Lieutenant William T. Ryder became the first person to parachute from a moving aircraft while in the service of the U.S. Army. Ryder was a pioneer of American airborne development.

the Command and General Staff College in Fort Leavenworth, Kansas, conducted exercises and in-depth discussions that led to the development of an embryonic airborne doctrine. No doubt, the Americans were aware that other armies were already examining the viability of airborne forces.

Perhaps the greatest advancement in airborne doctrine during the 1920s and 1930s occurred in the Soviet Union. The first parachute unit of the Red Army, the *Parashutno Desantniy Otriad* (PDO), was authorized during the period in the Leningrad Military District under the command of Marshal Mikhail Tukhachevsky, a strategic visionary better known as a proponent of the Deep Battle theory of combat. On August 2, 1930, Soviet airborne troops executed their first jump from 1,500 feet (460m) near the city of Voronezh. Five years later, 2,500 airborne troops parachuted and landed in gliders during military exercises.

German officers, including Luftwaffe chief Hermann Göring, observed these maneuvers with great interest. An inspired Göring facilitated the conversion of a police unit into the first airborne formation of the Nazi military machine and called for volunteers to populate the new force. In January 1936, a nucleus of 600 officers and soldiers formed the first German parachute and glider companies. Under the command of General Kurt Student, these troops came to be known as the Fallschirmjäger.

Amid the escalation of tensions with Japan in 1939, Soviet airborne troops were deployed to the Far East and fought as light infantry. The Soviets seized Bessarabia from Romania in the summer of 1940, and airborne units jumped unopposed to occupy their objectives during the brief operation. The outbreak of World War II focused global attention on the combat prowess of German airborne forces. The Luftwaffe executed the world's first large-scale airborne combat operations on April 9, 1940, during the conquest of Norway. Elements of a Fallschirmjäger battalion seized key airfields in the vicinity of the capital city of Oslo, enabling ground troops to complete a swift victory.

Below: General Billy Mitchell, better known for his advocacy of strategic and tactical airpower between the world wars, also envisioned an airborne operation that was considered during the final months of World War I.

A month later, German glider troops stunned the world again with their lightning seizure of Fort Eben-Emael on the Belgian border with the Netherlands. Fort Eben-Emael was thought to be nearly impregnable; however, during the execution of Case Yellow, the invasion of France and the Low Countries, these elite troops leveraged the element of surprise, landing silently on and around the fortress and subduing its defenders in a mere 30 hours.

Emboldened by their early successes, German war planners determined that the Greek island of Crete in the Mediterranean Sea could be seized rapidly in a combined operation. The vanguard of the Nazi onslaught was a 15,000-man airborne contingent that began parachuting in the vicinity of tactically important locations on the island on the morning of May 20, 1941. Although the Germans were eventually successful, casualties were alarmingly high among both men and precious Junkers Ju-52 transport aircraft, which fell victim to accurate ground fire from British and Commonwealth troops defending the island. Nearly 300 planes were lost, and estimates of German casualties approached 7,000. Many of the fallen were elite Fallschirmjäger. Hitler was taken aback by the cost and suspended further airborne operations.

Meanwhile, British Prime Minister Winston Churchill was dazzled by the lightning-fast and highly effective German airborne operations in France and the Low Countries. His demand that a

Airborne Visionary?

Nearly 160 years before the U.S. Army's airborne forces were authorized, Benjamin Franklin, patriot, author, statesman, and inventor, was serving as America's commissioner to France. While observing a demonstration of hot air balloons in Paris, Franklin remarked, "Where is the prince who can afford to cover his country with troops for its defense as that 10,000 men descending from the clouds might not in many places do an infinite deal of mischief before a force could be brought together to repel them?"

Perhaps Franklin's question was prophetic, and he had seen the future of warfare—one that included airborne troops. He may also have been aware of the parachute, which made the concept viable. The oldest known image of a parachute-type contraption dates to the late 1400s in Italy, and Renaissance artist and inventor Leonardo da Vinci designed a parachute suspended by a wooden frame during the same period.

Right: Benjamin Franklin witnessed the flight of a balloon like this one during a visit to France in the 1700s. More than 150 years later, the U.S. Army began training airborne forces.

British airborne force of 5,000 men be equipped, trained, and ready for action by the end of 1940 spurred the formation of the airborne forces that later came to be known as the Parachute Regiment. From this grew the famed 1st and 6th Airborne Divisions that constituted the 1st Airborne Corps, which fought bravely in World War II.

Airborne Awareness

With interest in airborne doctrine and operations growing, the U.S. Army's command establishment closely observed the results of the German operations. The Americans were impressed—although they remained unaware of the extremely high casualties the Germans had sustained in Crete—and the Army's efforts to establish operational airborne units gained new impetus.

Above: During training exercises in the 1930s, paratroopers of the Soviet Red Army prepare to board an aircraft. The Red Army was among the first armed forces in the world to recognize the potential for airborne forces in warfare.

During the course of World War II, five airborne divisions—the 82nd, 101st, 11th, 13th, and 17th—were formed within the U.S. Army, along with several independent parachute battalions and regiments. The development of training, doctrine, and equipment to support such formations took place rapidly once the highest echelons of the Army's command structure committed to the effort. Four days after Lieutenant Ryder made his milestone jump in Georgia, General George C. Marshall, Army Chief of Staff, issued orders to begin formal staff studies into the components of an operational airborne command.

CI-320/9685 1st Ind.
(9-28-40)
Constitution of 501st Parachute Battalion

HEADQUARTERS THE INFANTRY SCHOOL, Office of the Commandant, Fort Benning, Georgia, October 9, 1940—To: The Chief of Infantry, War Department, Washington, D. C.

1. With reference to paragraph 2, basic letter, the estimate of funds required and the details of the housing plan for the 501st Parachute Battalion were sent direct to the Quartermaster General on September 16th. He has acknowledged receipt and stated that the project will be given early consideration. The total estimate of funds was $317,250.00. To provide shelter for this battalion pending the construction of barracks, the sum of $7,950.00 is needed. Request for that amount has gone forward (copy inclosed).

2. The area selected as the jumping field is shown on the photo map accompanying letter, this headquarters, to the Chief of Infantry, dated September 4, 1940, Subject: "Preparation of Jumping Field for Parachute Troops". The estimate accompanying that letter showed a total of 27,340 man days of work required to complete the preparation of the field. CCC units are arriving without equipment but hand tools are available and steps are being taken to procure trucks, tractors, and the other heavy equipment required. Work has been started with troop labor. Four hundred and fifty CCC enrollees have arrived and 350 additional are scheduled to arrive this week. It is expected that 200 will be available to begin work on the clearing project on October 14th. The full force will not be available until the erection of their barracks is complete. However, this project is being given priority and four of the six companies will work on it until completed. Unless there is serious delay in procuring heavy equipment it is believed the work can be completed by December 1, 1940.

A report with reference to the location of towers, accompanied by marked photo map, was forwarded by 9th Indorsement 580 (5-28-40), dated October 5, 1940.

3. Lieutenant Colonel Ross O. Baldwin is charged with the conduct of relations between the Infantry Board and the Commanding Officer, 501st Parachute Battalion.

For the Commandant:

/s/ Frank Lockhead
/t/ FRANK LOCKHEAD,
Lieutenant Colonel, Infantry,
Act'g Adjutant General.

3 Incls: withdrawn
1 Incl. added
Copy Letr. Hq. TIS, 10-9-40.

-3-

Left: This 1940 document officially constituted the 501st Parachute Battalion at Fort Benning, Georgia. The first unit of its kind to be activated, the battalion consisted of 446 officers and men.

Ryder's 50-man test platoon made a larger platoon-sized jump on August 29, 1940. On September 16, the first unit of the U.S. Army specifically organized for airborne operations, the 501st Parachute Battalion, was activated at Fort Benning with a cadre of 34 officers and 412 enlisted men, all of them volunteers.

Leaping Bill Lee

For nine months, the 501st was the sole formation of its type; however, as the Army grew to nearly half a million personnel, another battalion, the 502nd, was authorized. By the end of 1941, the 503rd and 504th Battalions were also organized. In the summer of that year, the Provisional Parachute Group was established as the airborne administrative headquarters, and Lieutenant Colonel William C. Lee was given command.

The 46-year-old Lee was an ROTC (Reserve Officers' Training Corps) graduate of North Carolina State University and a World War I veteran. During the 1930s, he had seen German airborne exercises firsthand. Later, as a staff officer serving under General Lesley McNair, chief of Army Ground Forces, he remained captivated by the potential of airborne warfare.

One story, perhaps apocryphal, is recounted that, while still a major on McNair's staff, Lee shared an office with his superior officer, a colonel, and talked incessantly about airborne operations. The exasperated colonel once turned to him and said, "Major, I am sick and tired of hearing your nonsense about airborne warfare. No American soldier is ever going to have little enough sense to jump out of an airplane even in a parachute, and I don't want to hear the word 'airborne' spoken in this office again."

Some time later, the phone rang in the shared office, and a terse voice on the other end of the line asked bluntly, "What are you folks doing toward developing airborne warfare?" Lee handed the phone to the colonel, who then gave permission for Lee to speak freely with the caller, who had identified himself as a representative of President Franklin D. Roosevelt. Soon enough, Lee was at the White House, briefing the president on what he had seen in Germany. From that time forward, Roosevelt was a staunch supporter of the Army's airborne initiative.

In succeeding years, Lee secured his place in Army history and became known as the "Father of the U.S. Airborne." One of his innovative contributions to the training of individual paratroopers was the installation of 250-foot (75-m) towers at the Fort Benning jump school, from which soldiers experienced a parachute-assisted free fall. Lee had seen such a tower hoisting customers aloft by cable and then dropping them by parachute during the 1939 World's Fair in New York and recognized their practical application in airborne training.

Problems with transport aircraft and coordination with ground units handicapped the development of airborne tactics during exercises and maneuvers in 1941. Still, higher-level planning continued. In direct response to the German

One of Lee's contributions was the installation of 250-foot (75-m) towers at the Fort Benning jump school.

conquest of Crete, the 550th Infantry Airborne Battalion, the first air-landing unit of the army, was formed in Panama in July. The first air-landing unit formed in the United States was the 88th Infantry Airborne Battalion, organized in September. Throughout the summer, directives were issued. Studies of glider transportation, the development of new transport and cargo planes, and the ability to deliver the unassembled 75mm-pack howitzer artillery piece to the battlefield were undertaken as planners considered the concept of an airborne combat team complete with medical personnel, an antitank company, field artillery, and an infantry battalion.

By early 1942, it was clear that the organization and staffing of an airborne command structure had outgrown the strategic and tactical capabilities of the Provisional Parachute Group. The three existing parachute battalions in the United States and the single battalion stationed in Panama were reorganized. The 501st Parachute Battalion became the 1st Battalion, 501st Parachute Infantry Regiment. On March 23, 1942, a dedicated Airborne Command was created, and Provisional Parachute Group

Left: As a 46-year-old Lieutenant Colonel, William C. Lee was given command of the Provisional Parachute Group in late 1941. Lee is remembered today as the father of the U.S. Army airborne forces.

personnel formed its headquarters with Colonel Lee as its first commander.

After the U.S. entered World War II on December 7, 1941, six airborne regiments were authorized. As the regimental organization was solidified, the structure would facilitate the activation of the first airborne divisions. Parachute infantry battalions were activated at Fort Benning, Georgia, Camp Toccoa, Georgia, and Camp Mackall, North Carolina. With the authorization of new airborne divisions, the strength of each battalion was augmented prior to incorporation into a parachute infantry regiment.

Originally an infantry division that had fought with distinction during World War I, the 82nd was reactivated on March 25, 1942, with Major General Omar Bradley, who later became commander of the XII Army Group in Europe during World War II, in command. On August 15, the unit was redesignated the 82nd Airborne Division. Major General Matthew B. Ridgway took command, and training began at Camp Claiborne, Louisiana.

On the same day that the 82nd Airborne Division was created, the 101st Airborne Division was activated at Camp Claiborne. Originally formed as an infantry division in July 1918, the 101st did not see action during World War I. It was reformed in 1921, but existed primarily on paper for the next 20 years. In 1942, William C. Lee, now a major general, was placed in command. During the ceremonies that activated the unit, he told the assembled troops, "The

Below: A paratrooper trainee descends from one of the practice towers installed at Fort Benning. Those who engaged in such training found out quickly whether they were airborne material, and a number of soldiers washed out of the rigorous program.

Right: General Matthew B. Ridgway, remembered as one of the most effective airborne commanders of World War II, poses for a photographer during the prewar years. Ridgway commanded the 82nd Airborne Division and the XVIII Airborne Corps.

101st has no history, but it has a rendezvous with destiny."

The 11th Airborne Division was activated on February 25, 1943, at Camp Mackall. The 17th and 13th Airborne Divisions followed at Camp Mackall on April 15 and August 13, 1943, respectively. Each was originally assigned the same mix of parachute, glider, and support units.

Glider pilots received specialized training, and the first qualified group completed its course in June 1942. Three months later, the first glider infantry battalions were authorized. Unlike the parachute troops, glider infantrymen were not volunteers, and although parachutists initially received $50 per month hazardous duty or "jump" pay, glider pilots and troops, nicknamed "Glider Riders," were not compensated with such a pay increase until the summer of 1944.

Injuries and deaths occurred during parachute training. However, glider training was hazardous in its own right. During the 10 months from May 1943 to February 1944, a total of 162 men were injured and 17 killed in glider accidents.

Paratrooper Preparation

On May 20, 1942, the Army issued FM 30-31, matter-of-factly titled *Basic Field Manual: Tactics and Techniques of Air-borne Troops*. The handbook included information on everything from parachute packing to weapons, unit structure, and ground deployment. Parachute troops, it declared, were the "spearhead of a vertical envelopment or the advance guard element of air landing troops or other forces." In other words, the primary mission of airborne troops was to take control of landing areas and hold them until relieved by stronger forces brought in aboard gliders or other aircraft. Such a premise held sway until combat experience dictated a review. Released on October 9, 1943, Training Circular No. 113 asserted that airborne and troop carrier units were to come directly under the control of theater commanders until deployed. Once committed to an operation, they would devolve to the control of the senior officer in the area of deployment. These forces were to be utilized as an element of a combined effort, operating in close cooperation with other military assets.

The commitment of airborne forces was guided by several maxims. These included the following:

- The element of surprise must be present.
- Parachute troops should not be used for missions that can be performed by other troops.
- The decision to use parachute troops should be made well in advance of the scheduled date of the operation.
- A comprehensive knowledge of the terrain involved in the operation is essential.

Wearing their jump gear, troopers of an airborne infantry battalion parade along the streets of Washington, D.C. The dome of the Capitol Building looms in the background, and spectators line the parade route.

- A long-range forecast of meteorological conditions should be carefully considered during the planning phase.
- Because of technical requirements, all parachute troop missions should start from a base that affords the required facilities for packing of parachutes and for making minor repairs. From this base, parachute units may be flown directly to their objective or transported by any available means to a designated airfield, to be picked up by their transport airplanes.
- Terrain objectives to be seized and held should lie in the path of the contemplated advance of friendly forces.
- Local air superiority must exist.
- Combat aviation is essential for the protection of parachute troops while in flight and during landing, and for supporting fires before, during, and after landing.
- Parachute troops should be relieved and withdrawn to their base as soon as practicable after the arrival of supporting ground forces.
- All principles of offensive and defensive action applying to infantry combat are equally applicable to parachute troops.

By the date of issuance of Training Circular No. 113, the hard lessons of North Africa, Sicily, and Italy were being absorbed. A deeper understanding of the critical elements involved in a successful airborne combat operation had fostered the need for more in-depth assessment of factors such as the prevailing weather conditions, particularly wind, and the selection of landing sites.

Further, an overriding concern persisted that airborne troops were essentially light infantry once on the ground. As such, the weaponry, essential equipment, and supplies they could carry were limited due to weight and size restrictions. In the face of overwhelming enemy firepower, the results could be catastrophic.

Training Circular No. 113, therefore, read, "Airborne troops should not be employed unless they can be supported by other ground or naval forces within approximately three days, or unless they can be withdrawn after their mission has been accomplished. No fire support, except from combat aviation, can be expected until contact is made with other forces."

Below: This photograph shows the officers of the 88th Infantry Airborne Battalion at Fort Benning, shortly after the United States entered World War II in December 1941. The insignia includes the motto "Ride the Storm."

Under either protocol, the individual airborne infantryman was tasked with executing the mission at hand. He was expected to carry out orders without hesitation, and his elite status was confirmed through a rigorous course of training that produced a significant failure or "washout" rate among the trainees.

"Airborne troops should not be employed unless they can be supported by other ground or naval forces within three days..."

Prospective paratroopers could be disqualified for numerous reasons, as noted in FM 30-31. These included:

- One refusal to go aloft for a scheduled jump.
- One refusal to jump from the plane in flight.
- Tendency toward airsickness, hysteria, or extreme nervous condition prior to the jump.
- Use of liquor, drugs, or any other artificial nerve sedative.
- Continued hesitancy or weak exits.
- Repetition of erroneous jumping technique on successive jumps.
- Failure to observe the prescribed rules of packing and jumping.

The regimen was divided into four phases: basic training, individual technical parachute training, unit training, and combined training. Basic training was virtually identical to that of a foot soldier, while parachute training acquainted the airborne recruit with the necessary specialized equipment for delivery from the air, and combined training involved exercises with aircraft, air-landing, and glider troops.

Right: Lined up to board their C-47 transport plane, anxious paratrooper trainees anticipate the exhilaration of their impending practice jump. Intense training prepared airborne troopers for the rigors of combat.

96
63TG

Elite Training

Unit training provided paratroopers with a degree of expertise in several areas that was significantly beyond that of the infantryman. Each trooper was required to learn to operate all weapons at the platoon level and care for, maintain, and pack a parachute. He was also taught demolitions, and those who were proficient with explosives were to be available for special missions requiring those skills.

A trainee who completed five successful jumps was awarded the coveted silver jump wings for his uniform and participated in a ceremony called the Prop Blast. During this, his success was toasted with a drink concocted from a secret recipe that was then secreted into an obsolete M-94 encryption machine. The keyword for the encryption was the familiar jump cry of "Geronimo."

Graduates of jump school certainly had reason to be proud of themselves, but getting there was a monumental undertaking—one of the sternest tests the American military could offer. Field Manual 30-31 stressed the importance of physical fitness. "Concurrent with the technical and tactical training of parachute units," it read, "an intense and continual physical training course must be conducted. This training tends to minimize the number of landing injuries and prepares the unit for arduous field service normally incident with parachute operations."

Lieutenant Ryder developed the physical training program that the paratroopers were required to complete. He was also responsible for the erection of a 34-foot (10-m) tower, nicknamed "Ryder's Death Ride," from which the trainees were required to jump. The tower portion of airborne training alone lasted nine days.

Opposite: A stick of paratroopers hits the silk above its training ground at Fort Benning, Georgia. Hesitation at the door or a refusal to jump marked a soldier for almost certain dismissal from the airborne service.

Above: Standing ready at the edge of a training tower, a paratrooper waits for the order to jump. This photo was taken in 1943, at the height of training and deployment activity of airborne formations in the U.S. Army.

For the paratroopers, the most harrowing aspect of the training was the jump itself, from the safety of an airplane high above the ground into the atmosphere while relying on the proper performance of the parachute for a safe landing. Private George Graves began airborne training at Fort Benning, Georgia, in the summer of 1942. In a letter to his parents dated July 21 of that year he described the anxiety and the exhilaration of his first training jump.

"Well, Monday the 20th of July was certainly an exciting day in my young life," Graves wrote. "We sat around the field for about three hours watching the three other companies making their first jumps, as we were the last company of four to jump. They came out in eight-man masses, so when four or seven or something like that came out we could tell that someone had refused... I found to my great horror that I was the No. 1 man out of 16 out of the plane. We sit opposite each other in the plane and naturally can observe all the movements of our fellow travelers. Well, I had to sit right next to the damned open door, and I couldn't help looking out from time to time at the ground getting smaller and smaller.

"...On the ground I had told myself over and over and over 1,000 times," continued Graves, "There's nothing to this. You'll be the first out and have to set a good example for those other guys. Well, looking at the sweating faces opposite me, all just as white as a ghost, just bloodless, made it 1,000 times worse! God knows what I looked like. Then I looked at the 'jump master' who gives us our orders and picks the place for us to land...He looked to me like a devil or an executioner in his big wind goggles. I got no encouragement whatsoever looking at him."

Graves obeyed the jump master's order to stand up and hook up. "I only had to take a half step from where I was, but I got the wrong foot in the door," he wrote his parents. "I didn't lean out the door into the prop blast as I had my hands incorrectly inside the door. He gave me a good crack behind the knees and out I went. I vaguely remember seeing the tail flash over my head, and I must have had a good body position as I had a very gentle opening jerk. Suddenly, I felt a wonderful glow of excitement come over me, like a baby when he sees a new toy. You just can't describe it. Luckily, I came in with the wind at my back and made a swell landing."

Left: In this staged training photo, a paratrooper has just come to earth and brandishes his Thompson submachine gun as the parachutes of other trainees billow in the background.

Silver Wings

In the early days of the U.S. Army's airborne service, virtually everything was new. Uniforms, specialized equipment, and insignia were adapted to the airborne role. The distinctive jump boots and uniform that became recognized trappings of the American paratrooper were designed by William P. Yarborough, a young officer who had graduated from the U.S. Military Academy in 1936. Although these items are iconic in their own right, the most recognizable contribution that Yarborough made to the outfitting of a qualified paratrooper was his design of the silver Parachutist Badge with its familiar pair of wings surrounding a parachute (see above). The "jump wings" have been worn with pride since Yarborough offered the design, which was approved in March 1941.

While posted at Fort Benning in late 1940, Yarborough volunteered for airborne service. He was given command of Company C, 501st Parachute Battalion, and rose to prominence. In the summer of 1942, he was appointed airborne advisor on the staff of Brigadier General Mark Clark. He led the planning of the airborne phase of Operation Torch, the Allied invasion of North Africa on November 8, 1942, and commanded airborne units in Sicily, Italy, and southern France.

Yarborough reached the rank of lieutenant general and retired from the Army in 1971 after 40 years of service. He is recognized as the "Father of the Modern Green Berets," the U.S. Army's Special Forces. Yarborough died on December 6, 2005, at the age of 93.

Currahee

In a corner of northeastern Georgia, laborers of the Works Projects Administration (WPA), a creation of President Franklin D. Roosevelt's New Deal, built Camp Toccoa in the late 1930s to serve as a training facility for the National Guard. With the coming of World War II, the site hosted airborne recruits, complementing the bustle of activity at Fort Benning and Camp Mackall.

The first would-be paratroopers, 5,000 of them, arrived at Camp Toccoa in July 1942; eventually, 17,000 men would train there. When they departed, they would have every twist and turn and every rock and pine tree along the roads up Currahee Mountain seared into their collective memory. Four parachute infantry regiments, the 501st, 511th, 517th, and the 506th—immortalized in Stephen Ambrose's book *Band of Brothers*—endured rigorous training there.

The facility was originally named Camp Toombs in honor of Robert Toombs, a politician and Confederate general in the American Civil War. However, the name was changed to Camp Toccoa after one of its early commanders noted that prospective troopers passed by the Toccoa Casket Company and an old cemetery before arriving at Camp Toombs to learn the art of jumping from airplanes. The combination was simply too eerie.

Currahee Mountain, rising 1,735 feet (529m) above sea level, was the most imposing geographic feature at Camp Toccoa. The trainees regularly ran and hiked to the summit and back, resulting in the famous slogan, "Three miles

Above: Three miles up; three miles down. Troopers of the 506th Parachute Infantry Regiment run the road on Currahee Mountain, a 1,735-foot (529m) promontory at the training camp in Toccoa, Georgia.

up; three miles down!" The word "Currahee," which became the war cry of the 506th Parachute Infantry Regiment, is said to be Native American, translating to English as "stand alone." For those who trained at Camp Toccoa, that translation was most fitting.

Organization

The strength of the airborne divisions authorized in 1942 totaled roughly 8,500 men, somewhat more than half that of a standard infantry division. Although their complement was altered during World War II, the original divisions included a parachute infantry regiment, two glider infantry regiments, up to three parachute field artillery battalions, a battalion of airborne engineers, and signal, medical, and quartermaster companies. By 1944, airborne divisions expanded to include three parachute infantry regiments at peak strength.

The basic parachute infantry squad consisted of 12 men, two noncommissioned officers, usually a sergeant and a corporal, and 10 riflemen. It was armed with rifles, a submachine gun, and a light machine gun. The platoon consisted of a command group that included the platoon leader, assistant platoon leader, platoon sergeant, signal corporal, radio operator, and two messengers, along with two rifle squads and a 60mm mortar squad. Total platoon strength was about 37 troopers. The parachute rifle company consisted of a command group that included the company commander, assistant commander, and a small group of enlisted men to facilitate tactical control of the company, operate communications equipment, and provide security for the command post—about 130 men.

The basic tactical unit of the airborne forces was the parachute battalion. Consisting of headquarters and headquarters company personnel divided into combat and administrative echelons, the battalion also contained three rifle companies, an 81mm mortar platoon, and a .30-caliber (7.62mm) machine gun platoon. Total battalion strength was roughly 530 troopers: 35 officers and 495 enlisted men.

In 1942, the parachute infantry regiment included three parachute battalions, headquarters, headquarters company, a service company, and other attached components. Altogether, a full-strength regiment numbered more than 2,000 troopers.

Field Manual 30-31 stressed that once an airborne formation was inserted on the ground it was to function as infantry. The regimental commander, along with the commanders at lower levels, was "charged with the duties of the commander of an infantry rifle regiment... In addition he is responsible for parachute activities and maintenance, and training peculiar to parachute troops."

The Outfit

Parachute troops were issued special jump boots and two-piece jump suits. Outfitted in full combat and jump gear, the trooper carried an incredible array of weapons, supplies, and equipment; FM 30-31 provided explicit instructions for the proper placement of each item. These included everything from his rifle to hand grenades, helmet, parachute, reserve parachute, extra ammunition, rations, map and compass, gloves, pocketknife, and toilet tissue.

Field Manual 30-31 stressed that once an airborne formation was inserted on the ground it was to function as infantry.

Altogether, an average enlisted paratrooper carried 70 pounds (32kg) of additional weight; an officer carried 90 pounds (40kg). At times, specialized tasks might be assigned to an individual trooper, and the equipment needed to complete the job might raise the additional weight to 120 pounds (54kg). Fully laden paratroopers often required assistance to stand and board transport aircraft.

"Items that may be carried in addition to those shown," read the field manual, "include demolition equipment, signal equipment, bayonet, extra ammunition, medical equipment, and the carbine. The amount of equipment carried is limited to that which allows a safe rate of descent. The type of equipment is limited by the fact that any protruding angular objects may foul the suspension lines of the canopy, and the possibility that such objects may cause serious injury to the parachutist, who may have to roll or tumble on landing."

Additional equipment and supplies were parachuted from aircraft in a variety of containers, depending on the size and weight of the contents. These were often tied together in a configuration called a daisy chain.

Standard airborne weaponry included the M1 Garand rifle, the smaller M1 carbine that was often carried by officers, rear echelon, and staff personnel, the Thompson submachine gun, which added some automatic firepower at the squad level with a rate of fire of approximately 700 rounds per minute, the Mk 2 hand grenade (pineapple), T2 rifle grenade, 60mm and 81mm mortars, the Browning M1919 .30-caliber (7.62mm) light machine gun, the Colt Model 1911 .45-caliber (11.43mm) pistol, the M1 rocket launcher, popularly known as the Bazooka, and the 75mm pack howitzer light artillery piece, which could be parachuted or delivered via glider in pieces and assembled in the combat zone.

Brave Young Men

Even as they trained, the mystique, elite status, and élan of the airborne troops were growing. The American public embraced heroes, and the rugged persona of the paratrooper was ideal as a morale booster on the home front. One magazine published an early assessment, stating that paratroopers "...in the first place are perfect specimens. They have to be, because their work is rough, tough, and full of excellent opportunities to get hurt. Mentally they're quick on the trigger, again because their job demands it, because split seconds can make the difference between instant death or a successfully completed job."

Indeed, from the earliest days there was no illusion among senior Army commanders that airborne troops would pay a severe price while serving as the "tip of the spear." They were expected to sustain heavy casualties while performing a variety of roles that included conducting raids, capturing a specific target and holding until relieved, attacking rear areas to facilitate the success of offensive ground operations, and harassing the enemy at every opportunity. Airborne units were also counted on to operate as independently as they were able with limited organic resources.

Many of the finest young officers and soldiers in the U.S. Army gravitated toward airborne service. Among them was Captain James M. Gavin, a 1929 graduate of the U.S. Military Academy at West Point. While the German juggernaut swept across Europe in the early days of World War II, Gavin returned to the Academy as an instructor in tactics and read reports of the spectacular successes that the Nazi airborne units had achieved.

Above: Wearing the two stars of a major general, James Gavin commanded the 82nd Airborne Division during much of its combat service in World War II. For a time, Gavin was the youngest general officer in the U.S. Army.

In the spring of 1941, Gavin applied for a transfer to airborne service. The request was denied, prompting him to write letters to influential friends such as Lieutenant Ryder, who was already serving in the Parachute Test Platoon at Fort Benning. Gavin traveled to Washington, D.C., several times to personally request the change. Finally, in July his reassignment was approved. Gavin was among those who graduated from jump school in August. One of the trailblazers who shaped the future of U.S. Army airborne operations, Gavin went on to command the 505th Parachute Infantry Regiment and the 82nd Airborne Division during World War II.

Years later Gavin wrote of those heady days as American airborne forces were coming together—elite but destined to face a rugged, experienced enemy. "A quantum jump, technologically speaking, had been made by the Germans," he observed. "It would not be enough to copy the Germans. We had to strike boldly into the areas of innovation. From what we had seen so far, it was clear that the most promising area of all was airborne warfare, bringing the parachute troops and the glider troops to the battlefield in masses, especially trained, armed, and equipped for that kind of warfare."

When American airborne troops deployed during World War II, they proved resourceful, resilient, and tenacious in combat, earning the respect of both allies and enemies. The diary entry of one German general described them as "Devils in baggy pants." Their training and esprit de corps had prepared them to the extent possible, and in the heat of battle they produced a combat record that resonates in military history to this day.

Below: Fully loaded for a mission, these paratroopers of the 101st Airborne Division board a Douglas C-47 transport aircraft prior to a training jump. The 101st Airborne became legendary in its defense of Bastogne during the Battle of the Bulge.

CHAPTER 2

OPERATION TORCH

Only two years after the U.S. Army officially sanctioned the formation of an airborne arm, American paratroopers were committed to a vast offensive against Axis forces on the coast of French North Africa.

Operation Torch, a highly complex endeavor scheduled for November 8, 1942, involved Allied forces on land, sea, and air.

Conceived in an effort to open a second front and assist the Soviet Union in its immense struggle with German forces in the East, Torch evolved as a viable alternative to an invasion of Nazi-occupied Northwest Europe, for which the Western Allies were unprepared in 1942. Never before had armed forces planned and executed an offensive on such a grand scale. Troops were to land near three key cities on the North African coast: Casablanca, Oran, and Algiers.

In addition to diverting German resources from the Eastern Front, the ultimate goal of the offensive was to eliminate the Axis presence in North Africa: Allied forces pressed eastward from the Torch foothold, while the British Eighth Army, under General Bernard Law Montgomery, relentlessly pushed the enemy, commanded by Field Marshal Erwin Rommel, westward following the great victory at El Alamein on the Egyptian frontier in October 1942.

Aside from the logistical challenges they faced, the most immediate concern for Torch planners was the possibility of resistance from the substantial Vichy French ground and air forces based in North Africa. Nominally under the control of the collaborationist French government that emerged as the Germans overran France and the Low Countries in the spring of 1940, armed opposition from Vichy forces would jeopardize the success of the landings.

Opposite: His hand on his line, a paratrooper prepares to exit a C-47 transport aircraft in this posed photo taken during a practice exercise. Note the broom and other items in the background that indicate that this image was taken on the ground.

Tactical Torch

On the tactical level, uncertainty as to the Vichy response to the Torch landings prevailed until Allied troops actually set foot on North

Left: General Lloyd Fredendall, commander of the American II Corps in North Africa, examines a map while French General Edouard Welfert (light cap) looks on and Lieutenant Henri Thewes acts as the interpreter for the officers.

African soil. Therefore, the complex blueprint for Operation Torch was obliged to recognize the potential threat that more than 500 French aircraft posed to the landings and to the supporting naval vessels off the North African coast.

Plans for airborne troops to participate in operations against Casablanca and Algiers were briefly considered and then dropped. However, in the vicinity of Oran, a major port city on the Algerian coast 230 miles (370km) east of the British bastion at Gibraltar, two Vichy French airfields, Tafaraoui and La Senia, were of particular concern. These included the only runways in western Algeria that were considered adequate for sustained operations, while Tafaraoui was the only one with a hard surface. Vichy fighter aircraft were within easy striking distance of the Center Task Force, one of three poised to hit the North African beaches, which included 18,500 troops of the U.S. 1st Infantry and 1st Armored Divisions under the command of Major General Lloyd Fredendall.

Parachute Possibilities

Tafaraoui was only 15 miles (24km) south of Oran, and La Senia a mere five miles (8km) distant. To secure these airfields, removing the threat of Vichy airstrikes against Oran and facilitating the introduction of reinforcements and supplies, it was decided that the inherent risks of an airborne operation were worth taking. The 509th Parachute Infantry Regiment (PIR) was placed under Fredendall, and its 2nd Battalion was slated to make the first American combat jump in history.

The 509th had been authorized on March 14, 1941, originally as the 504th Parachute Infantry Battalion, and activated on October 5 of that year at Fort Benning, Georgia. In February 1942, the battalion relocated to Fort Bragg, North Carolina, and joined the 503rd Parachute Infantry Battalion to form the newly created 503rd Parachute Infantry Regiment. In June, the 503rd was detached for service in Scotland and became the first American airborne unit to deploy overseas during World War II.

The American paratroopers trained with their counterparts of the British 1st Airborne Division and took on a decidedly British flair in the process. In the course of this training, the regiment participated in the lowest large-scale parachute drop in history, jumping from an altitude of a mere 143 feet (43m). On November 2, 1942, less than a week prior to Operation Torch, the 503rd was redesignated once again as the 2nd Battalion, 509th Parachute Infantry Regiment.

Oran and Environs

The occupation of Oran presented its own hazards. Vichy fortifications ringed the cliffs that surrounded the harbor, discouraging an attempt to capture the port city by frontal assault. Instead, amphibious landings at Arzeu, 30 miles (48km) east of the targeted airfields, and Les Andalouses, 35 miles (56km) from La Senia and 45 miles (72km) from Tafaraoui, were planned. Carrier-based air support would have to be withdrawn within two or three days of the landings, and land-based Allied planes needed airfields before they could deploy to North Africa. The distance from the beaches to Tafaraoui and La Senia gave rise to discussions of a parachute operation to secure the bases until the airborne troops were relieved by the invasion forces advancing overland.

Two months prior to Torch, General Dwight D. Eisenhower, Supreme Allied Commander in the Mediterranean Theater, gave the go-ahead for an airborne assault on Tafaraoui and La Senia. The 2nd Battalion, 509th Parachute Infantry Regiment—the only American unit of its kind then in Europe—was designated for the drop, and its delivery was assigned to the 60th Troop Carrier Group. The two units had already been

Below: A formation of the 509th Parachute Infantry Regiment stands at attention in North Africa. Elements of the 509th executed the first wartime airborne jump in the history of the U.S. Army during Operation Torch on November 8, 1942.

training together for about three weeks when these orders were received in early September.

On September 12, a command group called the Parachute Task Force was established with Colonel William C. Bentley in charge. Bentley had served previously as an Army Air Forces' attaché in Morocco and was familiar with the area to an extent. A cadre of 77 officers and enlisted personnel formed the command structure of the Parachute Task Force, and Bentley was in command during the preliminary phase and while the paratroopers were in the air. Lieutenant Colonel Edson D. Raff commanded the 2nd Battalion, 509th, and went directly to General Mark W. Clark, a member of Eisenhower's staff and a close friend and advisor of the supreme commander, to request that the paratroopers remain under his own direct command once they were on the ground. Raff was a respected officer, who had trained his men relentlessly and earned the nickname "Little Caesar" both for his hard-nosed approach to command and his stocky build. His perspective was appreciated, and Clark granted the request.

Some concerns were raised during the planning of the airborne operation. Chief among the dissenters was Air Marshal William L. Welsh, the highest-ranking member of the air forces section of Eisenhower's planning cadre for Torch. Welsh recommended that the airborne troops should be held back and committed after the Torch landings during the drive to capture Tunisia's capital city, Tunis. His assertion received only passing consideration, and the preparations went forward.

Daunting Distance

The first American airborne combat operation remains the longest mission of its kind in the history of warfare. The entire invasion was planned under a supposed veil of secrecy. To diminish the possibility of the airborne force being discovered, the Douglas C-47 transport planes that were to carry the paratroopers had to be located as far as possible from German intelligence operatives, radar stations, and fighter bases in occupied France. The fuel

Below: Relaxing during their weeks of airborne training in New Jersey, troopers of the 503rd Parachute Infantry Regiment pause for a group photograph. The 503rd PIR went on to earn accolades for its role in several engagements during World War II.

Right: Lieutenant Colonel Edson Raff commanded the 2nd Battalion, 509th Parachute Infantry Regiment, during action in North Africa. He is pictured here with U.S. First Lady Eleanor Roosevelt.

capacity of the C-47s further dictated that the planes should be based as close to the African continent as possible. Survey crews criss-crossed Land's End at the southwestern tip of England, and the small airfields at St. Eval and Predannack were chosen. An original force of 36 planes was increased to 39, and these were divided between the two bases.

Of equal importance was the determination of the best air route for the assault. Hazardous flight paths across Vichy France in the east or the open Atlantic Ocean in the west were quickly dismissed. The most direct route was through Spanish airspace. Although ostensibly neutral, the Spanish government was viewed with suspicion by Allied commanders. Its fascist head of state, Generalissimo Francisco Franco, was known to be pro-German. The possibility that Spain might enter the war on the Axis side was real, and the overflight could be considered enough provocation to hasten that event. Spanish fighters and antiaircraft guns might also take a toll among the transports. Also, the prospect that the Spanish could alert the Germans early might spell disaster for the enterprise.

Nevertheless, the airborne mission was approved to fly across Spain, a daunting distance of 1,100 straight-line air miles (1,770km). There would be no interim stop at Gibraltar. The risk of discovery by the Germans was too great. The flight was understood to be one-way, and the C-47s would be required to land in the wastes of the North African desert if airfields were unavailable.

The introduction of a fighter escort for the transports was initially discounted due to the hazards of landing at night and the overcrowding of the small airfields at Land's End. However, repeated requests from the transport commanders were finally heeded, and Royal Air Force Fighter

Command put together plans for direct escort and diversionary missions. Three days before the mission embarked, six Bristol Beaufighters based at Predannack and a flight of Supermarine Spitfires from Portreach were assigned as escorts. Once the escorts were aloft, the commander of the Beaufighters would determine how long his planes would stay with the C-47s, droning slowly at just 135 miles per hour (217km/h), while the Spitfires were ordered to turn for home at dusk.

A complement of 531 paratroopers was slated to load and lift off at 5 p.m. on November 7 and drop near the target airfields at 1 a.m.

For most of its duration, the eight-hour flight would be conducted under cover of darkness; this offered some protection from enemy eyes and antiaircraft defenses, although it also obscured landmarks and other visual navigational aids. A hoped-for solution lay in the disposition of the Royal Navy antiaircraft ship HMS *Alynbank*. This was equipped with a beacon that would begin sending radio signals from a position about 35 miles (56km) off the African coast near Oran at 11:30 on the night of November 7. The signal was to be broadcast at 440 kilocycles, a frequency that would simulate an Italian transmission. If all went according to plan, the radio compasses aboard the C-47s would pick up the ship's beacon and ride the signal on the proper course to the airfields. To help ensure success, as soon as the transport planes were visible at a distance of 20 miles (32km), the *Alynbank* would also begin flashing a V from its signal light, maintaining this sign for five seconds at 30-second intervals until all the planes passed overhead.

As the transports crossed the North African coastline, they were also expected to pick up a radar signal planted near Tafaraoui by an agent

codenamed Bantam. Bentley's plane and those of group commanders and squadron leaders were to carry receivers known as "Rebecca" that would enable them to home in on Bantam's signal. It was hoped that operatives on the ground might also fire flares to illuminate Tafaraoui once surprise was assured.

A complement of 531 paratroopers was slated to load and lift off into the afternoon sky at 5 p.m. on November 7 and drop near the target airfields at 1 a.m. Intelligence reports indicated that antiaircraft guns defended both Tafaraoui and La Senia, and, due to their proximity to Oran, French troops from the city might rapidly counterattack the lightly armed paratroopers. La Senia was deemed the most difficult objective due to its shorter distance from Oran, and it was also

Above: Douglas C-47 transport planes tow gliders during airborne exercises in the United States. Glider operations were an integral part of American airborne efforts during World War II, and glider regiments were organic to American airborne divisions.

deemed the least valuable of the two airfields. Tafaraoui was an all-weather field, slightly further away from the city, and considered easier to capture. The flight path to Tafaraoui, across a large dry lakebed called the Sebka d'Oran, was also less likely to attract attention.

The parachute drop itself would take place at Tafaraoui. Once that objective was secured, a company of the 2nd Battalion would be detailed to march on La Senia, destroy its facilities and any aircraft that were on the ground, and withdraw. Another small force would disrupt Vichy communication lines near an airfield to the northeast at Lourmel, which would assist the ground troops advancing from Les Andalouses. Once these two missions were accomplished, the concentrated airborne force was to hold at Tafaraoui until relieved.

The mission of the 2nd Battalion, 509th PIR, was nearly canceled in late October after General Clark returned from a clandestine meeting with Vichy officials with promising news that the Torch landings might be unopposed. Eisenhower considered canceling the airdrop and saving the paratroopers for operations in Tunisia, as Air Marshal Welsh had suggested. Clark met with Bentley and Raff on October 28, and the three offered contingency plans to Eisenhower. Should negotiations prove fruitless and the Vichy French

Above: During a training exercise at Hungerford, 67 miles (107km) west of London, paratroopers tumble to the ground. Although time and equipment were always in short supply, continuous training was critical to the success of airborne combat operations.

appeared likely to resist the Allied invasion, the original "Plan A" would go into effect as the signal "Advance Alexis" was broadcast. If the Vichy French agreed to cooperate with the Allies, an alternative "Plan B" would be implemented with the broadcast of the signal "Advance Napoleon." Plan B called for the airborne force to land in daylight on D-day, November 8, at La Senia and stand ready to undertake a mission against airfields in Tunisia.

Serious Shortage

Throughout the early days of the U.S. airborne forces, a lack of transport aircraft plagued their progress, limiting training time, deployment, and eventually negatively impacting combat operations. During the 1930s, the U.S. Army Air Corps had led the world in the development of air transport capability; however, no formal organization had been established. On April 30, 1942, Air Transport Command was authorized, and on June 20, just five months prior to Operation Torch, Troop Carrier Command was designated with the primary mission of carrying parachute and glider troops as directed.

Exacerbating the early lack of structure and direction was the simple fact that air planners believed transport planes could be readily purchased when the need arose. This attitude prevailed from 1939 through mid-1940 as the U.S. military rearmed for the possibility of war,

Wartime Workhorse

When he wrote his memoir of World War II, titled *Crusade In Europe*, General Dwight Eisenhower, Supreme Commander of Allied Forces in Europe, credited the Douglas C-47 Skytrain transport aircraft, the bulldozer, the two and one-half ton truck, and the landing craft with enabling the Allies to gain the final victory.

The C-47 was indeed a war-winning machine. More than 10,000 of the versatile transport planes, capable of carrying men and equipment, were produced during the war.

A military modification of the civilian Douglas DC-3 passenger plane that first flew in 1935, the C-47 was the primary carrier of American and British airborne troops during World War II. The first C-47s were delivered to the U.S. Army Air Forces in September 1941, and other aircraft types were rapidly phased out of airborne operations.

The C-47 was capable of carrying up to 18 combat-loaded paratroopers or a two and one-half to three-ton cargo payload. The 75mm pack howitzer was the heaviest weapon it could transport, and subsequently this versatile gun became the standard issue of American airborne artillery units. The four-man crew of pilot, co-pilot, navigator, and radio operator appreciated the ease of flying and maintaining the C-47, which the British referred to as the Dakota. It could sustain heavy combat damage and remain aloft. It was capable of taking off with a full load from an unpaved runway only 3,000 feet (900m) long. With supplemental fuel tanks topped off, its range was an impressive 1,500 miles (2,400km). Although it was a slow aircraft, with an average cruising speed of only 150 miles per hour (240km/h), it was capable of dropping to 110 miles per hour (175km/h) and maintaining altitude during an airborne operation, allowing paratroopers to jump from a stable platform. The fuselage door was seven feet (2m) wide, which facilitated the quick exits of combat-loaded troopers. Limited numbers of the C-53 transport, a variant of the C-47 that was not configured to carry cargo, were also built during World War II.

Although only slightly more than 500 C-47s and C-53s had been delivered to the U.S. military by August 1942, American industry was producing more than 100 per month by mid-1943, finally alleviating a shortage in transport aircraft.

Below: A military variant of the famed Douglas DC-3 civilian passenger plane, the C-47 was a transportation wonder during World War II, carrying men and materiel during operations around the globe. The C-53 Skytrooper, a modified C-47, was manufactured exclusively to carry paratroopers.

and virtually no orders were placed for new transport aircraft during that period. Only five new transport planes were delivered in 1940, and in 1941 only 133 entered service. At the end of 1940, the Air Corps had only 122 obsolete but serviceable transport aircraft.

On the eve of Torch, the entire American troop carrier capability in the European Theater belonged to the 51st Troop Carrier Wing.

The realization that its initial assessment was wholly inaccurate prompted the Air Corps to place orders for nearly 12,000 transport planes between June 1940 and the end of 1942. Although steps had already been taken to augment the number of transport squadrons and groups, the effect of the shortage of planes was keenly felt as Operation Torch approached. On September 1, 1942, the 51st Troop Carrier Wing headquarters detachment arrived in Scotland. Its 60th and 64th Troop Carrier Groups came within days, followed later by the 62nd.

On the eve of Torch, the entire American troop carrier capability in the European Theater belonged to the 51st Troop Carrier Wing. Training had been further restricted by lengthy modifications that were being done to the 60th Group's C-47s in preparation for the Torch mission. These included the installation of formation lights, rheostats to control electric current, flame dampeners, jump bells to complement the red and green indicator lights, and VHF radio sets for communication between planes. The modifications themselves were not complicated, but the workload strained the depot facility at Burtonwood beyond capacity.

Bad weather interfered with the forward movement of the 60th's planes to the airfields at St. Eval and Predannack, and 25 C-47s arrived on November 6, just hours before the mission was to begin. Fourteen planes were released from modifications on the afternoon of November 6, and their pilots and crews spent a sleepless night preparing for relocation the next day.

Briefings were held at both airfields on the morning of November 7, but these were of little value. No mention was made of the most prominent terrain features the pilots might encounter over Morocco, and weather reports were later proven somewhat inaccurate. A briefing at Predannack was a waste of time. The officers conducting those proceedings had assumed the objective was Gibraltar rather than Oran and provided useless information to their audience. The pilots of the 14 late planes received only cursory overviews of the mission, and when they took to the air in the late afternoon of November 7 they could barely stay awake at the controls.

Into the Sky

Plan A, anticipating a hostile reception in Africa, was in effect until the afternoon of November 7. With planes and paratroopers assembled, the signal for Plan B, "Advance Napoleon," was received, and takeoff was delayed for four hours to allow aircraft to land in daylight at La Senia. Due to the late hour at which the change was communicated, some troopers had already been in the cramped quarters of their planes with full combat loads for two hours when word reached their officers.

At 9:05 p.m., the first C-47s rose into the air and formed into four flights, a lead flight of nine planes and three more of 10 each. Final assembly took place above Portreach, and the force flew south on a heading of 225 degrees. Strong winds were encountered over the Bay of Biscay, where a turn was made to 177 degrees. Almost immediately some planes fell behind the leaders, and as the wind speed increased, the number of stragglers grew.

Cloud cover and rain squalls forced some planes to divert from their intended course, and when the formations neared the coast of Spain they encountered rough weather due to an incoming front that meteorologists had warned the pilots to expect. As the planes climbed to 10,000 feet (3,000m) to clear coastal mountains, some lost airspeed and fell further behind. Others attracted sporadic antiaircraft fire. The weather remained rough, and aircraft became widely scattered.

Pilots later reported that they were unable to see the formation lights of other planes. These had been previously dimmed for the mission, but were supposedly visible if the planes remained in close proximity to one another. As gaps widened to more than 200 yards (180m), some of the aircraft were essentially flying alone. Attempts to maintain radio contact were frustrated as operators were unfamiliar with the new VHF sets and reception was poor.

Below: Douglas C-47 transport planes under construction. Thousands of C-47s were manufactured, but transport aircraft were always in short supply. Note the wide fuselage doors to facilitate the rapid exit of paratroopers from the plane.

Cloud cover hampered attempts to navigate by the stars, while only a few planes had American instruments for the purpose. Others had been supplied with British tools just prior to takeoff. Clouds also obscured landmarks, although some pilots were able to identify the city of Madrid in the distance. Most of the pilots flew over Spain and the Mediterranean by dead reckoning. Many were thrown miles off course by an unexpected wind blowing from east to west, and, as they made landfall over Africa at dawn, low-hanging fog covered the terrain for miles.

In the confusion, several pilots became disoriented. One plane ran out of gas and landed at Gibraltar. Three others landed in Spanish Morocco, 180–250 miles (290–400km) west of Oran. Two planes landed in French Morocco, and Vichy French fighters either shot down or forced three more to land. Antiaircraft guns barked along the African coastline, and those pilots who managed to reach La Senia expecting a peaceful landing were surprised when they took even more antiaircraft fire.

Those pilots who had managed to stay somewhat on course received little help from the *Alynbank*. Broadcasting on 460 kilocycles rather than the correct 440, its beacon was unintelligible. On the ground at Tafaraoui, Bantam was unaware that Plan B was in effect. He anticipated the arrival of the transports overhead at 1 a.m. When none appeared, he destroyed his radar equipment.

Below: At an airborne training facility in North Carolina, paratroopers participate in a takeoff drill. Continuous training was necessary to allow thousands of airborne troops to board transport aircraft efficiently and maintain mission schedules.

Join Up and Jump

Colonel Bentley and five other planes crossed the African coastline about 100 miles (160km) west of Oran; moments later, five more C-47s

Above: Paratroopers carried an array of equipment, sometimes weighing more than 100 pounds (45 kg). Among the items in this display are hand grenades, a .45-caliber Colt pistol, primary and reserve parachutes, canteen, a spoon, and an M1 Garand rifle.

appeared nearby. When he was unable to locate a landmark, Bentley landed and ascertained his position through questioning some nearby Arabs. After one of his group's planes had flown on alone, Bentley took off again. Two more C-47s joined up during the ensuing flight.

Just after 8 a.m., Bentley spotted eight transports that had landed at the edge of the Sebka d'Oran. He was informed that Vichy snipers were taking shots at the men on the ground and that a column of vehicles was approaching. If these were French, a full-scale firefight might erupt. A quick radio discussion with Lieutenant Colonel Raff ended with the decision to drop paratroopers along a ridge that commanded the approaches to the northern edge of the dry lakebed about 35 miles (56km) from Tafaraoui. In short order, paratroopers jumped from at least nine C-47s.

While the other aircraft landed, Bentley continued with an air reconnaissance. He observed the smoke of battle around Tafaraoui and dodged antiaircraft fire before landing with engine trouble and raising Fredendall's II Corps headquarters on the radio. While Bentley worked with the radio, one of the C-47s that had flown to Spanish Morocco landed nearby. The pilot had dropped his troops off to save gasoline and flown on toward Oran until he ran out of fuel. Minutes later, Vichy troops reached the scene and took Bentley's entire party prisoner.

Flying the third C-47 in the lead flight, Major Clarence Galligan may have been the first American pilot to land troops in enemy territory. He flew through antiaircraft fire along the coast

Geronimo!

Early in the development of American airborne forces, the cry of "Geronimo!" became familiar as paratroopers leaped from the doors of transport planes. The origin of this now famous cry remains something of a mystery.

Geronimo, a famed chief of the Native American Apache tribe, was once imprisoned at Fort Sill, Oklahoma, and his grave is located nearby. One account says that the paratroopers adopted the cry after hearing that, with U.S. troops in hot pursuit, Geronimo once leaped from a steep cliff while on horseback. It was a feat the soldiers were reluctant to duplicate, and Geronimo temporarily made good his escape.

Another explanation seems somewhat more plausible. In his 1979 book *Paratrooper!* Gerard Devlin mentions that the origin of "Geronimo!" dates to the early days of the parachute test unit at Fort Benning in 1940. On the night before their first jump, a group of paratroopers enjoyed a few beers and took in a movie. Although the name of the film is unknown, it might well have been *Geronimo*, which had been released in 1939.

When the movie was over and the men were walking back to their barracks, Private Aubrey Eberhardt asserted that he had no fear of the coming jump. His friends jeered and said that Eberhardt would be so frightened that he would not remember his own name.

"All right, damn it!" Eberhardt shot back. "I tell you jokers what I'm gonna do! To prove to you that I'm not scared out of my wits when I jump, I'm gonna yell 'Geronimo!' loud as hell when I go out that door tomorrow!" Eberhardt did just that, and the cry caught on. Both the 501st and 509th Parachute Infantry Regiments placed "Geronimo" on their early unit patches.

Below: Adopted after World War II, the insignia of the 509th Parachute Infantry Regiment bears the word "Geronimo" that has become synonymous with the airborne soldiers of the U.S. Army. The cry was often heard as a trooper jumped from his transport.

and was attacked by a French fighter plane above the Sebka d'Oran. RAF Spitfires chased the French fighter away. Galligan landed his damaged plane on the dry lakebed about five miles (8km) from La Senia and marched with his crew and 14 paratroopers to its rim, where he ordered them to dig in and wait. French fighters appeared overhead, but did not strafe the group.

A company of French troops with a 75mm artillery piece in tow approached menacingly, but did not attack, probably awaiting the arrival of Colonel Bentley, who was already a prisoner. Bentley advised Galligan to surrender, and the major complied.

By 9 a.m., 33 planes had reached the vicinity of Oran.

Meanwhile, Raff had broken several ribs during the parachute jump and relinquished command of his troopers to his executive officer, Major W.P. Yarborough. These men set out to identify the column that was advancing toward approximately 250 more paratroopers and troop carrier personnel who had taken cover from the sniper fire behind a low stone wall. The best news of the day so far was received when the approaching column was identified as American troops driving inland from the beach at Les Andalouses.

Once the snipers were driven away, an attempt was made to load the paratroopers who had been pinned down back aboard the planes and ferry them across the Sebka d'Oran to mount an attack against Tafaraoui. The drive was aborted when the landing gear of several aircraft became stuck in thick mud.

With the sun high in the sky, Yarborough ordered his command to rest. While these troopers were eating lunch he received a message that American columns advancing from the beachhead at Arzeu had captured Tafaraoui.

Yarborough sent a message back to the area where the C-47s were located, asking for volunteers to pick up three planeloads of paratroopers to garrison the Tafaraoui airfield. At 4 p.m., these planes reached Yarborough. A few minutes later, they were again airborne with their cargoes of 2nd Battalion troopers. Five miles (8km) from Tafaraoui, half a dozen French fighter planes jumped the transports and forced them to land. The three C-47s were badly shot up and were later scrapped.

On the ground once again, Yarborough and his troopers continued on foot toward Tafaraoui and reached the airfield as the sun rose the next morning. Trucks picked up wounded men and the crews of the three planes that had been left behind and delivered them to the airfield.

Around noon on November 8, word reached the transport crews and airborne troopers who remained at the edge of the Sebka d'Oran that Tafaraoui might be secure. Lieutenant Colonel Thomas Schofield, commander of the 60th Troop Carrier Group and the ranking officer on the scene, dispatched Major John Oberdorf in a single C-47 to reconnoiter the airfield.

In less than an hour Oberdorf became the first American pilot to land at Tafaraoui. As his wheels touched down, French 75mm artillery peppered the field and raked his C-47 with shrapnel. A few minutes later, two more transports came in to land. When Schofield confirmed that the shooting had at least temporarily stopped, he allowed the remaining C-47s to load and fly to the airfield. As the afternoon wore on, 25 C-47s and two planeloads of paratroopers were delivered to Tafaraoui. The French artillery still fired an occasional harassing shot until the following morning. One shellburst severely damaged a C-47 and wounded a crewman.

As the first combat operation in the history of American airborne forces came to a close, there were five dead and 15 wounded.

Four French Dewoitine fighters lined up for strafing runs against the Americans on the ground at Tafaraoui, but these were blasted out of the sky by Spitfires of the 31st Fighter Group, relocating to their new base from Gibraltar. Some aircraft and paratroopers were still scattered around North Africa by the time Oran fell on the morning of November 10.

Taking Stock

As the first combat operation in the history of American airborne forces came to a close, casualties had been surprisingly light. Among the paratroopers and troop carrier personnel, there were five dead and 15 wounded. Lieutenant Dave Kunkle, killed while aboard one of the C-47s, was the first U.S. Army airborne officer to die in battle. Private John T. Mackall of Company E, 2nd Battalion, 509th PIR, was seriously wounded during a French fighter plane's attack on his transport. Mackall died in a Gibraltar hospital on November 12, and Camp Hoffman, North Carolina, was renamed in his honor. A sprawling 62,000-acre (25,000-hectare) complex where airborne troops trained, Camp Mackall included an airfield with three 5,000-foot (1,500-m) runways, 1,750 buildings, 65 miles (100km) of paved roads, five movie theaters, beer gardens, and a 1,200-bed hospital, all constructed in the amazing span of four months.

Most of the Americans who had missed their objectives were eventually reunited with the 509th. The Vichy French released their prisoners. Those aboard the two C-47s that landed in French Morocco were detained until November 13 and performed some transport duty for the Western Task Force of Operation Torch before flying to Tafaraoui on November 20. The planes and paratroopers that landed in Spanish Morocco were interned until February 1943.

The first U.S. Army airborne combat mission had come to an anticlimactic end. It was true that both the airfields at La Senia and Tafaraoui had been captured, and Oran was in American hands. However, the airborne troops had played only a minimal role in these successes. Several factors contributed to the generally disappointing results of the heroic but unproductive foray.

Right: The airborne training facility at Camp Mackall, North Carolina, opened in 1943 and is commemorated with this historical marker. The Camp was named in memory of Private John T. Mackall, mortally wounded in North Africa.

The entire mission had been authorized in an effort to take objectives that were within range of ground forces landing on the beaches near Oran. The 1,100-mile (1,770-km) distance was too great for the transports to fly cohesively, particularly with much of the trek in darkness. Communications were hampered by the failure of the beacons and the blunder that led the *Alynbank* to broadcast on the wrong frequency, along with the unfamiliarity of aircrews with their equipment. Bad weather, some of it unforeseen, contributed to the loss of formation in flight as winds scattered C-47s over hundreds of miles. Confusion regarding the response of the Vichy French to Operation Torch complicated matters. Some of the Americans expected a peaceful mission, while others clashed briefly with Vichy forces. The lack of information presented during the preflight briefings, including the totally erroneous information offered during one of these, was virtually inexcusable.

Some observers have concluded simply that senior Allied commanders, including General Eisenhower, had authorized the deployment of the airborne troops with unnecessary haste. Air Marshal Welsh was probably not alone in his opinion that the goals of the mission did not warrant the hazards that were surely to be encountered. The Allies were fortunate that casualties were not considerably higher and that the mission did not end in complete disaster. Had the Vichy forces responded with coordinated and determined resistance, such was a real possibility.

Jump Revisited

There were lessons to learn and errors to be corrected in the aftermath of that first mission, but in mid-November the Allies were engaged in a high-stakes race with the Germans to occupy and control Tunisia. Airborne forces were in theater, and they appeared to offer the best option to accelerate the effort to capture key positions.

On November 10, General Jimmy Doolittle, commanding the American Twelfth Air Force, ordered the 60th Troop Carrier Group to Maison Blanche, an airfield near Algiers, to join the 64th Group, which flew in on the 11th. About 300 paratroopers of the 509th PIR reached Maison Blanche aboard the 60th Group's planes, while the transports of the 64th and subsequently the 62nd Groups supported the operations of the British 2 and 3 Parachute Battalions.

Lieutenant Colonel Raff and Major Martin E. Wanamaker, the senior officer of the 60th Group at Maison Blanche, were ordered to capture the crossroads town of Tebessa, where several overland routes into central Tunisia converged. Time was critical, and few good maps were available. Intelligence reports were sketchy, and planning was minimal due to the urgency of the situation. German forces had been reported on the march just a few miles from Tebessa.

While the troop carrier men performed maintenance and refueled, straining French gasoline through chamois to remove impurities, the paratroopers packed chutes and prepared for another combat jump. The best drop zone near Tebessa was identified as an old French airfield at Youks-les-Bains, 10 miles (16km) west of the town.

At 7:30 a.m. on November 15, 20 planeloads of 2nd Battalion paratroopers took off from Maison Blanche for the 300-mile (480-km) flight. Raff, in pain from his broken ribs, flew in the first transport, which Wanamaker piloted. Six RAF Spitfires came along as escort; these were later joined by six Hawker Hurricanes. Around 9:30 a.m., the airborne troops jumped from altitudes of 300 to 400 feet (90–120m).

Above: General Jimmy Doolittle commanded the U.S. Twelfth Air Force in North Africa. Doolittle is famous for leading a daring bombing raid against the Japanese capital of Tokyo in April 1942.

Anxious moments occurred as the paratroopers descended. Trenches filled with combat troops and heavy weapons were visible. The Vichy 3rd Zouave Regiment was directly below them. Luckily, the Vichy soldiers proved friendly, and no shots were exchanged. Raff later commented that the "landing pattern over the target was perfect and well timed" and that the jump at Youks-les-Bains was the most successful of his career.

Raff sent a strong contingent forward to occupy Tebessa and was soon informed that the way was open to Gabes on the Mediterranean coast. If the paratroopers were allowed to advance that distance, they might prevent the retreating Germans under Rommel from linking up with other enemy forces already operating in Tunisia. Raff radioed General Clark for

The parachutes of American airborne troops billow in the wind as C-47 transports disgorge their human cargoes somewhere over Europe. The U.S. Army's airborne forces participated in numerous major operations in the European Theater during World War II.

permission to make the stunning advance, but was warned to go no further than Gafsa, 75 miles (120km) north of Tebessa. Clark's decision was wise. The paratroopers were lightly armed, and providing adequate support for them at a distance would have been problematic. Nevertheless, Raff's initiative secured the right flank of the Allied advance toward Tunis through the critical month of February 1943.

On November 29, the British 2 Parachute Battalion jumped at Depienne to destroy German airfields and supply bases. German troops and tanks attacked them near the village of Oudna, and the British paratroopers fought a running battle across the desert, eventually covering a distance of 60 miles (95km) and losing half their number killed or captured.

The last Allied airborne mission in North Africa took place on December 23, 1942, when 30 American paratroopers carrying 500 pounds (225kg) of explosives dropped near El Djem to destroy a bridge. The planes flew low to avoid detection, and visibility was good with the illumination of a full moon. The drop went flawlessly, but the troopers became disoriented on the ground and marched away from their objective rather than toward it. Most of them were captured by the Germans.

While the troop carrier groups remained active with logistical support, the Allied airborne units were utilized as infantry for extended periods during the remaining days of the North Africa campaign. Senior commanders discussed additional parachute operations, but these proved unnecessary as Allied ground troops made progress, eventually trapping the Germans against the Mediterranean coast of Tunisia and forcing one of the largest mass capitulations of the war.

As the fighting in North Africa came to an end, the number of airborne troops based on the continent increased in preparation for their anticipated role in the next Allied offensive, the invasion of Sicily.

Below: Glider troops of the U.S. 82nd Airborne Division prepare to board their CG-4 Waco glider during training for the airborne phase of Operation Husky, the Allied invasion of Sicily. The Sicily operation took place in July 1943.

US

CHAPTER 3

SICILY AND ITALY

The engines of the C-47 droned monotonously through the darkness as Colonel James M. Gavin, commander of the 505th Parachute Infantry Regiment, 82nd Airborne Division, strained to glimpse the turning beacon on the island of Malta. He never saw it.

Airborne operations were risky in the best of conditions. On the night of July 9, 1943, however, Gavin was leading 3,405 men into combat, and the high-stakes mission was fraught with peril. Among the first Allied soldiers to set foot on Axis territory during Operation Husky, the invasion of Sicily, Gavin's troopers were ordered to seize high ground several miles beyond the invasion beaches, where American troops were to come ashore within hours.

Husky Takes Shape

Even as the battle for control of North Africa raged, Allied planners were considering their next move against the Axis forces in the Mediterranean Theater. Some senior officers advocated a strike against the Balkans. Others believed Sardinia or even southern France would be a promising target. After contentious debate, though, it was determined during the Casablanca Conference in January 1943 that an invasion of Sicily offered the best prospects for success and would perhaps pay the greatest dividend for the investment of blood and treasure required to take the island.

Allied victory in Sicily would mean that approximately 300,000 German and Italian troops might be neutralized. The fascist government of Benito Mussolini was already believed to be unstable, and a major defeat on Italian soil might even knock Italy out of the war. Hitler might also be compelled to divert troops from the Eastern Front to bolster the defenses of the Italian mainland, easing the pressure on the Soviets. Sicily, a landmass slightly larger than the state of Vermont, would also serve as a springboard for further operations in the Mediterranean.

Opposite: Paratroopers of the 82nd Airborne Division prepare for Operation Husky. Much larger than previous missions in North Africa, the airborne phase of Husky was fraught with risk, and paratroopers were widely scattered across Sicily.

Above: Colonel James M. Gavin, commander of the 505th Parachute Infantry Regiment, briefs officers prior to departure for Sicily. Gavin came to the ground in Sicily unsure of his exact location – or even whether he was on the island.

After several revisions, the plan for Operation Husky dictated that the British Eighth Army, commanded by General Bernard Law Montgomery, would land four infantry divisions, the 5th, 50th, 51st, and the Canadian 1st, along with a contingent of Royal Marine Commandos, on a 40-mile (65-km) front in the southeast corner of the island from the Pachino Peninsula to the Gulf of Noto, south of the port of Syracuse. The American Seventh Army, under General George S. Patton, Jr., would put three infantry divisions, the 1st, 3rd, and 45th, ashore to the west of Montgomery at the Gulf of Gela. These were to be followed as soon as practicable by the 2nd Armored Division. With the Americans protecting his left flank, Montgomery was to drive northward, capture the city of Messina, and cut off the evacuation route of the Axis forces defending Sicily. Both amphibious landings were to be preceded by airborne operations.

Airborne Emphasis

Montgomery and Patton considered an airborne prelude essential to the success of their landings, and the best atmospheric conditions were expected on the night of July 9–10. A quarter moon, forecast to set half an hour after midnight, would provide an appropriate amount of natural light to assist in the American parachute drop and a British glider mission.

Opposite: Paratroopers board their C-47 transport plane prior to takeoff from their base in North Africa. Although many of the planes missed their drop zones and suffered heavy casualties, the airborne troops fought well and achieved their objectives in Sicily.

Just after dinner that evening, the troopers of the 505th PIR and the attached 3rd Battalion, 504th PIR, 456th Parachute Field Artillery Battalion, and Company B, 307th Airborne Engineer Battalion began boarding 222 C-47s of the U.S. 52nd Troop Carrier Wing at a cluster of airfields around the village of Kairouan in Tunisia. Between 11:40 p.m. and 12:30 a.m., the Americans were to jump into Sicily, landing in designated drop zones on the high ground known as the Piano Lupo five miles (8km) from the town of Gela. Holding their positions, they were ordered to support the landings of the 1st Infantry Division by cutting the roads to the north and east of the invasion beaches, denying their use by German forces that were expected to counterattack from nearby Caltagirone. After linking up with the advancing 1st Division, the paratroopers would fight as infantry, assisting with the capture of an airfield at Ponte Olivo, about five miles (8km) further northeast.

Training had been limited but intense, with little of it involving night jumps, and it had achieved mixed results. The transport pilots were inexperienced, and although the flight plan seemed straightforward enough to those on the ground it was complicated by nocturnal conditions and the fact that much of it was over the waters of the Mediterranean Sea. The pilots were to assemble in unfamiliar V of V formations and fly a straight line to Malta, where a strong beacon would assist their navigation in a turn toward Cape Correnti, east of the American landing beaches. At Cape Correnti another turn would take the planes slightly offshore to follow the Sicilian coastline nearly to Gela. Yet another turn inland would position the C-47s over the drop zones on time. In retrospect, one troop carrier group commander lamented, "I do not believe it feasible to even try to fly again such a course...."

A month earlier, Gavin had decided to make a run along the proposed air route and experienced his first enemy fire. During a stop along the way, a Luftwaffe air raid scattered bombs and shrapnel, sending the colonel's party scurrying for cover. He wrote in his diary, "At about 10:05 we were hit with an air raid of nice proportions, thus breaking a record of years of never having heard a hostile shot."

Before they clambered aboard the C-47s, Gavin, with his brief exposure to enemy action

Right: Colonel James M. Gavin commanded the 505th Parachute Infantry Regiment in Sicily and led his troops through heavy fighting. This photograph was taken some time later, with Gavin wearing the stars of a major general. He is also proudly wearing the distinctive patch of the 82nd Airborne Division.

in the back of his mind, distributed a written message to his paratroopers. "SOLDIERS OF THE 505th PARACHUTE COMBAT TEAM," it read, "Tonight you embark on a combat mission for which our people and the free people of the world have been waiting for two years.

"You will spearhead the landing of an American Force upon the island of SICILY. Every preparation has been made to eliminate the element of chance. You have been given the means to do the job and you are backed by the largest assemblage of air power in the world's history.

"The eyes of the world are upon you. The hopes and prayers of every American go with you.

"Since it is our first fight at night you must use the countersign and avoid firing on each other. The bayonet is the night fighter's best weapon. Conserve your water and ammunition.

"The term 'American Parachutist' has become synonymous with courage of a high order. Let us carry the fight to the enemy and make the American Parachutist feared and respected through all his ranks. Attack violently. Destroy him where ever found.

"I know you will do your job.

"Good landing, good fight, and good luck
COLONEL GAVIN"

As the planes climbed into the darkening sky, salt spray from the churning Mediterranean misted across their windshields. They encountered high winds, blowing steadily at 30 miles per hour (48 km/h), gusting almost to gale force, and much stronger than considered safe for a parachute drop. Since this was a combat mission, there was no turning back. Formations became ragged as the pilots continued in the darkness, searching for familiar landmarks, but finding none. Smoke from the preinvasion bombardment, increasing antiaircraft fire, and low-hanging haze obscured the final checkpoints—Biviere Pond and the mouth of the Acate River—that should have helped guide the pilots to the drop zones. They had been briefed on the air route, but had only seen daylight aerial reconnaissance photos of the Sicilian terrain and approached the coast of Sicily from multiple directions.

"The eyes of the world are upon you. The hopes and prayers of every American go with you."

More than 200 C-47s scattered their paratroopers across southeastern Sicily. One transport crashed into the sea, and two others became hopelessly lost, their pilots electing to return to Tunisia with their troops still aboard. Despite their difficulties, the pilots landed in North Africa with reports of successful drops. One historian characterized these optimistic statements as "a prodigious overestimate."

Taking the Offensive

Thirty-three sticks of American paratroopers came down in the British zone, while 53 were in the area of the 1st Division near Gela, and 127 dropped behind the invasion beaches assigned to the 45th Division between the towns of Vittoria and Caltagirone. The 2nd Battalion, 505th PIR, under Major Mark Alexander, managed to land somewhat intact, but it was 25 miles (40km) from its assigned drop zone. Eight C-47s in the second serial dropped Company I, 505th, on target south of a road junction that it was ordered to seize, while 85 men of Company G came down about three miles (5km) distant, and the headquarters and two platoons of Company A dropped in their assigned zone north of the road junction along with the command section of the 1st Battalion.

The rest of the 82nd Airborne Division was widely dispersed across the Sicilian landscape. Three planes near the end of the aerial caravan were blown far off course, missing Malta and the southern coast of Sicily entirely. The pilots circled

back and made landfall above the coast of eastern Sicily near Syracuse. Aboard were the troopers of the demolition section assigned to blow up the railroad bridge across the Acate River, and the pilots believed they were on target. The paratroopers were dropped near a bridge south of Syracuse, 65 miles (100km) from their actual objective.

Most of the 313th Transport Group veered widely off course, one squadron missing Malta by at least 20 miles (32km) and also reaching Sicily over its eastern beaches. Twenty-three C-47s dropped their human cargoes around the town of Avola in the British zone, 50 miles (80km) from their intended objective. Approximately 65 of these wayward troopers found each other in the darkness and then managed to link up with British ground troops, assisting in the capture of the town.

Taking the initiative as best they could, airborne officers gathered and organized small bands of paratroopers, located enemy positions, disrupted communications, and started the battle where they were. Only about 200 reached the American objective of the high ground at Piano Lupo. They miraculously held the position with no heavy weapons until 9 a.m., when two battalions of the 16th Regiment, 1st Division, linked up with the beleaguered troopers of Company I, 505th PIR.

Lieutenant Colonel Arthur "Hardnose" Gorham, commanding the 1st Battalion, 505th PIR, was one of the few American officers near the Piano Lupo on the morning of July 10. With the help of Captain Edward M. Sayre, one of his company commanders, Gorham scraped together about 100 paratroopers. He had no idea where the rest of his battalion had landed. Nevertheless,

Left: Seated on long benches aboard their C-47 transport, paratroopers of the 82nd Airborne Division smile apprehensively en route to Sicily and combat with the German and Italian forces defending the island.

Left: Paratroopers aboard a C-47 await orders from an officer to make final preparations for the jump into Sicily on July 9, 1943. Although they were scattered across the island, small groups of American troopers hit the enemy hard during the opening hours of Operation Husky.

Gorham instructed the men to dig in along a road leading toward the town of Niscemi. As the sun rose, German tanks and supporting infantry rumbled into a deadly trap. Flanking fire decimated the German soldiers who were caught without cover, and bazookas took out four of the tanks before the survivors fled in disorder. The following day, Gorham took on a German tank with a bazooka. Stepping out alone, he was killed by enemy fire.

Captain James McGinity led the 85 men of Company G in capturing their objective at Ponte Dirillo across the Acate. As the sun rose, troops of the 180th Regimental Combat Team, 45th Division, made contact with McGinity. Leaving some men to guard the bridge, the combined force advanced north to high ground that commanded the approaches along the coastal highway.

Sixty paratroopers from the 3rd Battalion, 505th PIR, joined Lieutenant Colonel Earl Taylor's 3rd Battalion, 45th Division, along with three 75mm pack howitzers of the 456th Parachute Field Artillery Battalion, which reached the coastal highway and turned toward Vittoria at daybreak.

Meanwhile, Alexander's 2nd Battalion steadily silenced enemy positions along the coast near Santa Croce Camerina. Narrowly averting a disastrous drop over open water, Alexander had forced his way back from the open door of his C-47 when he saw only ocean below him. Anxious to turn for home, the pilot and navigator had flipped on the green light prematurely. When the light came on again, Alexander jumped, only to realize immediately that the plane had been too low. He crashed to the ground and temporarily lost consciousness.

When he came to, Alexander realized that his men had been taking fire from five enemy pillboxes since the moment they had jumped. The troopers rallied, silencing each pillbox in succession, and then counting 12 dead among their number. More than 500 men of Alexander's 2nd Battalion converged and set off toward Gela. The major directed the capture of an Italian battery at the coastal town of Marina Di Ragusa along the way. A single pack howitzer of the 456th Parachute Field Artillery was wheeled into position and began to pummel the concrete blockhouse with scarce 75mm rounds. Only 30 were at hand, but the few that were fired had the desired effect. The Italians surrendered moments before Alexander ordered a direct assault.

Fatigued from their jump, march, and fights with the pillboxes and the battery, Alexander's troopers dug in for the night. Sniper shots rang out and kicked up dust around them. While his men searched for the source of the bothersome shots, a young officer flashed Morse code to a British cruiser lying close to the shore. A few naval shells promptly crackled overhead, and the sniper beat a hasty retreat. The following morning, the Americans set out again toward Gela and took Santa Croce Camerina, an objective of the 45th Division, along the way.

Planes of the 313th Troop Carrier Group's 49th Squadron found Lake Biviere and dropped a portion of Company A about two miles (3km) northeast of their assigned drop zone. These troops came under fire quickly, but as daylight approached approximately 100 had gathered. They captured an enemy position and then established a roadblock on the Niscemi Road, using their bazookas and small arms to turn back a German counterattack that included half a dozen tanks. Continuing south to capture the junction of the Niscemi Road and the coastal highway, one of the primary objectives of the entire airborne operation, they ran into substantial defenses. Halted momentarily, the Americans demanded the surrender of the Italian troops inside the bunkers, warning that heavy naval gunfire would be called down on them if they refused. No contact with the navy had actually been established, but the bluff worked and the

Below: Parachutes billow as troopers of the 82nd Airborne Division descend on Sicily, a few hundred feet below. High winds, enemy antiaircraft fire, and general confusion plagued the Sicily airdrop, but the paratroopers fought heroically.

Italians came out with their hands up. An hour later, the paratroopers made contact with soldiers of the 1st Infantry Division advancing inland.

Jump into Jeopardy

The 316th Troop Carrier Group brought in 505th regimental headquarters personnel, signalmen, medical personnel, engineers, and artillerymen. Gavin was in the lead plane, and he had become concerned with the failure to spot the turning beacon on Malta. The colonel stood up, walked back to another officer, and calmly whispered that he believed serious problems lay ahead.

The pilot made another turn. Another hour went by. When the jump signal was given, Gavin was the first man out the door of his plane. He shook off the effects of a hard landing, gritted his teeth against a sharp pain in one of his legs, and began backtracking from the direction in which the C-47 had flown. He came across a couple of his staff officers and rounded up about a dozen men. By then, he realized that he was far from his assigned drop zone.

Years later, Gavin wrote that he had "some doubt as to whether we were in Sicily, Italy, or

Below: Paratroopers of the 82nd Airborne Division pause along a railroad track in Sicily. Hours after landing in hostile territory, the Americans were engaged in heavy fighting with German and Italian units on the island.

the Balkans, although the odds strongly favored the first."

The colonel led his small force toward the flashes and sounds of gunfire. What Gavin heard was most likely the attack of about 40 troopers of the 505th Headquarters Company, commanded by 1st Lieutenant H.H. Swingler, on Italian pillboxes that covered a crossroads on the highway south from Vittoria. They briefly detained an Italian soldier but were unable to glean any information from him before he managed to slip away. The pace of Gavin's march caused some men suffering from jump-related injuries to fall out along the way. At daylight the little band ran into a concealed Italian position. The lead paratrooper was killed by machine-gun fire, and one of Gavin's men cut down an Italian officer with his Thompson submachine gun.

Overmatched, the Americans scrambled to safety and waited until dark, when they resumed their quest to find the bulk of the 505th. About 2:30 a.m. on July 11, they reached 45th Division lines near Vittoria. Once in the town, Gavin found an abandoned jeep, hopped aboard with several other men, and went searching for more of his command. At dawn, the colonel came across 180 troopers of the 3rd Battalion commanded by Major Edward C. "Cannonball" Krause, who had camped overnight in a tomato field.

Gavin asked Krause what he had done to achieve his battalion objective, and the response was essentially "nothing." The general got the 3rd Battalion up and moving and appropriated a platoon of the 307th Engineers to renew his own search in the direction of Gela. A few minutes after parting company with Krause, the Americans came across a German motorcycle speeding along a dirt road. To avoid being shot dead, the officer in the sidecar raised his hands in surrender and tried to explain that he and the driver were medical personnel. Gavin did not believe the German, and the men were taken prisoner.

Biazza Ridge

Passing a railroad junction, the Americans stumbled upon a ridgeline rising about 100 feet (30m) directly in their path. Olive groves spread along the grassy slope that appeared to have caught fire and then burned itself out.

Although he was still somewhat unsure of his position, Gavin believed the high ground might be tactically valuable and ordered Lieutenant Ben Wechsler, the engineers' commanding officer, to take a platoon up the ridge. As soon as they came within sight of the enemy soldiers along the heights, bullets began to fly. Gavin sent a runner hustling rearward to bring Cannonball Krause and the other 3rd Battalion troopers up.

The lead paratrooper was killed by machine-gun fire, and one of Gavin's men cut down an Italian officer with his Thompson submachine gun.

Wechsler's engineers reached the crest of Biazza Ridge and came under intense fire from the enemy soldiers they had just driven off and a German battalion that had not been visible down the reverse side of the slope. With his men in a tight spot, Gavin slipped back across the railroad junction in search of the badly needed reinforcements. He spotted Major William Hagan, the 3rd Battalion executive officer, with 250 paratroopers, a few men from the 180th Regimental Combat Team, and a platoon from the 45th Division. Sprinting to the relief of the hard-pressed engineers, these men ignored the enemy fire that clipped branches and kicked up clouds of dust around them, bowling into the Germans and forcing them back down the ridge until mortar and artillery fire began falling among them, compelling a halt. Tiger tanks with menacing 88mm guns were reported in the vicinity as well.

Above: Lying prone to avoid attracting enemy gunfire, American paratroopers contemplate their next move during the fighting at Biazza Ridge in Sicily. Colonel James M. Gavin led the paratroopers and elements of other units in the tactical victory.

It was up to Gavin to decide what to do next. The enemy force in front of him was substantial, and it was now obvious that Biazza Ridge, eight miles (13km) east of Vittoria, dominated a substantial length of the coastal highway. Despite being outgunned, Gavin concluded that he had found the flank of the 45th Infantry Division and stepped into the path of the Hermann Göring Division, an elite German armored formation that included Luftwaffe field troops, attempting to reach the beach and exploit the gap between the 45th and 1st Division landing zones.

Gavin ordered his command to dig in and defend the high ground. For a while the heaviest weapons on hand were bazookas, which fired antitank rounds that proved incapable of penetrating the heavy armor of German tanks. A pair of 75mm pack howitzers from the 456th Parachute Artillery Battalion turned up and became a welcome addition to the defenses.

Throughout the day, German artillery pounded the Americans on Biazza Ridge. Tanks crept closer to the thin defensive line. One Tiger rolled up between two buildings and began searching for a target. Artillerymen rolled a howitzer forward just in time to see the ground in front of them erupt with the explosion of an 88mm shell. Undeterred, the American gunners replied. Their 75mm round hit the Tiger, but failed to penetrate its thick armor. However, it was enough to persuade the German tank commander to pull back.

By 3 p.m., Gavin's command had taken heavy losses. Small parties of American soldiers had heard gunfire and rushed forward to join the fight, but two-thirds of the defenders were killed or wounded, including two men who had driven a captured Italian armored personnel carrier to an exposed position and died when the vehicle took a direct hit. Their bodies hung limp inside the demolished carrier for the rest of the day – in plain view of those fighting for their lives against long odds.

Late in the afternoon, as German tanks had advanced to within 50 yards (45m) of Gavin's command post, word reached II Corps headquarters that the Americans on Biazza Ridge were hanging on by their fingernails. Fire support requests were quickly relayed to corps artillery and the ships of the Western Task Force offshore. Within minutes, heavy guns barked on shore and at sea, shattering the German advance. About 7 p.m. Lieutenant Swingler arrived with 100 more paratroopers, and 11 tanks detailed from the 45th Division came on the scene.

While some commanders would have been content to hold their ground, Gavin decided to attack. At the colonel's order, the mixed bag of

Below: A medic dispenses life-giving blood plasma to a wounded American soldier in Sicily while civilians watch from a doorway. Casualties were high among the troopers of the 82nd Airborne, and high-level discussions took place concerning future airborne operations.

American troops swept down the ridge. The Germans fell back in disorder, abandoning the positions that had pinned down the paratroopers with mortar and machine-gun fire for much of the day. The advance was swift, and Lieutenant Swingler came across a lone Tiger tank, its crew milling about outside. He flipped a grenade into their midst, killing the Germans on the spot. The Americans dug in, prepared to hold the ridge against a counterattack. Gavin settled at his command post in an olive grove and slumped to the ground exhausted. He later received the Distinguished Service Cross for his heroism at Biazza Ridge and a Purple Heart for his painful leg injury.

As they had been trained to do, the paratroopers of the 82nd Airborne Division fought with whatever they had and wherever they were. Small bands of troopers ambushed enemy patrols, cut telephone lines, and created confusion among the defenders. Their widely dispersed drops had convinced senior German commanders, including General Paul Conrath, whose Hermann Göring Division had been halted at Biazza Ridge, that they were under attack by 20,000 to 30,000 American paratroopers. In actuality, only 3,400 had jumped into battle.

Along with the notable successes at Biazza Ridge and Santa Croce Camerina, a few three-plane elements had succeeded in dropping their sticks of paratroopers in clusters that amounted to roughly platoon strength. Behind enemy lines in the 45th Division sector, these intrepid paratroopers were responsible for the capture of

Below: American paratroopers advance cautiously toward a treeline somewhere behind the beachhead near Gela during the opening hours of Operation Husky. The troopers of the 82nd Airborne Division overcame strong enemy resistance to capture their objectives in Sicily.

Right: On the outskirts of the village of Ribera, Sicily, General Matthew Ridgway, commander of the 82nd Airborne Division, confers with members of his staff. Ridgway was soon elevated to higher command, and Colonel James Gavin was promoted to lead the division.

Vittoria, destroying two Italian field artillery batteries in the process. Lieutenant Peter Eaton of the 3rd Battalion, 504th PIR, gathered a platoon-sized unit that captured two Italian vehicles towing antitank guns. Blocking the road, Eaton's men took up defensive positions, and soon a German tank leading a column of infantry rumbled into view. The paratroopers disabled the tank and shot up the enemy foot soldiers, who scattered among the mines the Americans had buried along the approach route.

Despite their widely dispersed drops, the troopers of the 82nd Airborne achieved their Operation Husky objectives, although the forces that managed to accomplish these tasks were only fragments of those intended for the purpose. A force slightly larger than a company had captured the Niscemi Road junction with the coastal highway. Gavin's opportunistic seizure of Biazza Ridge had occurred somewhat by accident, and his command had nearly been overrun by German armor.

General Matthew Ridgway, commanding the 82nd Airborne Division, received incomplete reports throughout the early hours of Operation Husky. He was virtually unaware that his division was performing so well in the face of such difficulties. At 7:55 a.m. on July 12, he reported to Patton's Seventh Army headquarters that he still had "no formal element of Combat Team 505 under my control." The extent of Ridgway's consolidated force at the time consisted of about a company of paratroopers and a single battery of 75mm pack howitzers.

Glider Catastrophe

General Montgomery changed the British airborne mission from a parachute drop to a glider operation with the objective of securing the bridge at Ponte Grande across the Apano River, south of Syracuse. The paratroopers of the 1st Airlanding Brigade were to hold the bridge until infantry of the 5th Division covered the seven miles (11km) from their landing beaches near the coastal town of Cassibile.

Two hours ahead of the Americans, the 2,075 British airborne troops, the vanguard of Operation Husky, lifted off from North African airfields aboard 144 American-made Waco and British Horsa gliders towed behind 109 C-47s and 35 British-built Armstrong Whitworth Albemarle transports flown by aircrews of the U.S. 51st Troop Carrier Wing.

As difficult as the American airborne operation had proven, the experience of the British glider

Above: Ready for takeoff, C-47 Skytrain transport planes and Waco gliders line the airfield at Comiso, Sicily. Many transports and gliders were shot down or damaged during Operation Husky, exacerbating an already acute shortage of aircraft.

troops was much worse. Buffeted by high winds, the gliders bucked in the air, and formations loosened. Six Albemarles and their Wacos never got out of North African airspace. Five of these returned to base when the gliders were found to be loaded improperly or not airworthy. Three more turned around with glider problems. These later returned to the air, two with replacement gliders attached. Yet another transport was forced to land in Tunisia when a jeep that its glider was carrying broke loose inside.

The transport pilots were ordered to fly low to avoid radar detection, and their windshields were whipped with steady streams of ocean spray. At least two more pilots became lost over the Mediterranean and turned back, and three more found Sicily, but failed to locate the proper landing zones. These planes turned around as well. One Horsa glider snapped its towline over the sea and was lost, while a Waco was prematurely released early in the flight. Five gliders managed to set down about 15 miles (24km) south of Ponte Grande between Cape Passero and Avola. Six more gliders were released in the vicinity, but crashed into the water. Another glider landed 15 miles (24km) north of Syracuse near Augusta. About 130 transports did find the Sicilian coastline above Cape Passero, but many more of these simply disappeared or crashed into the dark Mediterranean. It is estimated that 70 gliders were either released too soon or in the wrong area. Troop Carrier Command concluded that only 58 gliders landed in Sicily at all.

Lieutenant Lennard Withers of the 2nd Battalion, South Staffordshire Regiment, led

General Matthew B. Ridgway

When Major General Matthew B. Ridgway took command of the 82nd Airborne Division in August 1942, he had never jumped from an airplane. His men, however, had already completed parachute training. No doubt some of them thought Ridgway would always be a "leg," too old at 47 to qualify for his parachute wings and content to stay on the ground.

A 1917 graduate of the U.S. Military Academy, Ridgway had other ideas. His first task was to oversee the conversion of the 82nd, originally an infantry division with a solid combat record, to full battle-ready airborne status. Some time after the transition was completed, the general did in fact earn his wings as a qualified airborne trooper. Ridgway went on to lead the division through some of its most difficult days during World War II. He was involved in the planning of the airborne phase for Operation Husky, the invasion of Sicily, and jumped into Normandy on D-Day with his division in June 1944. In the autumn of that year, he was given command of the XVIII Airborne Corps, which included the 82nd and 101st Airborne Divisions and later encompassed all airborne units of the U.S. Army. Ridgway's command participated in Operation Market Garden, the Battle of the Bulge, and Operation Varsity, the airborne crossing of the Rhine River during the last weeks of World War II in Europe. He briefly commanded troops on the Philippine island of Luzon prior to the surrender of Japan.

In 1950, Ridgway was sent to Korea to take command of the U.S. Eighth Army following the death of General Walton Walker in an accident. He restored the morale of his command and turned the tide of the Korean War with victories at Chipyong-ni and Wonju, blunting a Chinese offensive. In April 1951, President Harry S. Truman named Ridgway to replace controversial General Douglas MacArthur as commander of all U.S. and United Nations' forces in Korea. He directed a steady counteroffensive that regained much of the territory previously lost to the communists.

Above: General Matthew Ridgway commanded the 82nd Airborne Division and the XVIII Airborne Corps during World War II. He attained the rank of full general (shown here) and went on to command United Nations' forces in the Korean War.

Ridgway went on to succeed General Dwight D. Eisenhower as Supreme Allied Commander in Europe for the newly formed North Atlantic Treaty Organization (NATO). He served a term as Army Chief of Staff and was often at odds with then-President Eisenhower over military policy. Ridgway retired from the Army in 1955 and served as chairman of the Board of Trustees of the Mellon Institute and as a director of Gulf Oil Corporation. He wrote two books, *Soldier: The Memoirs of Matthew B. Ridgway* and *The Korean War*. He died in 1993 at the age of 98.

104 glider men toward Ponte Grande. Only 73 reached the bridge, and most of these were killed or wounded during the successful fight for control of it. The British troopers defused explosives the Italians had set to demolish the bridge and held grimly to the hard-won span. They withstood counterattacks and sporadic fire well into the afternoon, when it appeared inevitable that they would be overrun.

The glider men suffered 605 casualties; among them were 326 missing and presumed to have drowned.

With only 18 men capable of shouldering a rifle and ammunition nearly exhausted, Withers surrendered to an Italian force that was nearly battalion strength. Minutes later, elements of the 5th Division approached, recaptured the bridge, and freed the glider men.

Montgomery flatly stated that the bold action at Ponte Grande saved his ground troops a week of fighting. The price, however, had been high. The glider men suffered 605 casualties; among them were 326 missing and presumed to have drowned. The 1st Airlanding Brigade had suffered 29 percent casualties, while only about five percent of the original force allocated had participated in the capture of Ponte Grande.

Fatal Friendly Fire

During the run-up to Operation Husky, senior Allied commanders developed several contingency plans for the introduction of airborne reinforcements once a beachhead was established. However, one of the primary concerns such an effort presented involved the possibility of friendly fire as transport planes flew over concentrations of warships and supply vessels.

Securing the cooperation of the U.S. Navy was problematic. General Ridgway formally requested the establishment of an air "corridor" through which transport planes could fly without fear of being fired upon by gunners aboard the ships below. At a meeting held three weeks before Operation Husky began, Navy officials refused. Ridgway took his request all the way to Seventh Army Chief of Staff, General Geoffrey Keyes, who related the difficulty to General Patton. Then the situation changed rapidly. Within three days, the flamboyant commander of the Seventh Army had the necessary approval to secure a corridor above the Western Task Force when Patton called for his airborne reinforcements.

By mid-morning on July 9, Operation Husky was well established in southeastern Sicily, and Allied forces were moving inland. Resistance had been substantial at times, and the center of Patton's line had been particularly heavily engaged. After a full day of combat, he decided that the 2,000 airborne reinforcements of the 1st and 2nd Battalions, 504th PIR, along with the 376th Parachute Field Artillery Battalion and the 307th Airborne Engineer Battalion were needed to bolster his offensive capability.

An airborne reinforcement mission was scheduled for the night of July 11. Assembling over the Kuriates Islands and then flying around Malta to the assigned drop zones near an abandoned airfield at Farello, the transports were slated to reach the coast of Sicily above the village of Sampieri, 30 miles (48km) east of Gela, at 10:30 p.m. The last leg of the air route was through a corridor two miles wide and two miles inland (3km by 3km), considered the best path to avoid the convoys and warships below. Once their paratroopers had dropped, the C-47s were to fly another three miles (5km) inland toward the town of Licata at the western edge of the landing beaches, then turn for their bases in North Africa.

Four days ahead of the reinforcement mission, an alert was delivered to the Navy command

and to Army corps and division headquarters for further distribution. On the same day, naval personnel acknowledged receipt of the message through embarkation headquarters in Tunis.

General Ridgway was anxious. On the afternoon of the mission, he flew from North Africa to Sicily, visiting six antiaircraft batteries in their positions near the 1st Infantry Division command post. When Ridgway asked the crews whether they were aware of the directive to hold fire, five of them responded in the affirmative. The sixth had not received notification. The general brought the situation to the attention of officers of the 103rd Coast Artillery Antiaircraft Battalion and was reassured that during a later meeting the pending airborne flyover would be stressed to those present.

The pilots and crews of 144 transports of the 51st Troop Carrier Wing received mission briefings on the afternoon of June 11, and the first planes took off at 7 p.m.

Mistaken Identity

For a while, the flight was uneventful. Then, north of Malta, some of the transports flew above a convoy, and scattered antiaircraft fire arced skyward. No aircraft were hit; however,

Below: The bodies of dead paratroopers of the U.S. 82nd Airborne Division are lined up for identification and temporary burial in Sicily. These casualties may have been the victims of a horrific friendly fire incident that occurred over the Sicilian coastline.

the message was clear. The gunners aboard ships—and probably those manning antiaircraft batteries on shore—were jittery. Axis aircraft had been active over the landing zones, and they had been particularly busy above the Seventh Army invasion beaches throughout July 11.

As the sun came up, a dozen Italian planes attacked along the beaches, compelling vessels to take evasive action and dropping bombs that damaged two ships with near misses. Around 2 p.m., four fighters strafed the beaches at Gela and a single enemy bomber dropped five bombs in the area. At 3:40 p.m., 30 German Junkers Ju-88 bombers pressed home attacks that bracketed the cruiser USS *Boise* and scored a direct hit on the Liberty ship *Robert Rowan*. Loaded with ammunition, the ship erupted like a volcano.

Air Raids

An even larger air raid swept in just before 10 p.m., and the *Boise* was bracketed a second time while nearby destroyers dodged bombs and several ships sustained damage. After an hour the enemy planes departed, leaving the American gunners shaken and on edge as the air transports crossed the Sicilian coastline. Some reports indicate that the landing beaches and ships offshore had endured as many as 23 separate air attacks during the harrowing day.

Five minutes ahead of schedule, the first two flights of the 313th Troop Carrier Group flew over the airfield at Farello and dropped their paratroopers at 10:40 p.m. The next flight had come within sight of Lake Biviero, the final checkpoint on the flight path and well within the supposedly safe corridor, when a single machine gun began to chatter. In a flash, a storm of antiaircraft fire streamed skyward at the slow C-47 formations. The pilots of the 313th tried to stay within the corridor, but the fire was so intense that many of them veered toward the town of Licata and were set upon by the guns of more ships clustered offshore.

Between five and 10 miles (8 and 16km) off the coast, the planes of the 61st Troop Carrier Group were turning into the corridor when their rear squadrons were caught in the contagious swirl of antiaircraft guns unleashing a torrent of steel into the sky. Planes scattered, and pilots attempted to regain formation; however, cohesion was irretrievably lost. Eight C-47s turned back to North Africa with their paratroopers still aboard. Others jettisoned their cargoes where they were. A few sticks of paratroopers were released over the sea.

"It was an uncomfortable feeling knowing that our own troops were throwing everything they had at us," recalled Captain Adam A. Komasa, commander of Headquarters Company, 504th PIR. "Planes dropped out of formation and crashed into the sea. Others, like clumsy whales, wheeled and attempted to get beyond the flak which rose in fountains of fire, lighting the stricken faces of men as they stared through the windows."

As one transport flew over the bow of the troop ship *Susan B. Anthony* and near the attack cargo ship *Procyon*, guns aboard both ships blazed. Whether recognition lights were visible is unknown. The C-47 caught fire and crashed near the stern of the cruiser USS *Philadelphia*.

The plane carrying Colonel Reuben H. Tucker, commander of the 504th PIR, was unable to maintain the proper course and became separated from other aircraft. Flying alone over beaches in the 1st Division sector, it took heavy fire. Tucker ordered the pilot to fly west until a landmark could be identified. When Licata was sighted, the plane turned back toward Gela. Sensing that open air was as safe as remaining aboard the plane, Colonel Tucker ordered his men to jump in the midst of heavy antiaircraft fire. After

Opposite: The Liberty ship *Robert Rowan*, loaded with ammunition, erupts in a terrific explosion after being hit by German dive bombers off the coast of Sicily.

hitting the ground, Tucker hurried toward five nearby tanks that were firing their .50-caliber (12.7mm) machine guns at the planes overhead and convinced them to stop.

Friendly fire raked the transports mercilessly. Some planes reported that they were under attack for 30 miles (48km) after departing the Sicilian coastline. When the ordeal was finally over, 23 C-47s had been shot down and 37 seriously damaged. The 316th Troop Carrier Group, flying last in the long transport line, lost 12 planes and sustained 37 casualties. Six C-47s were shot down before they discharged their paratroopers. Forty-four men died when their planes crashed. Four more were found dead aboard aircraft that returned to their bases in North Africa. Overall casualties topped 400 airborne and troop carrier personnel. One transport managed to stay in the air; it returned to its base in North Africa, where ground crewmen counted 1,000 bullet holes in its wings and fuselage.

Above: Paratroopers of the 82nd Airborne Division advance along a road in Sicily. Following their airdrop, the troopers battled their way toward the city of Palermo. The offensive role of the division in Sicily ended on July 24, after two weeks of fighting.

During the inquiry that followed the tragedy, it was apparent that the beleaguered gunners aboard ships and on shore had been heavily taxed by the Axis air raids earlier on July 11. While some units obviously did not receive word of the air mission, it is likely that many of those that did nevertheless opened fire when the transports appeared overhead. General Eisenhower himself pointed out that the risky flight path, “followed the actual battlefront for

35 miles; and the antiaircraft gunners on ship and shore had been conditioned by two days of air attacks to shoot at sight."

Appalled at the needless loss of life, General Ridgway later remarked that blame was widespread: "The responsibility for loss of life and material resulting from this operation is so divided, so difficult to fix with impartial justice, and of questionable ultimate value to the service because of the acrimonious debates which would follow efforts to hold responsible persons or services to account, that disciplinary action is of doubtful wisdom... The losses are part of the inevitable price of war in human life."

Yet Another Incident

On the evening of July 13, the British forces in the southwest began a concerted effort to reach the town of Catania, and an airborne operation codenamed Fustian was initiated to capture the Primosole Bridge spanning the Simeto River seven miles (11km) south of the objective. Yet again, friendly fire disrupted an airborne operation in an active combat zone. Half the pilots carrying 1,900 men of the British 1st Parachute Brigade encountered heavy antiaircraft fire.

Two transports were shot down, nine turned around and headed back to North Africa, and 87 ran the gauntlet. Of these, only 39 dropped their paras within a mile of the designated drop zones. Four planeloads came down within 10 miles (16km) of the Primosole Bridge, and four more were 20 miles (32km) away, scattered on the slopes of Mount Etna, the famous volcano that dominated the roads north to Messina, the prize of the campaign. Only 200 paras reached the bridge, and their heaviest weapons were three antitank guns. These valiant men managed to seize the span and disable explosives the Italians had set, but their hold on the key bridge was tenuous at best.

Complicating matters, the primary British airdrop was virtually simultaneous with that of the machine-gun battalion of the German 1st Parachute Division, and many of the British paratroopers came down in the midst of the enemy. A heated firefight ensued, but the British held the Primosole Bridge throughout July 14. The advancing 50th Division threatened to outflank the German parachute battalions in the vicinity, compelling them to withdraw, and the infantrymen linked up with the British paratroopers at the southern end of the Primosole Bridge late in the day.

Opportunistic Patton

The reassignment of Highway 124, a key route toward Messina on the left flank of General Montgomery's British Eighth Army, had been originally assigned to General Patton's Seventh Army in its supporting role. When Field Marshal Sir Harold Alexander, commander of the Allied 15th Army Group, redrew the boundaries between the British and American forces and gave the road to Montgomery, Patton was furious. However, in his anger Patton also saw opportunity. His forces had already pushed out to the west in force, and without Highway 124 much of the Seventh Army would essentially be out of a job.

Patton persuaded Alexander to sanction a strong "reconnaissance" to the west; however, Alexander soon had misgivings and ordered Seventh Army to reorient to the north, again to protect the Eighth Army flank. Patton essentially ignored the revised directive and divided his command into two forces: General Omar Bradley's II Corps, and a Provisional Corps under General Keyes, which included the 2nd Armored, 3rd Infantry, and 82nd Airborne Divisions along with elements of the 9th Infantry Division and supporting artillery units.

Patton's eyes were firmly fixed on the port of Palermo, the Sicilian capital and the largest city on the island. In 72 hours, the Provisional Corps raced 100 miles (160km) to the west and captured Palermo. Within 10 days, the Seventh Army was in control of the western half of Sicily, having captured 53,000 Italian prisoners and 400 vehicles with the loss of only 272 casualties.

The thrust to Palermo met stiff resistance in only a few places. Approaching from the south on July 19, Colonel Tucker's 504th PIR was two hours ahead of schedule as it passed through the lines of the 39th Infantry Regiment, crossed the Platani River, and covered 17 miles (27km) in six hours. Tucker brought up 75mm pack howitzers and deployed squads of troopers to dislodge the few pockets of Italian resistance.

By nightfall, the 504th had advanced 25 miles (40km). The most significant engagement of the day occurred at the Verdura River, where an Italian pillbox opened fire on an American halftrack mounting a 75mm gun. With the first unexpected Italian shot, the halftrack backed away and slid into a ditch. Luckily, the vehicle halted with a perfect field of fire for its gun, which promptly opened up on the Italians as troops deployed and began peppering the structure with 37mm and machine-gun fire. Within minutes, 70 Italian soldiers surrendered.

Convinced that Italian resistance was crumbling, Keyes ordered the 82nd Airborne to screen the assembly of the 2nd Armored Division along the Belice River in preparation for a quick armored strike that would take Palermo. In the event, both the 2nd Armored and the 3rd Infantry Divisions entered the city, which surrendered without much of a fight on the evening of July 22.

Subsequently, Keyes ordered Ridgway to capture the town of Trapani at the western tip of Sicily. On the 23rd, Gavin loaded the 505th PIR aboard trucks and headed west with virtually no opposition through a succession of towns and along Highway 113. At Santa Ninfa, the advance resembled a victory parade as civilians threw flowers, fresh fruit, and chocolates to the Americans.

Around 4 p.m. as the 505th PIR reached the outskirts of Trapani, diehard Italian defenders opened fire from a roadblock, and a minefield stalled the advance. While the paratroopers deployed to clear the road, Italian artillery began firing from the surrounding hills. The battle lasted about three hours as the roadblock was subdued and the guns of the 376th Parachute Field Artillery and the 34th Field Artillery Battalion answered the sporadic Italian shelling. The paratroopers infiltrated behind the Italian positions in the hills, and Contrammiraglio Giuseppe Manfredi, commanding the Trapani Naval District, surrendered the city.

While Gavin and the 505th took Trapani, the trucks that had transported them turned back to pick up Tucker's 504th, which was ordered to take the town of Alcamo on the northern coast. With that accomplished, the 504th advanced to Castellammare by the late afternoon of July 24, completing the last offensive action of the 82nd Airborne Division in Sicily.

Sicilian Postscript

In the immediate aftermath of the Sicilian Campaign, which ended in August 1944 with the Seventh Army's capture of Messina and the unfortunate withdrawal of large numbers of German forces to the Italian mainland, the performance of the airborne troops was evaluated. The paratroopers had fought heroically and contributed to the success of Operation Husky, but there were issues.

Navigation beacons and pathfinder activities were in need of improvement. Simple air routes and thorough training in formation flying at night were necessary. Relying on recognition lights, formation flying, safe corridors, and passing the word that planes were coming seemed futile in

Opposite: American soldiers in the Sicilian city of Palermo stand guard amid a pile of discarded weapons and other equipment surrendered by Italian troops.

an effort to avoid horrific friendly-fire incidents. Secretary of War Henry L. Stimson questioned the use of crack troops, who obviously fought like tigers on the ground, in large-scale airborne operations that put them at even greater risk.

General Lesley McNair, commander of U.S. Army Ground Forces, was skeptical as well. He wrote, "After the airborne operations in Africa and Sicily, my staff and I had become convinced of the impracticability of handling large airborne units. I was prepared to recommend to the War Department that airborne divisions be abandoned in our scheme of organization and that the airborne effort be restricted to units of battalion size or smaller."

General Ridgway disagreed and argued forcefully for a major airborne role in Operation Avalanche, the looming invasion of Italy.

Italian Conundrum

The fall of Benito Mussolini's fascist government in Italy took place on July 25, 1943, in the midst of Operation Husky. The new Italian government, led by Marshal Pietro Badoglio, began negotiating with Allied leaders in mid-August, and through a series of meetings eventually offered to surrender and even enter the war against Nazi Germany, its former Axis partner. The Italians agreed to surrender on September 1 and signed a formal armistice two days later. The surrender was to be announced to the world on September 8.

Planning for a parachute drop on the Italian capital, codenamed Giant II, began.

General Eisenhower called the political wrangling "...a series of negotiations, secret communications, clandestine journeys by secret agents, and frequent meetings in hidden places that, if encountered in the fictional world, would have been scorned as incredible melodrama."

In exchange for their cooperation, the Italians required one proviso: that a substantial Allied force race for Rome, the Eternal City, capital of Italy, and a center of inestimable culture, art, and history, to defend it against the vengeful Germans.

Allied planning for the invasion of Italy had begun in earnest in the spring of 1943, and the conquest of Sicily fueled the effort. In Operation Baytown, Montgomery's Eighth Army was to land at Reggio Calabria on the toe of the Italian boot. Operation Slapstick included the landing of the British 1st Airborne Division from cruisers at the port of Taranto. Both of these actions were in southern Italy. Subsequently, a third amphibious operation, Avalanche, was added. Clark's Fifth Army would land at Salerno, 30 miles (48km) southeast of Naples, and move to capture the large port city.

With the addition of Avalanche, the possibility of supporting airborne operations gained momentum. At first, a glider landing that would hold key bridges and prevent the Fifth Army from being flanked by the Germans was considered and then discarded.

A larger operation, Giant I, was soon being formulated. Truly ambitious, Giant I involved inserting two regimental combat teams of the 82nd Airborne Division by glider on the night of September 8, prior to the Salerno landings the following day, with orders to cut the main highway across the Volturno River north of Naples to prevent German counterattacks from reaching the invasion beaches. Giant I was modified several times. The capture of the town of Cancello was an added objective, and the glider regiment of the 82nd Airborne was slated to make an amphibious landing at the mouth of the Volturno, fight overland, and link up with the air-dropped regiments.

Reconnaissance, however, revealed that the shallow waters and sandbars at the mouth of the Volturno made an amphibious operation impossible. Further, the necessity of employing up

to 145 C-47s for the mission—a full 45 percent of all air transport available in the Mediterranean, the lack of fighter aircraft due to obligations to cover the Salerno beaches—and the potential requirement of resupplying the paratroopers fighting 40 miles (64km) inland by air, rendered the mission highly risky.

Eisenhower ordered Giant I scaled back to two battalions that would seize limited objectives around Capua. However, the operation was canceled completely during the first week of September – not because of military concerns, but due to the tantalizing prospect of the Italian surrender offer.

To facilitate the Allied end of the bargain, the swiftest method of delivering a substantial number of troops to the vicinity of Rome was obviously through the air. Hence, planning for a parachute drop on the Italian capital, codenamed Giant II, began.

Above: Among thousands of Italian soldiers who surrendered to the Allies on Sicily during Operation Husky, these men wave white flags and appear to be relieved that their fighting days are over.

Innocuous

Although the Italians suggested five airfields near Rome for Giant II, three of these were deemed unacceptable due to heavy German antiaircraft batteries located nearby. The two acceptable airfields, at Furbara and Cerveteri 25 miles (40km) northwest of Rome, were relatively small and led Ridgway to suggest that a single parachute combat team could realistically be

Above: Troopers of the 82nd Airborne Division proceed along a street in the Italian city of Naples past an idle British Bedford light truck. The retreating Germans left booby traps throughout the city, compelling Allied troops to advance with caution.

inserted. Therefore, the Giant II plan included two battalions of the 504th PIR, elements of its headquarters company, a battery of antiaircraft guns, and other support troops that would be carried to the target airfields in 135 C-47s on the night of September 8.

The success of Giant II and hundreds of men's lives depended on the guarantees of Italian cooperation, and many senior Allied officers were uneasy. Eisenhower took action that would hopefully alleviate much of the anxiety. General Maxwell D. Taylor, the artillery commander of the 82nd Airborne Division and a liaison officer at Allied Force Headquarters, and Colonel William T. Gardiner of the U.S. Army Troop Carrier Command were dispatched by Eisenhower on a dangerous mission to Rome on September 7 to evaluate the risk associated with the planned drop. Taylor was instructed to send a message containing the single word "innocuous" if he judged that the plan should be scrapped.

The American officers reached the shore near Gaeta after being transferred from a British motor torpedo boat to an Italian Navy corvette. Their uniforms were splashed with water and mud to give them the appearance of airmen who had been shot down and rescued. Following a ride in a car and then an ambulance, the Americans reached Rome. They were offered a fine dinner, but became agitated when no high-ranking Italian official appeared to discuss the situation with them.

Eventually, they were brought to Badoglio, who reiterated his pro-Allied stance and his concern that German forces would occupy Rome. Still, given the circumstances, Badoglio sent a message to Eisenhower effectively canceling his earlier commitment for an immediate armistice. Both Taylor and Gardiner believed the "situation invited disaster."

Taylor sent three messages to Allied headquarters, just to make sure that his assessment of the Giant II was understood. The first was received at 8 a.m. on September 8. The third, which came through later that morning, read tersely, "Situation innocuous." Eisenhower had received the first of the communications around noon and ordered a two-hour postponement of Giant II.

Eisenhower ignored Badoglio and announced the Italian surrender on September 8, prior to the Salerno landings. Badoglio had no choice but to follow suit and made his announcement of the surrender just after 5 p.m. Badoglio's proclamation was supposed to signal the beginning of Giant II, and the airborne commanders proceeded.

When word of Eisenhower's postponement finally reached the airfields on Sicily, some C-47s were loaded and taxiing toward takeoff, and 62 transports were actually circling the airfield at Licata waiting to form up for the run to Rome. Had the message been received an hour later, it is doubtful that the planes could have been recalled.

By September 9, it had become apparent that the Badoglio government had no control over the situation in Rome. Eisenhower canceled Operation Giant II, averting a probable disaster.

Beachhead Reinforcement

Due to its expected participation in the subsequently aborted Giant II, the 82nd Airborne was unavailable to immediately participate in the Salerno landings once the Rome operation was canceled. Two days after the Fifth Army hit the beaches at Salerno, control of the 82nd Airborne reverted to General Clark.

Several options, including an amphibious deployment and the resurrection of a modified Giant I airdrop were considered, but the exigencies of war demanded a different role for the paratroopers. On September 13, a ferocious

Right: Prior to an airborne operation to reinforce the beachhead on the Italian mainland at Salerno, paratroopers of the 82nd Airborne Division check their gear. The action at Salerno was heavy, and for a time the issue was in doubt along the beachhead.

German counterattack threatened the very existence of the Salerno beachhead as tanks drove nearly to the Italian coastline at the confluence of the Sele and Calore rivers, partially driving a wedge between the British X Corps and the American VI Corps.

Massed American artillery, along with a collection of clerks, cooks, bandsmen, and others pressed into service as infantry to shore up the Fifth Army center, finally stopped the enemy advance. The situation remained serious. At the southern end of the beachhead only a handful of 45th Division troops and engineers held the front line. Reinforcements were desperately needed, and the airborne troops, who would have to be parachuted into the beachhead due to a lack of suitable airfields, constituted a rapid deployment force that could do the job.

"I want you to accept this letter as an order," Clark wrote to Ridgway, "I realize the time normally needed to prepare for a drop, but I want you to make a drop within our lines on the beachhead, and I want you to make it tonight. This is a must."

Using the logistical support that had been in place for an anticipated mission to Capua, the airborne troops boarded C-47s of the 313th, 314th, and 61st Troop Carrier Groups. There was little time to establish a safe flight corridor that would reduce the potential of another friendly fire incident, so the pilots were instructed to fly along the coast of Italy to a drop zone 1,200 yards long by 800 yards (1,100 by 730m) wide on the Sele Plain about five miles (8km) north of the town of Agropoli between the key coastal highway and the Tyrrhenian Sea. Radar beacons and special lights deployed by pathfinders were used to guide the aircraft to the drop zones along with five-gallon (20-liter) cans full of gasoline-soaked sand that were set alight by combat engineers already on the ground.

Around 11:30 p.m., the first troopers of Colonel Tucker's 504th PIR jumped from 35 planes at 800 feet (240m). Most of these came down within 200 yards (180m) of the drop zone, and all were within a mile (1.6km) of it. Some transports from a second flight experienced mechanical problems, delaying their arrival over the drop zone for some time. These pilots experienced some navigational difficulties, and one company of paratroopers came to earth about 10 miles (16km) off target.

Nevertheless, about 1,300 airborne troops had parachuted into the beachhead from 85 transports within 15 hours of Clark's urgent request for

reinforcements. At 3 a.m. on September 14, Tucker advised VI Corps headquarters that his two battalions were aboard trucks and heading to the front, where they reinforced the 36th Division near Monte Soprano.

The success of the first Sele airdrop ensured that a follow-up operation would take place there along with a contemplated mission to drop the 2nd Battalion, 509th PIR, at Avellino to bolster the X Corps. On the night of September 14, the 316th Troop Carrier Group loaded 2,100 troopers of the 505th PIR. These were successfully dropped inside the beachhead perimeter near Paestum and trucked to the front line around Agropoli, near the positions the 504th had occupied hours earlier.

Although there had been some delays, 125 of an original complement of 130 C-47s completed the second Sele mission, and 123 of these dropped

Below: General Mark Clark, commander of the Allied Fifth Army that executed the landings at Salerno on the Italian mainland, congratulates American troops following their heroic battle against strong German resistance.

Above: Paratroopers of the 505th Parachute Infantry Regiment, 82nd Airborne Division, trudge along a street in Naples after pushing northward from Salerno. By the time this photo was taken in the autumn of 1943, the 505th was a veteran outfit.

1,900 troopers within a mile and one-half (2.5km) of the drop zone. One observer remarked that the mission was "without a doubt the most successful jump the 505th CT has ever made."

The Avellino mission was plagued with difficulties. Clark had originally requested that the 2nd Battalion, 509th PIR, under Lieutenant Colonel Doyle R. Yardley, and 40 combat engineers jump at Avellino, 20 miles (32km) north of Salerno, on September 12 to delay German reinforcements, disrupt communications, and create general chaos for five days before withdrawing into the expanding Fifth Army perimeter.

The 64th Troop Carrier Group was to drop the 600 paratroopers about three miles (5km) from Avellino, and despite the delay there was little time for pilot briefings. Navigational errors, the failure of radar beacons, and the high altitude of 2,000 feet (600m) from which the jump was executed contributed to a wide dispersal of the troopers, some coming to earth from eight to 25 miles (13–40km) distant from their drop zone. Most of the antitank weapons and other equipment were lost in the jump. Bands of up to 25 paratroopers did their best to evade capture and eventually found their way to safety.

For several days, there was no contact with Yardley's command, and the troopers mounted small-scale raids as they were able. Eventually about 400 men of the 509th filtered back to Allied lines. Two planeloads of paratroopers were unaccounted for a month after the operation. By October a more complete accounting of the Avellino mission was compiled, and 118 men—nearly 20 percent of the force that had made the jump—were listed as killed in action, wounded, or missing.

The missions at Sele and Avellino were the last large-scale Allied airborne operations undertaken in the Mediterranean Theater until the invasion of southern France in the summer of 1944. Meanwhile, several small-scale missions were considered as the grinding Italian campaign progressed. These were never implemented.

The success of the Sele missions ensured that airborne operations would be considered during the planning for Operation Overlord, the Allied invasion of Western Europe scheduled for the spring of 1944. The 82nd Airborne Division was withdrawn to train for the upcoming assault on Hitler's Fortress Europe.

The M1 Carbine

Above: The M1 carbine was a versatile weapon issued to the airborne troops of the U.S. Army in great numbers due to its optimal length and weight.

Manufactured in great numbers during World War II, the M1 carbine was designed by a team of Winchester engineers during a three-year period, entered into a series of U.S. Army trials, and chosen from among 11 models following competition in the spring and fall of 1941. As the threat of war loomed, it became apparent that rear echelon troops and those in specialized roles would require a heavier weapon than the standard-issue pistols then in service. Officers, headquarters personnel, armored troops, and airborne units were eventually issued substantial numbers of the M1 carbine in addition to the famed M1 Garand rifle.

Weighing only 5.8 pounds (2.6kg) fully loaded, the carbine was considerably lighter than the Garand or the Thompson submachine gun. At 35.6 inches (900mm), it was approximately eight inches (20cm) shorter than the Garand. These two critical factors made the M1 carbine ideal for airborne troops, who hit the ground with force during parachute jumps and were sometimes injured by the stocks of the larger rifle. Like the Garand, the carbine was a semiautomatic, gas-operated, rotating-bolt rifle. From there, however, the similarity abruptly ended. While the Garand fired the .30.06-caliber Springfield round, the carbine fired a specifically designed .30-caliber (7.62mm) carbine cartridge from a detachable box magazine of 15 or 30 rounds. Contrary to popular belief, the M1 carbine was not simply a smaller version of the Garand. The two rifles shared only one common part, a buttplate screw.

Although it was not originally intended as a frontline weapon and was both praised and criticized for its perceived knockdown capability, the M1 carbine was often carried in combat areas. Its light weight and utilitarian length were praised by soldiers who were frequently on the move, such as airborne troops. A later variant, the selective-fire or fully automatic M2 carbine, was capable of firing up to 900 rounds per minute. The original M1 carbine remained in service with the U.S. military into the 1970s.

CHAPTER 4

D-DAY AND NORMANDY

From the mouth of the River Orne in the east to the doorstep of the Cotentin Peninsula, across more than 50 miles (80km) of the coastline of French Normandy and for several miles inland, the reports were confused and scattered.

German officers tried to make sense of what was happening, but to those in the midst of the crackling rifle fire and billowing parachutes of Allied airborne troops, the implications were clear: A major operation was underway.

At approximately 2 a.m. on June 6, 1944, six American C-47 transport planes flew low over the village of St. Moxel near the headquarters of the German 709th Infantry Division. Moments later, the sentries were engaged in a skirmish with paratroopers of the U.S. 101st Airborne Division. After two years of exhaustive planning and a 24-hour postponement due to bad weather, the liberation of Nazi-occupied Europe had begun.

Operation Overlord, the grand Allied plan to land more than 150,000 troops on five invasion beaches, codenamed Gold, Juno, Sword, Utah, and Omaha, was to be preceded by airborne operations involving three divisions—the American 101st and 82nd Airborne, and the British 6th Airborne—that would be inserted by glider or parachute to seize key objectives in support of the amphibious landings. While the glider-borne British troops secured the bridges over the Caen Canal and the Orne to anchor the eastern flank of the invasion beaches, the Americans were to jump near the western edge of the offensive.

Each of the American airborne divisions had been strengthened prior to Operation Neptune, the assault phase of Overlord. The 101st had come to England in the fall of 1943 with a single parachute regiment, the 502nd. In the following weeks, it was augmented with the 501st and the 506th, while it retained the 327th Glider Infantry Regiment. The 82nd had been withdrawn from Italy without one of its parachute regiments, the 504th, which remained in combat at Anzio, and did not return to England until May 1944.

Opposite: Paratroopers of the U.S. 101st Airborne Division pose with a trophy of war, a Nazi flag captured during recent combat. The 101st experienced its baptism of fire in Normandy.

The 504th would not be ready to take part in the Normandy invasion; however, the 82nd had received the 507th and 508th Parachute Infantry Regiment (PIR) in January to join the combat veterans of the 505th and the 325th Glider Infantry.

The westernmost landing beach, Utah, was to be assaulted by the U.S. 4th Infantry Division, which would then breach the German defenses on the beach itself, move inland, and protect the beachhead against the counterattacks that were sure to come. The 101st and 82nd Airborne Divisions were responsible for securing the western flank of the Allied lodgment. General Matthew Ridgway retained command of the 82nd, while General Maxwell Taylor had been placed in command of the 101st after General William C. Lee was incapacitated by a heart attack. While the 82nd was to capture the village of Ste. Mere-Eglise and hold bridges across the Merderet River, the 101st would facilitate the advance of the 4th Division.

Securing the Causeways

Immediately behind Utah Beach stretched a flooded, marshy plain with standing water more than three feet (90cm) deep in some places. Beyond the plain, the valleys of the Douve River and its tributary, the Merderet, had been flooded both by the Germans and by the natural drainage of the Cotentin Peninsula. A few feet above the flooded plain rose four narrow roads, or causeways. Control of the exits from these causeways was critical to the consolidation of the Utah beachhead and the conduct of future offensive operations, particularly against the major port of Cherbourg, which the Allies needed for resupply efforts in the anticipated offensive against Fortress Europe.

The 502nd and 506th PIR, with one battalion detached, were tasked with securing the causeways. The 502nd was to take the northernmost exits, Nos. 3 and 4, while the 506th was assigned the southern pair, Nos. 1 and 2. The 502nd and the 377th Parachute Field Artillery Battalion were to drop near the town of St. Martin-de-Varreville and destroy a battery of Soviet-made 122mm guns that were sighted toward Utah Beach. The 1st and 2nd Battalions of the 506th and the 3rd Battalion, 501st, were to drop between Ste. Marie-du-Mont and Hiesville, then advance to the area from Pouppeville to Audouville-la-Hubert.

The 1st and 2nd Battalions, 501st, were to capture the La Barquette lock on the Douve just outside the town of Carentan and blow up a

railroad bridge along with a pair of bridges on the road from St. Côme-du-Mont to Carentan. Two wooden bridges across the Douve between Carentan and the English Channel were to be captured by the 3rd Battalion, 506th, and either held or demolished if the Germans approached in force. Eventually, the 101st would link up with the advancing 4th Division, part of General J. Lawton Collins' VII Corps, and effect a junction with the V Corps, under General Leonard Gerow, advancing from Omaha Beach to the east.

Jumping astride the Merderet, the 82nd Airborne Division was to secure the area between the Merderet and the English Channel and from the Douve northward to Ste. Mere-Eglise. The 505th PIR was to capture Ste. Mere-Eglise and establish crossings of the Merderet at Chef-du-Pont and La Fiere, then maintain a defensive line from Neuville-au-Plain northward to Beuzeville-au-Plain, where it would link up with the 502nd PIR, 101st. The 507th and 508th PIR were to

Above: Pathfinders of the 3rd Battalion, 508th Parachute Infantry Regiment, pose beside a C-47 transport plane. The pathfinder job was extremely hazardous, marking drop zones for waves of paratroopers to come.

jump west of the Merderet and support the 505th in the bridgeheads across the river while preparing to fight their way westward at the appointed time. Their line was to extend three miles (5km) west and encompass a crossroads near Pont l'Abbé, arcing northward through the town of Beauvais. Defending the line at the Douve, the 507th was to blow up bridges at Pont l'Abbé and Beuzeville-la-Bastille.

To deliver the paratroopers to Normandy, more than 900 transport aircraft and 500 gliders were assembled under the auspices of the IX Troop Carrier Command, formed in October 1943. Brigadier General Paul T. Williams, who had led the transport effort in the Mediterranean, took command in February 1944. On D-Day and D+1, a total of 4,000 glider troops would be delivered to Normandy, carrying combat reinforcements, jeeps and artillery, medical, signal, and other support units. The total number of American airborne troops committed to the invasion of Normandy exceeded 13,000. Some of these were allotted to the seaborne landings and were to come ashore with the 4th Division.

Preparation

The marshaling and training of the Allied forces that were to strike Hitler's Fortress Europe on D-Day were collectively a massive undertaking. Airborne exercises took place throughout the winter and spring of 1943–44, including night jumps, since the operation was to take place in darkness roughly five hours ahead of the scheduled amphibious landings in Normandy. Exercise Eagle, conducted on May 11–12, was intended as a dress rehearsal for the bulk of the troop carrier groups and both airborne divisions. The results of Eagle and follow-on exercises that extended to the end of the month were encouraging, although a number of the troop carrier pilots had never flown combat missions or had limited experience.

Right: This trooper of the 101st Airborne Division is depicted in full combat gear, ready to board, stand up, hook up, and jump. Note the folding metal stock of his M1 carbine rifle.

The lessons gleaned in the Mediterranean shaped the flight paths of the troop carrier serials to avoid German antiaircraft fire and minimize the possibility of potential friendly fire incidents. The preliminary flight plan was approved in mid-April; however, intelligence reports necessitated significant changes. The primary German field opposition to the American airborne assault was expected to come from the 709th Infantry Division, the 91st Airlanding Division, the 1057th Grenadier Division, and the 6th Parachute Regiment. At the end of May, elements of the 91st Airlanding Division were detected perilously close to the drop zones of both the 101st and 82nd Divisions. The 82nd drop zones were pulled eastward, and Ste. Mere-Eglise, originally an objective assigned to the 101st, was switched to the 82nd.

The changes in drop zones required alterations to the flight

Devils in Baggy Pants

When the 82nd Airborne Division was withdrawn from the Mediterranean Theater, the 504th Parachute Infantry Regiment remained behind. Collectively, the 504th PIR, the 376th Parachute Field Artillery Battalion, and Company C, 307th Parachute Engineers were designated the 504th Parachute Combat Team.

Since the landings at Salerno, the paratroopers of the 504th PIR had fought as infantry during the rugged, costly advance of the Allied Fifth Army toward Rome. On January 4, 1944, the 504th was pulled from the front line to prepare for Operation Shingle, an amphibious operation that would land Allied troops at Anzio, 35 miles (56km) south of Rome, to outflank the stubborn German defenses at the Gustav Line further south.

Although the plan for the Anzio landings was risky, the logic appeared sound. Allied troops had made little headway against the Gustav Line, a string of fortifications in the mountains of the Italian boot that stretched from the Tyrrhenian Sea in the west to the Adriatic in the east. Stout enemy defenses at the town of Cassino had stymied the advance of the Fifth Army.

Originally, the 504th PIR had been scheduled to parachute into the Anzio area near Aprilia and capture the crossroads at Campoleone on January 22; however, probably influenced by the losses during the Sicily and Salerno drops, Operation Shingle planners shelved the idea. The 504th landed at Anzio from the sea, capturing the town of Borgo Piave on the 24th before German artillery and tanks forced them to withdraw. The regiment then held defensive positions along the Mussolini Canal until it was relieved on January 28.

Below: A German general referred to the 504th Parachute Infantry Regiment as "Devils in Baggy Pants," and the name stuck. The 504th later embraced the moniker with its regimental patch.

Following the pullout, the 3rd Battalion, 504th, was assigned to the 1st Armored Division and became the first U.S. airborne unit to receive the Presidential Unit Citation for its heroic stand against a German counterattack. Rather than a lightning strike, the Anzio operation devolved into a stalemate that was only broken months later in an all-out offensive known as Operation Diadem. The 3rd Battalion eventually rejoined its parent regiment, and the troopers continued to harass the enemy. One German general ruefully referred to the men of the 504th as "Devils in Baggy Pants," a nickname that has remained with the unit.

In March 1944, the 504th PIR was withdrawn from the Mediterranean, and on April 22 the troopship carrying the men arrived in Liverpool. The 82nd Airborne Division band was there to greet its returning battalion with martial tunes. While the anxious men of the 504th believed that they would rejoin the 82nd Airborne for the coming invasion of Western Europe, replacements were scarce and training time was short. A small number of 504th men were reassigned and took part in Operation Overlord as pathfinders.

plans. From various airfields around southern England, the first transports would rise into the night sky shortly after midnight on June 5. Flying a generally southern course, they were to proceed to a point over the open sea, execute a 90-degree left turn, and then fly 54 miles (87km) while passing between the Channel Islands of Alderney and Guernsey. Along the west coast of the Cotentin Peninsula at the Initial Point, codenamed Peoria, the troop carriers with the 82nd aboard would proceed straight to their drop zones 11 miles (18km) inland just north of the village of La Haye. The C-47s carrying the 101st were to make a slight left turn at Peoria and reach the drop zones 25 miles (40km) away.

Along the way, the transport planes would be aided by navigational beacons and the Rebecca-Eureka transponding radar system. Pathfinders would go in first and illuminate the drop zones. Once their drops were completed, the empty aircraft were instructed to turn and follow a reciprocal course back to their bases in England.

Commander-in-Chief

Senior Allied commanders acknowledged that the entire invasion plan was incredibly risky. At worst, failure meant losing the war. At best, it meant months—possibly years—of recovery in order to try again. The airborne phase was particularly worrisome. General Dwight D. Eisenhower, senior commander at SHAEF (Supreme Headquarters Allied Expeditionary Force), shouldered the ultimate responsibility for the success or failure of Operation Overlord.

Eisenhower accepted his role and wrote a brief statement that, in the event of the unthinkable, was to be released to the media. It concluded with the frank statement, "If any blame or fault attaches to the attempt it is mine alone."

Amid the ongoing risk assessment, the airborne phase of Overlord came under increasing scrutiny. Air Chief Marshal Sir Trafford Leigh-Mallory, commander of the Allied Expeditionary Air Force for the invasion, was pessimistic about its chances for success. Casualties were expected to run high: Some estimates concluded that half the planes carrying American paratroopers and 70 percent of the gliders would be shot down by German antiaircraft fire. Leigh-Mallory urged in writing that the American airborne plan should be scrapped.

Eisenhower weighed his options and decided that the effort should proceed; the airborne decision was just one of many that he wrestled with, taking advice from other members of the Combined Chiefs of Staff right up to the scheduled hour of departure.

When the worst weather in the English Channel in 50 years threatened to disrupt Operation Overlord, Eisenhower ordered a postponement from June 5 to the following day. According to a team of meteorologists headed by Group Captain James Martin Stagg, a narrow window of opportunity existed on June 6. The next available date with appropriate atmospheric conditions was two weeks later, June 19, and recalling the warships and vessels already loaded with troops while maintaining secrecy seemed impossible.

During a meeting at Southwick House just north of Portsmouth, England, in the early morning hours of June 5, Eisenhower asked the opinion of each of his lieutenants as to whether the invasion should proceed. When the last had expressed his thoughts, the commander-in-chief declared, "Okay, we'll go!"

Eisenhower cared deeply about the men he was sending into battle and knew that many of them would be killed or wounded. He initially intended to visit units of the 82nd Airborne on the eve of D-Day, but Generals Ridgway and

Opposite: Some of them sporting Mohawk cuts, paratroopers have shaved their heads in preparation for the parachute drop into Normandy on D-Day, June 6, 1944. Some American troopers also daubed their faces with war paint prior to takeoff.

HULL

Above: A first sergeant and a medical corpsman are among this group of paratroopers receiving last minute instructions on the ground prior to the airborne phase of Operation Overlord. Some of these troopers have camouflaged their helmets with vegetation.

Gavin asked him to stay away, saying their troops would be distracted. Instead, the commander-in-chief traveled from SHAEF headquarters to Newbury and visited with troopers of the 502nd PIR at Greenham Common Airfield. Laughing and joking with the paratroopers, he asked one of them where he was from. The trooper replied, "Michigan." Eisenhower beamed and replied, "Oh yes! Michigan—great fishing there—been there several times and like it."

Captain Harry Butcher, Eisenhower's naval liaison officer and a close friend, remembered, "We saw hundreds of paratroopers with blackened and grotesque faces, packing up for the big hop and jump. Ike wandered through them, stepping over packs, guns, and a variety of equipment such as only paratroop people can devise, chinning with this and that one. All were put at ease. He was promised a job after the war by a Texan who said he roped, not dallied, his cows, and at least there was enough to eat in the work."

When Eisenhower wrote his memoir of the war, *Crusade In Europe*, he recalled the evening. "I found the men in fine fettle, many of them joshingly admonishing me that I had no cause for worry, since the 101st was on the job, and everything would be taken care of in fine shape. I stayed with them until the last of them were in the air, somewhere about midnight. After a two hour trip back to my own camp, I had only a short time to wait until the first news should come in."

The Screaming Eagles, full of confidence, had trained for 22 months in anticipation of the moment. Their baptism of fire was at hand.

Airborne Insertion

The airlift missions for the 101st and 82nd Divisions were codenamed Albany and Boston respectively and included the 432 planes carrying the 101st and the 369 transporting the 82nd. The planes were further divided into serials of primarily 36 or 45 planes. Formations remained tight as the aircraft made landfall. However, cloud cover, strong winds, and increasingly heavy flak caused them to loosen substantially.

While some troop carrier groups placed the majority of their sticks on or near the drop zones, others were widely dispersed. The second flight in the second serial of the 436th Group, for example, dropped elements of the 377th Parachute Field Artillery five to seven miles (8–11km) northwest of their assigned drop zone. Among the planes carrying 82nd Airborne troopers, 118 sticks were intended for Drop Zone O. Of these, 31 came down within or close to the zone, while 29 more landed within a mile (1.6km), 20 within two miles (3km), 17 approximately five miles (8km) distant, three at least 14 miles (22km) to the north, and some were missing. Equipment was lost or damaged, some bundles sinking to the bottom of the flooded marshes.

One entire stick of paratroopers from Company A, 502nd PIR, was dropped into the English Channel and drowned. Others actually came down on Utah Beach or in the surf, shedding heavy equipment packs and swimming or wading to the shore. Some troopers came down in flooded areas and struggled with parachutes and gear in water over their heads.

Father Francis Sampson, regimental chaplain of the 501st PIR, came to earth in deep water and cut his equipment away before his parachute dragged him to a shallow spot. Ten minutes later, he swam back to his original drop point and made several dives to locate his Communion set. Radioman Hugh Pritchard came down with 140 pounds (63kg) of equipment and his radio in a leg bag. He went straight to the bottom of a marsh and was then dragged some distance by his billowing parachute. Only the collapse of the parachute saved him from drowning.

Fifty-one gliders assigned to the 101st were to land in darkness on the morning of D-Day,

Right: Their faces blackened for the coming jump into Normandy, paratroopers of the 101st Airborne Division gather around General Dwight D. Eisenhower, the Supreme Allied commander in Europe. Eisenhower feared that the airborne troops would sustain high casualties and wanted to wish them well prior to departure.

and Brigadier General Don F. Pratt, assistant commander of the division, was killed when his glider crashed.

Troopers of the 101st groped in the darkness individually or in small groups, click-clacking dimestore "cricket" toys that were distributed to the men for recognition purposes. The 82nd had declined to use the crickets and instead relied on the recognition sign "Flash," and the appropriate response, "Thunder."

General Taylor searched for half an hour before finding any of his fellow paratroopers. He stumbled across a lone private, and the two embraced with relief. Riding in with the 505th PIR, General Ridgway was making his fifth parachute jump, actually qualifying for his silver wings. General Gavin, accompanying the 508th PIR, came down in an apple orchard about two miles (3km) from his drop zone, with no idea where he was. It took him an hour to become oriented.

Screaming Eagles on D-Day

The commander of the 502nd PIR, Lieutenant Colonel Robert G. Cole, landed east of Ste. Mere-Eglise in an area assigned to the 82nd. After setting off in the wrong direction, Cole reached a

Below: A paratrooper of the 101st Airborne Division, the "Screaming Eagles," takes one last glance over his shoulder during boarding for the parachute drop into Normandy. Although they were scattered across the Normandy countryside, the 101st and 82nd Airborne Divisions performed admirably in the early hours of D-Day.

farmhouse on the edge of Ste. Mere-Eglise, where he was informed of his error. He turned around and headed toward his objective, the battery of six 122mm Soviet-made guns at St. Martin-de-Varreville. Along the way, he contacted individual troopers and groups of wandering men. With about 75 troopers, Cole ran into a convoy of German vehicles; 10 enemy soldiers were killed during the ensuing firefight.

When Cole's ad hoc command reached the supposed location of the enemy guns, he found that they had been removed. Preinvasion air attacks had damaged their fire-control equipment. Moving on to Causeway No. 3, Cole found the exit undefended and occupied the position without incident at around 7:30 a.m.

About two hours later, German troops were observed retreating from Utah Beach. Cole's troops lay in wait and gunned down as many as 75 Germans, with only one casualty. By 1 p.m., leading elements of the 8th Infantry Regiment, 4th Division, had reached Causeway No. 3 and linked up with the paratroopers.

Lieutenant Colonel Patrick J. Cassidy, commanding the 1st Battalion, 502nd, hit the ground on target near the village of St. Germain-de-Varreville. With a few men, he diverted from his assigned D-Day mission temporarily, advancing toward a group of stone buildings and a crossroads west of St. Martin. Reconnoitering revealed that the exits from Causeways 3 and 4 were clear. While he was unsure of what was happening to the west, he ordered 45 men to establish a defensive line at Foucarville to the north and took 15 men forward to clean out the stone buildings, labeled WXYZ on his map, which supposedly housed the German gun crews that manned the 122mm guns that Cole had already discovered were removed.

In the next few hours, one of the most extraordinary feats of individual arms in World War II took place. As they approached assault positions, Cassidy ordered Staff Sergeant Harrison Summers to take a squad and clear the buildings. To Summers, it was apparent that the other men, some of whom were not from the 1st Battalion, were reluctant to follow his order to move out.

Summers dashed forward alone, kicked open the door of the closest building, and shot dead four Germans with his Thompson submachine gun. He repeated the move at the second building, spraying the interior with bullets and killing six more Germans as the survivors fled through a back door. Somewhere along the way, Private William Burt joined in, firing a light machine gun in support. A young officer of the 82nd Airborne stepped up to assist, but was killed seconds later. Another officer was hit and fell. Then, Private John Camien came forward with his M1 carbine and the other squad members began firing from a ditch running parallel to the dirt road down which the sergeant had dashed.

Cole's troops lay in wait and gunned down as many as 75 Germans, with only one casualty.

Wounded in the thigh, Summers remained in the lead, and the building-to-building fight continued for five hours. The last building was set on fire with Bazooka rounds and tracer bullets. Summers barged in and found 15 German soldiers eating breakfast. His Tommy gun erupted, killing the startled men as they tried to get up from the table. Eighty German soldiers ran out into the open, and at least 50 of them were shot. Observers estimated that Summers was responsible for cutting down at least 36 German soldiers and the subsequent capture of many more. A total of 150 enemy troops were killed or taken prisoner at WXYZ.

When another soldier asked how Summers was feeling, the exhausted sergeant replied, "Not very good. It was all kind of crazy. I'm sure I'd

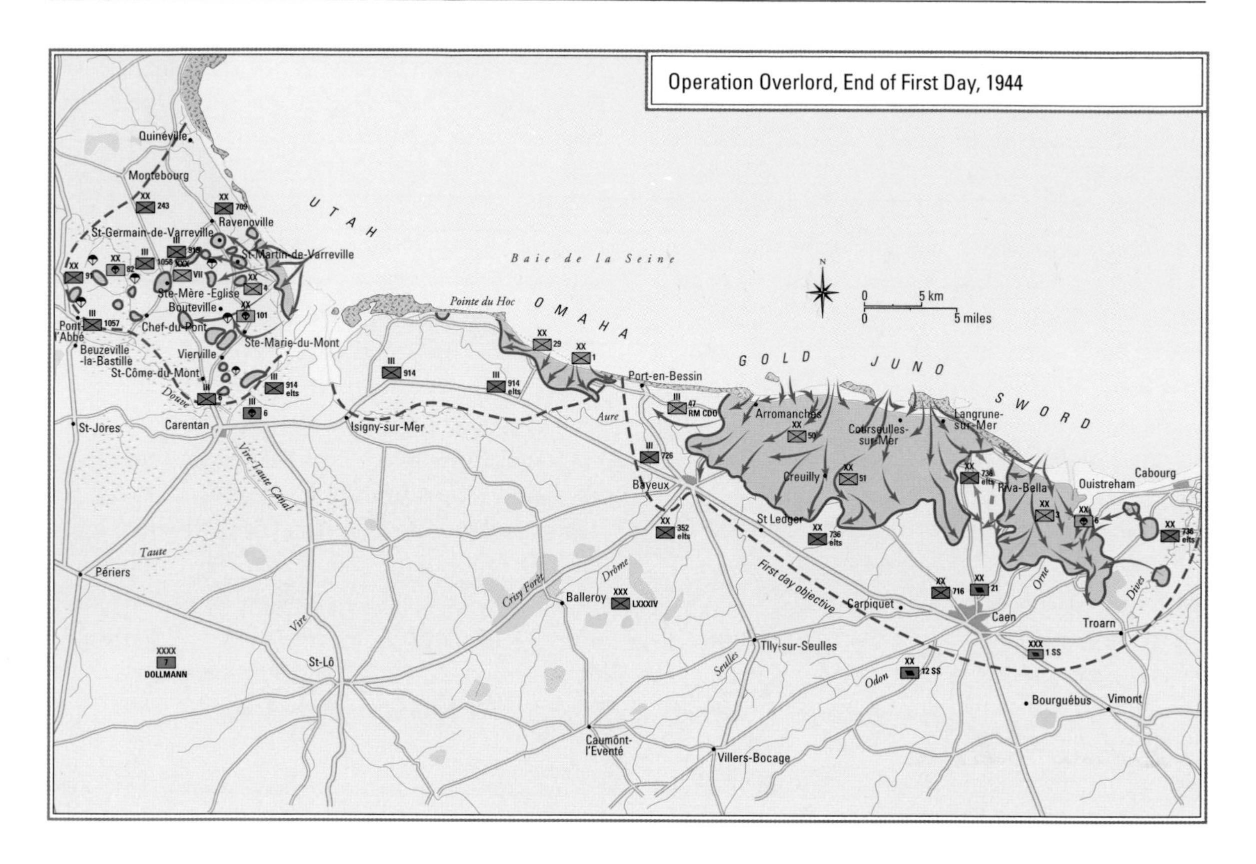

Above: Operation Overlord, the invasion of Normandy by Allied forces on June 6, 1944, included landing more than 130,000 men by sea and a further 24,000 by air.

never do anything like that again." Summers was recommended for the Medal of Honor, but received the Distinguished Service Cross for his heroism.

The 2nd Battalion, 506th PIR, under Lieutenant Colonel Robert L. Strayer, assembled and headed for Causeway No. 2 near Houdienville, arriving after 4th Division troops advancing from Utah Beach had already crossed.

Amid the confusion, dispersed groups of 101st troopers organized three separate efforts to capture Causeway No. 1 near Pouppeville. Although Strayer's advance was stalled in the face of stiffening German resistance, the regimental commander of the 506th PIR, Colonel Robert F. Sink, sent Lieutenant Colonel William L. Turner and 50 men of his 1st Battalion toward the exit. Meanwhile, General Taylor and Lieutenant Colonel Julian Ewell advanced with about 40 men on Pouppeville from the regimental command post at Hiesville, which was established in the correct location, with the 3rd Battalion, 501st.

Ewell's men were the first Americans to reach Causeway No. 1. They ran into about 70 defenders from the 1058th Regiment, 91st Airlanding Division, and took 18 casualties in the assault that secured the exit by noon. Before making contact with the 4th Infantry Division, the 3rd Battalion had killed or wounded 25 Germans and captured 38 prisoners.

As the area around the causeways was being cleared, Colonel Howard Johnson, commander of the 501st PIR, led 150 paratroopers of his own regiment and some joiners from the 506th in a rush to take the La Barquette lock. They brushed aside light resistance and took the lock intact, while combining with 50 other troopers under the command of Major Richard Allen, a regimental staff officer. Strong German units barred any further advance toward the Douve above Carentan on D-Day, and soon the Americans were fending off serious counterattacks. At times, the action around the La Barquette lock became so hot that the paratroopers referred to the position as "Hell's Corner."

While Colonel Johnson tried vainly to continue westward, the 2nd Battalion, 501st, led by Lieutenant Colonel Robert A. Ballard, approached its assigned objective, the Douve River bridges. German forces clustered around the village of Les Droueries put up fierce resistance. When Johnson sent orders to move toward La Barquette, Ballard was unable to completely disengage. His command spent the night of June 6 in sporadic firefights with probing German patrols. Actually, a battalion of the 91st Airlanding Division occupied St. Come-du-Mont, while the crack 6th Fallschirmjäger Parachute Regiment were firmly in control of Carentan and the rail and road bridges between the towns.

Johnson did what he could to consolidate his hold at La Barquette, pushing his perimeter southward and maintaining contact with the 3rd Battalion, 506th, on his left. Still, his hold on the lock was tenuous, with troop strength amounting

Below: American paratroopers secure an area in the village of St. Marcouf, France, during the early phase of the Normandy offensive. Nearby, a German shore battery threatened Utah Beach and sank an American destroyer. The battery was abandoned by the Germans on June 11.

only to about three companies rather than the planned full regiment. Had the Germans pursued a vigorous counterattack, they might well have retaken La Barquette, but no substantial offensive effort materialized in the area.

One of the key airborne contributions to the rapid advance of the 4th Infantry Division from Utah Beach on D-Day was made by a handful of troopers from Company E, 2nd Battalion, 506th PIR. This was immortalized in Stephen Ambrose's book *Band of Brothers*, later made into a popular Home Box Office television miniseries.

First Lieutenant Thomas Meehan III, commander of Company E, flew into Normandy with 16 members of the company headquarters section aboard a C-47 of the 439th Troop Carrier Group's 12th serial. Heading for Drop Zone C west of Ste. Marie-du-Mont, the plane was hit by German antiaircraft fire and crashed in flames, killing everyone aboard.

Command passed to First Lieutenant Richard Winters, who had lost his rifle and virtually all his equipment during the airdrop. Nevertheless, Winters assembled a cluster of paratroopers and reached battalion headquarters at Le Grand Chemin. The sound of heavy guns could be heard nearby, and Winters was ordered to silence a battery of what were believed to be 88mm cannon shelling the troops coming ashore at Utah Beach. In fact, the Germans had placed four 105mm guns with lines of fire directly down Causeway No. 2 three miles (5km) southwest of the beach at Brecourt Manor, a farmstead dominated by a large stone house.

Lieutenant Winters gathered a dozen men and set off around 8:30 a.m. Although these 101st

Below: Paratroopers of Company E, 506th Parachute Infantry Regiment, 101st Airborne Division, the famed "Band of Brothers," pause in a French village.

The Filthy Thirteen

"We weren't murderers or anything. We just didn't do everything we were supposed to do in some ways and did a whole lot more than they wanted us to do in other ways. We were always in trouble," explained Jack Agnew, a veteran of the 1st Demolition Section, Regimental Headquarters Company, 506th Parachute Infantry Regiment, 101st Airborne Division—known to history as the "Filthy Thirteen."

Twenty years after the end of World War II, stories of the Filthy Thirteen inspired author E.M. Nathanson to write the book *The Dirty Dozen*, loosely based on their wartime exploits. In 1967, a follow-up feature film, including an all-star cast, became a box-office smash.

The legend of the Filthy Thirteen grew from a combination of combat heroics, misadventures, and embellishment. Trained in the use of explosives, the Filthy Thirteen parachuted into Normandy on D-Day, June 6, 1944, tasked with securing bridges across the Douve River and destroying them if necessary. The men sported Mohawk haircuts and painted their faces with "war paint" in tribute to Jake McNiece, their first sergeant and leader through much of their combat experience, whose mother was partially descended from the Native American Choctaw tribe. A photograph of Filthy Thirteen members Clarence Ware and Charles Plauda painting each other's faces was published in the Army newspaper *Stars and Stripes*; in the June 9, 1944, edition of the newspaper, war correspondent Tom Hoge coined the nickname that stuck.

During training and deployment overseas, the Filthy Thirteen earned a reputation as hard-nosed, hard-fighting, and hard-drinking men, who did not bathe regularly, but knew the business of war and accomplished their missions. McNiece remembered being upbraided for missing reveille regularly and claiming that it was against his mother's Native American heritage. That excuse got nowhere, and McNiece expressed his displeasure with a drinking binge. He recalled, "I ended up beating the MPs with their own nightsticks. I spent a few days in the stockade...."

Above: Sporting their Mohawks haircuts and adorning their faces with war paint, these paratroopers of the Filthy Thirteen, the Demolition Section, Headquarters Company, 506th PIR, prepare for the Normandy airdrop.

Through the course of World War II as many as 30 men could rightly claim to have been members of the Filthy Thirteen. McNiece led several of the original men to the pathfinders and personally participated in four combat jumps during the war, including D-Day, Operation Market Garden, the relief of Bastogne during the Battle of the Bulge, and Operation Varsity, the airborne crossing of the Rhine River.

Right: First Lieutenant Richard Winters led a group of paratroopers from Company E, 506th Parachute Infantry Regiment, 101st Airborne Division, in the D-Day assault against German gun emplacements at Brecourt Manor. The guns threatened the American landings on Utah Beach, and the coordinated effort of Winters' command captured the positions with stunning efficiency.

troopers had been in combat for only a few hours, their training paid off with a textbook example of tactical operations that is still taught in military schools to this day. Winters deployed a pair of .30-caliber (7.62mm) machine guns to provide covering fire and utilized the Germans' own trenches to shield his advancing troopers.

German machine-gun positions were taken out with grenades, and three of the 105mm guns were disabled in succession with blocks of explosives dropped down their barrels that were then detonated with German grenades. A squad from Company D led by Second Lieutenant Ronald C. Spiers destroyed the fourth 105mm gun. The Americans wiped out a platoon of German troops, whom Winters believed had belonged to the 6th Parachute Regiment but may also have been troops of the 919th Grenadier Regiment, 709th Division. Fifteen Germans were killed and 12 captured, while four Americans died and two were wounded.

Before withdrawing under heavy machine-gun fire from the fortified manor house, Winters discovered a map that detailed German artillery and machine-gun positions across a wide area of the Cotentin Peninsula, which proved extremely valuable to intelligence. Winters received the Distinguished Service Cross for his leadership, while three 506th troopers were awarded the Silver Star, and 21 others the Bronze Star.

Describing the action at Brecourt Manor, Ambrose wrote, "The significance of what Easy Company had accomplished cannot be judged with any degree of precision, but it surely saved a lot of lives and made it much easier—perhaps even made it possible in the first instance—for tanks to come inland from the beach. It would be a gross exaggeration to say that Easy Company saved the day at Utah Beach, but reasonable to say that it made an important contribution to the success of the invasion."

Due to the fact that much of the 101st Airborne Division had been scattered across western Normandy during its airdrop and much of its equipment had been lost, only a fraction of the division's troop strength was initially able to fully participate in achieving its objectives on June 6, 1944. When D-Day was over, the 101st had sustained nearly 1,300 dead and wounded, but, in tandem with the 82nd Airborne, it had secured the western flank of the invasion.

All-American Division on D-Day

In the opening hours of Operation Overlord, the 82nd Airborne Division experienced more widely dispersed parachute drops than the 101st. Although they were told to fly straight, some inexperienced troop carrier pilots took evasive action as German flak intensified near the drop zones. High winds contributed to the disarray, and sticks of paratroopers were released well above and below the prescribed altitudes for good jumps.

Private Dwayne Burns of the 508th PIR recalled, "I could hear machine-gun rounds walking across the wings. It was hard to stand up and troopers were falling down and getting up; some were throwing up. Of all the training we had, there was not anything that had prepared us for this."

Approximately 30 paratroopers floated helplessly into the center of Ste. Mere-Eglise and were captured or shot dead in their chutes. Two men fell through the roof of a burning building. One trooper became stranded, dangling from the steeple of a church, and played dead for nearly three hours until German soldiers climbed up the tower and took him prisoner. The body of one trooper hung limply from a tree. A German soldier pointed to the lifeless American and

Below: In this scene from the acclaimed Home Box Office series *Band of Brothers*, Lieutenant Richard Winters and his paratroopers of Easy Company, 506th Parachute Infantry Regiment, prepare to assault the guns at Brecourt Manor.

The bodies of eight American glidermen, killed in the crash of their Waco CG-4 glider, lie covered with a parachute and awaiting temporary burial in Normandy. The wreckage of the overturned Waco lies in the background, mute testimony to the severity of its landing.

yelled, "All kaput!" to a group of townspeople who had ventured outside to see what was happening.

Aerial reconnaissance photos of the drop zones west of the Merderet at its confluence with the Douve, an area of about 12 square miles (31 square km) where the 507th and 508th PIR were to come down, had been deceptively reassuring. Images that appeared to reveal pastoral landscape perfect for airborne descent had been flooded more extensively by the Germans than anticipated, and vegetation had grown to cover the marshland, concealing the hazard. Complicating the drop was the presence of the German 1057th Grenadier Division in the area, preventing the pathfinders from marking the drop zones. Transport pilots searching for the markers delayed flipping the switches on their green lights until they were well past the appropriate positions, ultimately releasing the paratroopers over a wide area, many of them above the marshes.

Lieutenant Ralph De Weese of the 508th came down in three feet (90cm) of water and lying on his back. His parachute was caught by the wind, dragging him several hundred yards with his head underwater at times, although the equipment he carried on his chest prevented him from turning over and probably saved his life.

"Several times I thought it was no use and decided to open my mouth and drown," De Weese remembered, "but each time the wind would slack up enough for me to put my head out of the water and catch a breath. I must have swallowed a lot of water because I didn't take a drink for two days afterward."

Among the 82nd Airborne Division's D-Day casualties, 36 men were believed to have drowned. Sixty-three were taken prisoner, and 173 suffered broken arms or legs when they landed. The glider-borne troops of the 82nd Airborne lost 25 killed, 118 wounded, and 14 missing of the 957 men who rode the wood and canvas craft into Normandy. These were grievous losses, but far below the 70 percent casualty rate that Leigh-Mallory had predicted. All told, the 82nd Airborne Division lost 1,259 dead and wounded on June 6, 1944. Nearly two months later, an after-action report bluntly stated that an entire stick of paratroopers from the 507th PIR remained missing.

Gavin's Command

When General Gavin cut himself free from his parachute, he looked around the orchard and saw a familiar face: his aide, Lieutenant Hugo V. Olsen. Together they searched for the other

Left: This representation of a lone paratrooper of the 82nd Airborne Division who found himself hanging from the roof of the church in Ste. Mere-Eglise reminds citizens daily of the fighting that occurred in the town on June 6, 1944.

Above: A paratrooper of the 82nd Airborne Division takes time to assist French civilians in their evacuation from an area where fighting rages. The civilian population of Normandy welcomed the Allies as liberators after four years of German occupation.

men in their stick, finding all but one. Advancing warily about 400 yards (365m), the Americans spotted bundles of equipment in the midst of a flooded plain and gathered what they could. Then, the recognition lights for rallying points of the 507th and 508th PIR were spotted across the water. Olsen found these men and determined that Gavin's force was about two miles (3km) north of the La Fiere bridge, where the other groups were headed.

Gavin led his men another two miles (3km) toward La Fiere along the high embankment of the rail line that ran from Cherbourg to Carentan. The group came across the 1st Battalion, 505th, under Major Frederick Kellam, who was killed later in the day. Kellam had already taken action. "About a half mile from the La Fiere [bridge]," the general wrote, "I came across the 1st Battalion of the 505th Parachute Infantry, organized, under control, and already launching an attack of the La Fiere bridge. It was a most reassuring sight."

As the sun rose, about 600 men had congregated at La Fiere, where the crossing consisted of the bridge over the main channel and a narrow causeway extending another 500 yards (450m) across the marsh to the west bank and the bocage, or hedgerow, country beyond. Kellam's men of the 505th PIR were joined by a contingent of the 507th under Lieutenant John A. Wisner, and these men tried to storm the bridge—possibly thc action that Gavin observed on his arrival. Heavy German machine-gun fire broke up the attack.

Gavin sent 75 men south to look for another crossing point and received word that no Germans were guarding the bridge at Chef-du-Pont. He then took personal command of another 75 men and set off in that direction. General

Lying in a shallow ditch along a stone wall, American paratroopers watch intently for signs of enemy movement. The soldier in the foreground appears to be taking aim at a distant target. Small unit encounters marked the action as Allied troops pushed inland from the Normandy beaches.

Ridgway arrived at La Fiere and directed Colonel Roy Lundquist, commander of the 508th PIR, to take charge of the collection of paratroopers that had been inactive there for several hours.

West of the Merderet, approximately 50 troopers of the 2nd Battalion, 507th, under the battalion commander, Lieutenant Colonel Charles J. Timmes, advanced on Amfreville. Timmes believed gunfire he heard was an attack by other paratroopers against the town. He intended to support the effort, but was mistaken in his assumption: The German fire had been directed at Timmes' own men. He withdrew to a position east of Amfreville and sent 10 men to Cauquigny at the west end of the La Fiere causeway, an area the group had passed through during the night. By mid-morning, the patrol had placed its machine gun in the church at Cauquigny.

By this time, the paratroopers at La Fiere were launching a coordinated attack with three companies. One of these fought for two hours, crossed the causeway, and made contact with Timmes' patrol in Cauquigny with about 75 men. For a brief moment the consolidation of the bridgehead was at hand; however, there was no immediate follow-up to the success. The rolling landscape prevented clear observation of the assault's progress, and the extent of its success was unknown for a while. Most of the men who made the crossing, under the command of Captain F.V. Schwarzwalder, were ordered to continue to Amfreville to join their parent 2nd Battalion, 507th, rather than hold the western end of the causeway.

German Response

Although it was slow in developing, the German reaction at La Fiere was forceful. As Schwarzwalder headed toward Amfreville, German artillery rounds began to fall on Cauquigny. Machine guns chattered, and then a few tanks appeared. In the middle of the German counterattack, American reinforcements arrived—too little, too late. The paratroopers were compelled to give up the bridge, and German attacks pinned down the 507th troopers under Timmes and Schwarzwalder east of Amfreville for the next 48 hours. German counterattacks across the causeway were beaten back, but the Americans were forced to consolidate every available man, recalling troops that had been detailed to look for better places to cross the Merderet to the south.

"...an officer delivered a message from General Gavin: 'hold at all costs.'"

As the opportunity at La Fiere slipped away, Lieutenant Colonel Arthur Maloney, the executive officer of the 507th, was at Chef-du-Pont with about 175 troopers. Two attempts to take the bridge were repulsed by a small but determined band of German soldiers dug in along the sides of the approaching causeway. With the opposing forces in a standoff, Maloney was ordered to take every available man to reinforce La Fiere. Captain Roy Creek was left at Chef-du-Pont with only 34 paratroopers occupying ground surrounding a two-story creamery building.

Creek later wrote, "Concurrent with his [Maloney's] departure three things happened: One, direct artillery fire on our positions around the creamery reduced our strength to 20 men; two, an observation point in the creamery noted what was estimated to be a company of Germans moving around to our left rear. This threat never materialized, for they bypassed us in route to Ste. Mere-Eglise where, though not known to us at the time, a battle was being waged by elements of the 505th for that important objective; three, an officer delivered a message from Gen. Gavin, 'hold at all costs.'

"It was pretty obvious that it couldn't cost much more, but at the same time, it was

Above: A medic of the 82nd Airborne Division offers a drag from a cigarette to a wounded paratrooper in Normandy. Immediate medical care on the battlefield and in nearby aid stations saved the lives of many soldiers who were wounded during World War II.

doubtful we could hold something we didn't have. Reinforcements were requested, and as from heaven, C-47s began to appear, dropping bundles of weapons and ammunition. One bundle of 60mm mortar ammunition dropped right in our laps. Within 30 minutes, the officer who had previously delivered the 'hold at all costs' message returned with 100 men and a 57mm gun which was pulled into position on our side of the bridge. We started firing at the enemy field piece. I'm sure we didn't hit it, but we stopped the firing and that is what we had to do in order to survive."

Lieutenant Colonel Thomas J.B. Shanley, commander of the 2nd Battalion, 508th PIR, led one of the largest airborne forces, which initially assembled west of the Merderet River. Shanley hit the ground near the town of Picauville, but could not muster enough men to tackle his mission to destroy the bridge across the Douve at Pont l'Abbé. Although he had managed to establish radio communication with other clusters of paratroopers, sporadic pitched battles with German troops delayed a linkup of any consequence until late afternoon on June 6.

By that time, Shanley had correctly surmised that he was locked in a fight with at least a battalion of German infantry. He chose to consolidate his forces at the battalion assembly area on Hill 30, so named on American maps due to its height in meters. Shanley coordinated a spirited defense that delayed the advance of

elements of the 1057th Grenadier Regiment that had been ordered to clear the area west of the Merderet of American paratroopers.

Three intrepid men of the 508th, Corporal Ernest T. Roberts, Private John A. Lockwood, and Private Otto K. Zwingman, occupied observation posts in the small village of Haut Gueutteville and watched the Germans prepare an attack with a battalion of infantry and tank support. Against overwhelming odds, they held up the German advance for two hours while troop dispositions were completed at Hill 30. Shanley's forward position frustrated German attempts to bring the full weight of the 1057th Grenadier Division against either La Fiere or Chef-du-Pont, saving one or both of these positions from being overrun. During the next several days, the outpost on Hill 30 provided intelligence on German movements and boosted the renewed effort to establish a bridgehead across the Merderet.

While most of the 82nd airborne was scattered across Normandy, the bulk of the 505th PIR landed outside its primary objective, Ste. Mere-Eglise. Defensive lines were established to the north and south, and the 3rd Battalion, led by Sicily veteran Lieutenant Colonel Edward "Cannonball" Krause, hit the town with 108 assembled paratroopers, about one-fourth of its normal strength. Krause counted on swift movement and the element of surprise, instructing his men to use bayonets and hand grenades so that any weapon fired would be automatically presumed as hostile.

The capture of Ste. Mere-Eglise was accomplished rapidly, and the main road from Cherbourg to Carentan was cut. However,

Opposite: Soldiers tend to the bodies of American troops killed in action during the Normandy campaign in preparation for their burial. Although the 82nd and 101st Airborne Divisions took severe casualties on D-Day, their numbers were far below the projected 70 percent that it was feared they would sustain.

holding the town was difficult, and three hours later the Germans returned in force. At 9:30 a.m., a reinforced regiment advanced from the south to oust the Americans, but was repulsed in a sharp clash. About the same time, Lieutenant Colonel Benjamin H. Vandervoort was moving north from the vicinity with roughly half his 2nd Battalion, 505th, to establish a defensive line around the villages of Neuville-au-Plain and Bandienville.

Colonel William E. Ekman, commanding the 505th PIR, heard the clatter of small-arms fire during the German counterattack at Ste. Mere-Eglise and ordered Vandervoort to turn back to the town to bolster the 1st Battalion's defense. Fortuitously, Vandervoort ordered a platoon under Lieutenant Turner B. Turnbull to set up a blocking position at Neuville-au-Plain. Within minutes of their arrival, Turnbull's troopers were set upon by a German force that outnumbered them five to one. Tenaciously, the Americans held firm, fending off attacks for the next eight hours.

Ste. Mere-Eglise

A favorable unintended consequence of Turnbull's stand was the parry of the German thrust from the north against Ste. Mere-Eglise while the defenders of the town fought off a simultaneous attack from the south. The price in blood, however, was high. When Turnbull's battered platoon was withdrawn around 6 p.m., only 16 of the original 42 men were left alive.

Vandervoort reached Ste. Mere-Eglise at 10 a.m., and decided with Krause that his men would take the northern perimeter while the 3rd Battalion defended the southern half. Two companies were held in reserve, to serve as a fire brigade in case the defenses were pressed to breaking point. Soon enough, two companies of German infantry came up the road from the direction of Carentan while a few tanks rumbled along in support.

This German attack was beaten back handily, and Krause boldly ordered 80 troopers of

Company I to counterattack, hoping to catch the withdrawing Germans in their exposed flank as they withdrew. Company I managed to engage only a single enemy convoy, peppering it with grenades and small-arms fire. When no Germans were left alive, the Americans returned to Ste. Mere-Eglise and took up positions in anticipation of yet another German attempt to retake the town—but the enemy had had enough for the day and no further attempts were made on June 6.

"As we dug in, and made ourselves comfortable for a turn at short naps, the smell of death, which was to be with us for a long time to come, had begun to permeate the night air."

Back at Chef-du-Pont, Captain Creek's men and their reinforcements repulsed the German attack, crossed the Merderet, and dug in on the west end of the causeway; however, the position was a toehold, far too weak to be considered a bridgehead. Creek remembered the moment his men assumed the offensive once again.

"On a prearranged signal, all fires lifted and 10 men and one officer stormed the bridge and went into position on the western approach to guard the causeway," the captain wrote. "Five Germans made a run for it down the deathtrap causeway and were immediately shot down. That did it. The battle was over. The bridge was ours and we knew we could hold it.

"Just as with all victories in war," he continued, "we shared a let down feeling. We knew it was still a long way to Berlin. We began to organize and improve our position and tended to such pressing things as first aid to wounded, 25 in number who could not be evacuated because of a lack of any place to evacuate them. We gathered the bodies of the dead, Americans and Germans, and covered them with parachutes. D-DAY was almost over and it had gone fast and in a little while, it would be D+1. When would the beach forces come? They should have already done so. Maybe the whole invasion had failed. After all, we knew nothing of the situation except as it existed in Chef-du-Pont and Chef-du-Pont is a very small town."

Around midnight, Creek, who had been in charge since Lieutenant Colonel Edwin J. Ostberg, commander of the 1st Battalion, 507th PIR, had been wounded earlier in the day, realized his exhausted troopers were not alone anymore.

"At 2400 hours, our fears were dispelled," he recalled. "Reconnaissance elements of the 4th Infantry Division wheeled into our creamery yard complete with a few rations that they shared with us. As we dug in, and made ourselves comfortable for a turn at short naps, the smell of death, which was to be with us for a long time to come, had begun to permeate the night air. It was D+1 in Normandy... I reflected upon the details of the fighting and the bravery of every man participating in it. Some had lost their lives, some others had been seriously wounded and lay inside the creamery... We had done some things badly, but overall with a hodgepodge of troops from several units who had never trained together as a unit, didn't even know one another, and were engaged in their first combat, we had done okay. We captured our bridge and held it. We knew we faced D+1 with confidence and anticipation."

While the occupation of Ste. Mere-Eglise, the small lodgment at Chef-du-Pont, and the objectives of the 101st had been achieved, the American airborne divisions remained somewhat vulnerable as D-Day drew to a close. The 101st had linked up with the 4th Infantry Division, but the 82nd had only tenuous contact with either of these divisions. Initial reports from the field indicated that the Ridgway and his senior divisional commanders had control of only about 40 percent of the 82nd Airborne troop strength and just 10 percent of its artillery. The 325th Glider Infantry Regiment was slated to arrive the next morning.

Early estimates forwarded to VII Corps listed D-Day casualties in the 82nd Airborne alone at an alarming total of 4,000; however, most of these were missing troopers who began filtering in during the succeeding days.

On the Ground

In the center of the VII Corps line, contact had been established between the 82nd Airborne and the 8th Infantry Regiment during the night of June 6. Attempts to eliminate the German resistance south of Ste. Mere-Eglise met with some success, although the enemy continued to counterattack throughout the day on June 7, one attempt reaching to within 400 yards (365m) of General Ridgway's command post in the town.

One heavy German attack on Ste. Mere-Eglise was met by a task force of the 746th Tank Battalion, while the 8th Infantry Regiment advanced southward accompanied by two companies of the 70th Tank Battalion and entered the battle. The 2nd Battalion, 505th, then joined the 2nd Battalion, 8th Infantry, along with

Below: Following the fight to liberate the town of Ste. Mere-Eglise in Normandy, paratroopers of the 82nd Airborne Division grab a few minutes of rest. The 82nd and 101st Airborne Divisions secured vital exits from Utah Beach on D-Day and linked up with troops of the 4th Infantry Division coming ashore.

Above: During a firefight near the French village of Sauveur le Vicomte, an American soldier rises from cover to fire an anti-tank round from a bazooka. The bocage or hedgerow country in Normandy also provided concealment for German soldiers who contested the Allied advance inland.

approximately 60 tanks in a thrust to the north and west to eliminate the Germans threatening Ste. Mere-Eglise from that direction. Three hundred enemy troops were killed or captured during the operation.

Although the area around Ste. Mere-Eglise was now more secure, the arrival of the 325th Glider Infantry Regiment was welcome. Two serials landed in the prescribed zones, and the regiment was split, with one battalion supporting the 8th Infantry at Les Forges and the other heading north of Ste. Mere-Eglise.

Establishing crossings of the troublesome Merderet remained problematic. A ferocious German attack against the 82nd positions on the east bank of the river came very close to succeeding. Enemy tanks and infantry hit Company A, 505th PIR, hard at the river's edge and used the cover of one of their knocked-out tanks and other disabled vehicles to close the distance. German mortar and machine-gun fire reduced the platoon defending the right side of the bridge to just 15 men, but after the Germans asked for a half-hour truce to remove their dead and wounded they did not renew the engagement. Company A lost half its men killed or wounded.

On June 8, the troopers west of the Merderet remained isolated. Ridgway threw the 325th Glider Infantry into a hail of German machine-gun fire in an effort to reach the west end of the La Fiere causeway from Chef-du-Pont. Two tanks, one American and one German, were disabled and choking the bridge, and men who hesitated in the open were shot down. Casualties were high, but both Ridgway and Gavin personally encouraged the attackers. Eventually, four companies crossed the La Fiere causeway and linked up with Colonel Timmes' force and the 1st Battalion, 325th Glider Infantry.

To the south, Colonel Shanley and the beleaguered 2nd Battalion, 508th PIR, were relieved at Hill 30 after fighting virtually alone for three days. All American units west of the Merderet were brought within a single bridgehead emanating from La Fiere on the afternoon of June 8. This vital preliminary success helped set the stage for the VII Corps' westward offensive to cut the Cotentin Peninsula and capture Cherbourg.

On June 12, the reinforced 508th PIR, led by Brigadier General G.P. Howell, attacked across the Douve River to link up with the 101st Airborne at Baupte. German forces, which included large numbers of conscripted foreign soldiers, broke at first contact, creating a large hole in the defensive line that the 508th rapidly exploited. With the 82nd Airborne to the south and the 9th Division to the north, the American offensive moved westward.

By June 15, the 82nd Airborne Division was rolling forward against crumbling resistance. The 505th PIR reached Reigneville in relief of the 507th, and the 325th Glider Infantry advanced within 1,000 yards (915m) of St. Sauveur-le Vicomte. The following day, the 325th Glider and 505th reached the Douve River line at the edge of the village. Encouraged at the speed of the advance, Ridgway received permission to occupy St. Sauveur-le-Vicomte. The 508th PIR was released from a short stint in VII Corps reserve

Below: American paratroopers have taken possession of a small German tracked vehicle, a Kettenkrad, in the recently liberated town of Carentan.

and with the 505th established a bridgehead across the Douve up to 3,000 yards (2,750m) deep. The last German defenses east of the river were broken.

Three days later, control of the 82nd Airborne passed to the newly activated VIII Corps under General Troy H. Middleton. The VIII Corps was charged with organizing defensive positions from Carentan westward across the Cotentin Peninsula. The 82nd Airborne Division turned south and crossed the Douve at Pont l'Abbé with a bridgehead a mile and one-half (2.5km) deep, positioned to protect the southern flank of VII Corps in its westward drive.

By June 21, the three divisions of VII Corps, the 4th, 9th, and 79th, were poised to assault Cherbourg. After six more days of hard fighting, the Germans surrendered the great port city.

In early July, the 82nd Airborne Division was withdrawn to England. During 33 days in Normandy, the division had suffered 5,245 men killed, wounded, and missing in action. From the nocturnal airdrop to the defense of Ste. Mere-Eglise, the ultimately successful crossings of the Merderet River, and the westward drive across the Cotentin Peninsula, the 82nd had compiled another impressive combat record. In his after-action report, General Ridgway concluded, "...33 days of action without relief, without replacements. Every mission accomplished. No ground gained was ever relinquished."

Carentan

In the week following D-Day, efforts to link the VII Corps forces from Utah Beach and the V Corps from Omaha Beach were of primary concern. The village of Carentan was a focal point for that junction, and the town's capture became the primary objective of the 101st Airborne Division. On June 7, the day the divisional command was informed that Carentan was its sole objective, the 3rd Battalion, 506th PIR, and the 501st PIR were in a tight situation north of the Douve. Low on ammunition, they could not assume the offensive; however, they still managed to bag the entire 1st Battalion of the elite German 6th Parachute Regiment, which had been cut off around Ste. Marie-du-Mont.

Operating independently, Captain Charles G. Shettle of the 506th and Colonel Howard Johnson of the 501st caught the Germans in exposed positions along the marshes and the Carentan Highway. Many Germans were killed, and Shettle's men took 250 prisoners at Le Port while Johnson captured about 350 at La Barquette. Only 25 Germans managed to escape down the road to Carentan.

Heavy artillery fire and coordinated attacks by the 3rd Battalion, 501st, the 1st and 2nd Battalions, 506th, and the 1st Battalion, 401st Glider Infantry, succeeded in pushing the Germans out of St. Côme-du-Mont on June 7 as well. This drive cleared the Germans from the area north of the Douve and east of the Merderet.

Carentan, a vital crossroads and the key to the defense of the Cotentin Peninsula, proved to

Left: American paratroopers of the 101st Airborne Division prepare to take a ride in a captured German Kübelwagen following the hard fight to wrest control of Carentan from the Germans.

be a tough nut to crack. On June 8, the 506th, 502nd, and 327th Glider Infantry Regiment were poised for an assault. The plan was for a pincer movement that would envelop the city. While the 327th made the primary effort, the 502nd was to take high ground to the south.

On the afternoon of June 10, after a delay to repair one of four small bridges across the Carentan causeway, Colonel Cole's 3rd Battalion, 502nd, advanced single file and in the open. The paratroopers were obliged to cross the narrow, elevated causeway, which was six to nine feet (1.8–2.7m) above the flooded marshland and in plain view of the defending Germans. The attack bogged down under heavy enemy small-arms fire after three causeway bridges had been crossed.

At the fourth bridge, a heavy steel obstacle called a Belgian Gate blocked the advance so that only one man could squeeze past at a time. Six troopers made it across. When the seventh man was hit, Cole halted the effort. In darkness, three companies managed to cross the fourth bridge and deploy on both sides of the highway into Carentan.

Below: An assembly of paratroopers from the 101st Airborne Division stands at parade rest during a medal ceremony in the now quiet streets of Carentan. The battle for the town was among the most difficult that took place during the earliest days of the Normandy campaign.

By the next morning, Cole had decided to mount a bayonet charge against a farmhouse and enemy positions to the west, where German resistance had apparently concentrated. Cole and his executive officer, Lieutenant Colonel John P. Stopka, personally led the assault with about one-quarter of their 250 men following initially. Although the farmhouse was empty, German machine-gun nests and foxholes that had previously poured heavy fire into the Americans were silenced with bayonets and hand grenades.

Within hours the Germans had retired, leaving an estimated 500 dead and wounded in the fields southwest of the town.

While defenders were routed, the 3rd Battalion, 502nd, took heavy casualties. The Germans reorganized and repeatedly counterattacked the paratroopers along the highway. At times it appeared that Cole's thin line would rupture, but miraculously the Americans held their hard-won positions. The 2nd Battalion, 502nd came into the line during the night, but was as exhausted as Cole's command. Unable to advance any further, the 502nd was subsequently relieved by the 506th. Cole received the Medal of Honor for his bravery at Carentan; however, it was presented posthumously after he was killed during Operation Market Garden in Holland three months later.

While Cole heroically led his troopers across the Carentan causeway, elements of the 101st Airborne on their left flank managed to finally link up with V Corps advancing from Omaha Beach east the town.

In the predawn hours of June 12, the 2nd Battalion, 506th PIR, fought its way into Carentan after a night of intense artillery and naval bombardment. From the northwest, the 327th Glider Infantry quickly reached the center of town. Meanwhile, the 501st came in from the east and linked up with the 506th to take control of Carentan. The defensive perimeter was extended slightly to the south and southwest, although the 101st was unable to link up with the 82nd Airborne, which by then was heading across the Merderet toward the town of Baupte.

The Germans had actually pulled out of Carentan during the night of June 11, but they were not prepared to give up the crossroads town without a last, vicious effort to oust the Americans. On June 13, a fierce German counterattack by reinforced units of the 17th SS Panzergrenadier Division was repulsed by the 101st troopers with assistance from Combat Command A, 2nd Armored Division. Both the 501st and 506th were pushed back to within 500 yards (460m) of Carentan, but around 10:30 a.m., the tanks of Combat Command A arrived to stabilize the situation and assist in wresting the initiative from the enemy. The 502nd PIR counterattacked through the 506th, and the howitzers of the 14th Armored Field Artillery Battalion barked in support. Within hours the Germans had retired, leaving an estimated 500 dead and wounded in the fields southwest of the town. In the wake of the battle, the 101st established a solid defensive line along the road to Baupte and the Carentan highway. •

Until the end of June, the men of the 101st Airborne engaged in limited actions and occupied defensive positions south of Carentan. On the 29th, the 83rd Infantry Division relieved the 101st, which had sustained 4,670 casualties in nearly a month of fighting. General Taylor issued a statement that resonated with pride among the paratroopers.

"You hit the ground running toward the enemy," Taylor wrote. "You have proved the German soldier is no superman. You have beaten him on his own ground, and you can beat him on any ground."

Operation Dragoon: The Invasion Of Southern France

Although shortages in both fighting men and equipment thwarted original Allied plans to mount simultaneous invasions of northern and southern France in 1944, Operation Overlord proceeded on D-Day, June 6. The initial plan for the invasion of southern France, Operation Anvil, was suspended temporarily and then revived as Operation Dragoon.

Elements of the U.S. Seventh and the French First Armies landed along the coast of the French Riviera on August 15 with major objectives including the capture of the port cities of Toulon and Marseilles. Prior to the amphibious landings, Operation Rugby, an airborne insertion near the town of Le Muy northwest of the invasion beaches, was conducted by the Allied 1st Airborne Task Force, formed on July 11 as the Seventh Army Airborne Division and then renamed later that month.

Once Operation Dragoon was given the green light, only a few days of training were available, and most of it took place on the outskirts of Rome. With orders to secure the right flank of the invasion, seizing high ground and blocking roads over which German counterattacks were expected to advance, the 10,000 airborne troops of the U.S. 509th Parachute Infantry Battalion (PIB); the 517th Parachute Infantry Regiment; 1st Battalion, 551st Parachute Infantry Regiment; the 550th Glider Infantry Battalion; and the British 2nd Parachute Brigade jumped into southern France in the early-morning darkness of August 15.

The 509th PIB was a veteran outfit that had jumped in North Africa and fought in Italy at Anzio while also blunting a German offensive at Carano. The 550th and 551st were activated in the Panama Canal Zone, the 551st with a cadre of officers transferred from the 501st Parachute Infantry Regiment. Both units executed their first combat jumps during Operation Dragoon. The 517th PIR was activated in 1943 at Camp Toccoa, Georgia, and participated in the Italian Campaign before its transfer to Operation Dragoon. As independent battalions, these formations were attached to various larger units on numerous occasions during the war, and some were absorbed. The 509th remained independent throughout the conflict.

As the C-47 transport planes approached the coastline of southern France before daylight, thick ground fog rose to an altitude of 800 feet (240m), obscuring drop zones and rendering them either difficult or impossible for pathfinders to mark accurately. The resulting jump scattered some of the paratroopers widely, with many of the Americans coming to earth at distances of eight to 15 miles (13–24km) from their assigned drop zones; the British drop was reasonably accurate.

Despite their wide dispersal, most of the American paratroopers reached their assembly areas within a couple of hours. The 517th PIR occupied a series of hills five miles (8km) west of Le Muy with observation of the coastal route from Toulon to Saint Raphael. South of Le Muy, the 509th consolidated its positions on high ground with support from 11 75mm pack howitzers of the 463rd Parachute Field Artillery Battalion. Companies B and C of the 509th had parachuted near the city of St. Tropez and quickly took control there. Around 8:30 that evening, 509th troopers made contact with elements of the 45th Infantry Division advancing from the Allied beachhead.

A night attack against Le Muy by the 550th Glider Infantry Regiment was driven back, in part due to a lack of available artillery support. However, the effort was renewed the following day. By 3:30 p.m. on August 16, the town was clear of Germans and 170 enemy soldiers were captured. Allied

Above: Members of the 509th Parachute Infantry Battalion and their British counterparts rest in the town of Le Muy in southern France during Operation Dragoon. American and British airborne units combined to form the Allied 1st Airborne Task Force.

forces steadily moved inland, and on the morning of the 17th, troops of the 36th Infantry Division had entered Le Muy.

Following the initial success of Operation Dragoon, the 1st Airborne Task Force continued to cover the eastern flank of the Seventh Army while pushing northeastward to occupy Cannes and Nice. While cooperating with resistance fighters of the French Forces of the Interior (FFI), the paratroopers of the 509th moved on to La Courbaisse, Lantosque, and the ski resort of Peira Cava near the Italian border. The Germans defended the Fort Milles Fourches area vigorously, and heavy combat took place along with the delicate job of removing thousands of land mines that the enemy had buried. The airborne troops subsequently halted their advance in the Maritime Alps along the French–Italian frontier and assumed defensive positions.

In November 1944, several units of the 1st Airborne Task Force were withdrawn to Soissons, and the unit was officially disbanded later in the month. The 509th PIB was pulled back to La Gaude, east of Nice, until early December, when orders were received to move north to Villers-Cotterêts for duty with the 101st Airborne Division. During its short existence, the task force had spent approximately three months in the front lines.

CHAPTER 5

OPERATION MARKET GARDEN

General Omar Bradley, commander of the Allied 12th Army Group, was taken aback. "Had the pious teetotaling Montgomery wobbled into SHAEF with a hangover, I could not have been more astonished than I was by the daring adventure he proposed," Bradley remembered.

British Field Marshal Sir Bernard Law Montgomery—the hero of the pivotal Battle of El Alamein in North Africa, commander of all Allied ground forces for the D-Day invasion, and subsequently the leader of the 21st Army Group—was known as a meticulous master of the set-piece battle, one who would amass overwhelming superiority in men and equipment before committing to an offensive action.

Now, things had changed. As summer gave way to fall in 1944, Montgomery had been lobbying General Dwight D. Eisenhower, Supreme Commander of the Allied Expeditionary Force in Europe, to abandon or at least suspend the broad front strategy that had the Allied armies advancing inexorably toward the German frontier, where the fixed fortifications of the Siegfried Line, or West Wall, would be difficult to breach.

At times, stiff German resistance slowed the advance to a crawl—and there was another concern that Montgomery hammered home. Supply lines were stretching, and the availability of fuel, ammunition, foodstuffs, and all the elements that keep an advancing military force on the move, were becoming scarce. Montgomery continually argued that two Allied armies, the American Third and the Canadian First, should be halted and resupplied just enough to maintain a defensive posture. His own British Second Army and the American First Army would then receive the vast majority of war materiel, outflank the Siegfried Line, and mount a rapier-like thrust into the Ruhr, the industrial heart of Germany, crippling the enemy's capacity to wage war and prying open a direct route to the Nazi capital of Berlin.

On September 10, Montgomery met with Eisenhower in Brussels to outline his tactical

Opposite: As curious Dutch civilians look on, American paratroopers pull back through the ruins of the village of Nijmegen during the final phase of Operation Market Garden, a combined airborne and ground offensive in September 1944.

blueprint. Along with the big picture for the offensive, Montgomery proposed a preliminary action that was shocking in its boldness. It was dubbed Market Garden.

The Audacious Plan

A two-phase operation, Market Garden called for airborne troops to parachute into the German-occupied Netherlands and seize key bridges across the Maas, Waal, and Lower Rhine rivers. The paratroopers would hold the bridges, paving the way for ground troops to race swiftly through the Netherlands and into Germany. If all went according to plan, the war might even be won by Christmas 1944.

The seizure of the bridges and adjacent canals was essential for the ground forces to move swiftly along a single highway approximately 60 miles (96km) from the Allied lines in Belgium to the Dutch town of Arnhem. The veteran British XXX Corps would speed down the road from its bridgehead across the Meuse-Escaut Canal, brushing aside enemy resistance, relieving the paratroopers at the successive bridges, and serving as the vanguard of the larger force that would then push into Germany.

Montgomery's plan relied on the First Allied Airborne Army, activated just a month earlier, under the command of General Lewis H. Brereton. Under Brereton's direct control were the American XVIII Airborne Corps and the headquarters of the I British Airborne Corps. In early September, General Ridgway was elevated to command of the XVIII Airborne Corps, and General Gavin was promoted to command the

Below: Prior to their takeoff during the opening hours of Operation Market Garden, glider troops of the 101st Airborne Division and personnel of the IX Troop Carrier Command are briefed on what to expect during their deployment in the Netherlands.

Left: General Lewis H. Brereton commanded the First Allied Airborne Army, which included several divisions and independent formations of airborne and glider troops along with troop carrier units.

82nd Airborne Division. Along with the 82nd, the corps also included the 101st and 17th Airborne Divisions, and the IX Troop Carrier Command along with other independent units. The British I Airborne Corps, under General Frederick Arthur Montague "Boy" Browning, included the 1st and 6th Airborne Divisions, the Polish 1st Independent Parachute Brigade, some special operations troops of the SAS, and allocated air transport formations.

Since taking part in the D-Day invasion and subsequent fighting in Normandy, the 82nd and 101st Airborne Divisions had been refitting and absorbing replacements in England. The 17th Airborne Division, activated in April 1943, arrived in Britain at the end of August 1944, too late to prepare for Market Garden. The combat veterans of the 82nd and 101st were tabbed as the American contribution to Market, the airborne phase of Montgomery's plan. The British 6th Airborne had also taken part in Operation Overlord and did not return to England until early September, having suffered 4,500 casualties during three months of fighting.

When Eisenhower approved the significant departure from the broad front strategy that Market Garden entailed, the 82nd, 101st, and 1st Airborne Divisions, along with the attached Polish 1st Independent Parachute Brigade, were earmarked for the bold assault. As the overall plan was conceived, the 101st Airborne would secure the southernmost bridges, one over the Wilhelmina Canal at the town of Son, a pair spanning the Dommel River at St. Oedenrode, and then four more over the Aa River near the town of Veghel. The town of Eindhoven was also an objective, while the 101st held open 15 miles (24km) of the vital road toward Arnhem for XXX Corps use. By the end of their service in Market Garden, the troopers of the 101st would refer to this stretch of road as "Hell's Highway."

Farther north, the 82nd Airborne was ordered to capture the bridge at Grave, the longest in Europe at 1,960 feet (597m). The 82nd would also take one or more of the four bridges across the Maas–Waal Canal, another across the Waal at the town of Nijmegen, and the area around the village of Groesbeek. The final leg of the XXX Corps dash involved a drive from Nijmegen to Arnhem, where the 1st Airborne, commanded by General Roy Urquhart, was to seize three bridges across the Lower Rhine.

Market Garden was scheduled for September 17, just a week after Montgomery and Eisenhower met to discuss it. When various unit commanders were briefed on the operation, they were told that only light German opposition was expected. General Browning was said to have referred to it as a "party." Gavin was troubled as he analyzed the 82nd Airborne's role.

"The big Nijmegen bridge posed a serious problem," he said. "Seizing it with overwhelming strength at the outset would have been meaningless if I did not get at least two other bridges: the big bridge at Grave and at least one of the four over the Canal. Further, even if I captured it, if I had lost all of the high ground that controlled the entire sector, as well as the resupply and glider landing zones, I would be in a serious predicament. Everything depended on the weight and direction of the enemy reaction, and this could not be determined until we were on the ground. The problem was how much could be spared how soon for employment on the bridge."

Airlift Preparations

The largest airborne operation to date, Market Garden, came together in a remarkably short period of time. Realistically, it was not enough to address many of the nagging concerns regarding logistics, supply, and above all the level of German resistance that might be encountered.

Intelligence reports seemed to contradict the notion that the German Army was in full retreat. In fact, the Dutch resistance had warned that both the 9th and 10th SS Panzer Divisions were in the vicinity of Arnhem, recovering from the fierce fighting in Normandy. By coincidence, as Market Garden gained momentum, the German 59th and 245th Infantry Divisions were relocating from the area of the Fifteenth Army to that of the First Parachute Army, directly in the path of the offensive.

Eisenhower's chief of staff, General Walter Bedell Smith, relayed mounting concerns about the German military presence in the Netherlands to Montgomery. The response was dismissive. Smith wrote, "Montgomery simply waved my objections airily aside." Urquhart raised his own concerns to Browning and was told that tanks in reconnaissance photos were probably in need of repair. Urquhart was then told to take a short leave—to rest at home—just hours before the first transport planes lifted off.

Right: Posing in front of C-47 transports and gliders, members of the 101st Airborne Division anticipate the coming battle during Operation Market Garden. After landing in the Netherlands, the paratroopers fought as infantry for weeks.

Allied air supremacy that would minimize interference from German fighter planes, the desire for a strong drop pattern, coordination of air and ground movement, and the fresh recollection of the scattered Normandy jump outweighed the concerns of more intense enemy antiaircraft fire that would doubtless be encountered, and Market was declared a daylight operation. In its execution, more than 20,000 troopers would eventually be delivered to drop zones by parachute and more than 14,000 by glider along with 1,736 vehicles, 3,342 tons of ammunition, and 263 artillery pieces. To minimize exposure to antiaircraft fire and deliver

Above: Douglas C-47 transport planes carry American paratroopers to their designated drop zones in Holland during Operation Market Garden. The Market Garden airdrop was carried out in daylight and executed with accuracy.

the three airborne divisions most efficiently, it was decided that troop carrier groups would take the 1st and 82nd Airborne Divisions, landing to the north, on a flight path across the estuary of the Scheldt and Maas rivers, above roughly 80 miles (130km) of enemy-held territory. Those carrying the troopers of the 101st would fly a longer, southerly route that was mainly over Belgium and limited the flyover of enemy territory to 65 miles (105km).

Since Operation Overlord, the IX Troop Carrier Command had replenished its airlift capacity to roughly that of D-Day. The 101st Airborne was supplied with 424 C-47s for paratroopers along with 70 tow planes and gliders, while the 82nd received 480 troop transports and 50 gliders and tow planes. The 1st Airborne was allocated 145 C-47s and 358 gliders and tow planes.

Nearly 1,900 Allied fighter aircraft were committed to escort duty and antiaircraft suppression on September 17, while early that morning more than 1,400 bombers of the U.S. Eighth Air Force and Royal Air Force Bomber Command hit ground targets in the paths of transports and around the drop zones.

The Airborne Carpet

At 10:25 a.m. on September 17, the first American C-47s carrying pathfinders of the 101st Airborne Division began lifting off at 10-minute intervals. The airborne operation proceeded smoothly.

Headed to drop zones north of Eindhoven, the 442nd and 435th Troop Carrier Groups deftly got 45 planes into the air in five minutes and 32 planes aloft and in formation in 15 minutes

Above: Seated on benches in the fuselage of a C-47 transport, troopers of the 82nd Airborne Division await orders to prepare to jump into Holland during Operation Market Garden.

respectively. Carrying the 1st Battalion, 501st PIR, transports of the 424th Troop Carrier Wing dropped 42 sticks of troopers three miles (5km) northwest of their assigned drop zone, but a tight drop pattern allowed the battalion to assemble 90 percent of its men and equipment in less than 45 minutes.

The 442nd and 436th placed the 506th PIR right on target. One transport had been shot down along the way; however, the others delivered approximately 2,200 men with such accuracy that the regimental command post was functioning and 80 percent of the troopers were assembled within an hour. Only 24 jumpers had sustained injuries. The war journal of the 506th called the event "an ideal jump, better than any combat or practice jump executed." The 502nd PIR was also dropped accurately, assembling within an hour after coming down.

Six groups of the 50th and 52nd Troop Carrier Wings carried the 82nd Airborne Division, 7,250 strong, to drop zones near the Maas River south of Nijmegen. The 315th Troop Carrier Group dropped 78 sticks of paratroopers within 1,500 yards (1,370m) of its designated pathfinder beacons, and all of the 504th PIR except Company E, 1st Battalion, came to earth in the area.

C-47s of the 440th and 441st Troop Carrier Groups dropped two battalions and the headquarters of the 508th PIR just off the northern edge of its assigned drop zone, while the 3rd Battalion came down inside its eastern perimeter. In just over one and one-half hours, the regiment was 90 percent assembled. The commander of the 3rd Battalion later reported, "We could not have landed better under any circumstances."

Above: Their parachutes billowing, American airborne troops descend toward the Dutch countryside below. During Operation Market Garden, the 82nd and 101st Airborne Divisions were tasked with seizing key bridges on the road to Arnhem.

Tragic Valor

Meanwhile, the British 1st Airborne dropped along the north bank of the Lower Rhine, eight miles (13km) west of Arnhem. General Urquhart's Red Devils, as they were called, moved out swiftly toward their vital objectives. In a few minutes, sporadic sniper fire broke out. German resistance steadily mounted—and for good reason. The British had come to earth only two miles (3km) from the headquarters of German Army Group B. Field Marshal Walther Model believed he was the target of a kidnapping and hurried to the headquarters of General Wilhelm Bittrich, commander of the II SS Panzer Corps.

Bittrich was already responding with great insight. He ordered the tanks of the 9th and 10th SS Panzer Divisions to Arnhem and Nijmegen respectively. German troops cut the roads eastward to Arnhem and prevented the bulk of the 1st Airborne from reaching the city.

Only the 2nd Battalion, 1st Parachute Brigade, 500 men under Lieutenant Colonel John D. Frost, reached the northern end of the main bridge across the Lower Rhine at Arnhem. These were set upon by superior German forces, but held on grimly, waiting in vain for the arrival of the remainder of the 1st Airborne Division, stymied on the roads. Due to the stiff resistance encountered west of Arnhem, Operation Market Garden was doomed to fail.

The 1st Airborne Division fought gallantly for 10 days, but of the nearly 10,000 paratroopers Urquhart had taken into the vicinity of Arnhem, just over 2,000 evaded death or capture. Frost's valiant command held out at the Arnhem highway bridge for nearly four days before surrendering. Fewer than 50 men of the 2nd Battalion, 1st Parachute Brigade, managed to return to friendly lines.

Southern Exposure

Only two battalions of the 101st Airborne Division failed to land in or near their assigned drop zones on September 17. Dropping near Son, the 506th PIR, under Colonel Robert Sink, was to capture a bridge over the Wilhelmina Canal and continue south to Eindhoven. The 502nd PIR, commanded by Colonel John H. Michaelis, was to establish a perimeter around its drop zone just north of the 506th for later use as a glider-landing zone. Then, it was to capture more bridges over the Wilhelmina Canal near the town of Best and one of those spanning the Dommel. Farther north, Colonel Howard Johnson's 501st was to capture four road and rail bridges on the Willems Canal and the Aa River near Veghel.

The 501st PIR made rapid progress toward its objectives. Lieutenant Colonel Harry W. O. Kinnard, commanding the 1st Battalion, one of the two that had dropped in the wrong place, struck out toward Veghel as some of the troopers commandeered bicycles and trucks to speed the advance. When Kinnard reached Veghel, a handful of his troopers had already secured the railroad bridge over the Aa. The 2nd Battalion seized three bridges at Veghel, while the 3rd Battalion took the town of Eerde and cut the Veghel–St. Oedenrode highway, safeguarding the entire regiment's rear.

The 501st secured all of its September 17 objectives in the span of about three hours, capturing scores of prisoners in the process. In his haste to move against Veghel, though, Kinnard had not taken all his battalion's equipment along. He left 46 men under Captain W.S. Burd to bring the equipment and several paratroopers who had been injured during the jump forward at a slower pace. Burd's detachment was attacked by a strong German force and pushed back to a single building. When word of Burd's plight reached Kinnard, Colonel Johnson allowed him to send a platoon to the rescue. The attempt failed, and the survivors of Burd's group were captured.

The other battalion of the 101st dropped outside its zone was the 1st of the 502nd led by Lieutenant Colonel Patrick Cassidy. Cassidy's men nevertheless swept into St. Oedenrode, which commanded a major highway and a bridge across the Dommel, occupied the town, killed 20 Germans, and captured another 58.

General Maxwell Taylor, commanding the 101st Airborne Division, recognized the importance of the rail and highway bridges over the Wilhelmina Canal near Best. Although they were not on the direct XXX Corps line of advance, Taylor considered them significant in strengthening his defensive perimeter and knew that they could be used in the event that the route through Son was blocked.

Captain Robert E. Jones of Company H, 502nd PIR, started toward these bridges and immediately took heavy German fire. Jones sent a patrol under Lieutenant Edward L. Wierzbowski forward. The Americans came within sight of the highway bridge, but were forced to dig in, their strength reduced to three officers and 15 men.

Commanding the 3rd Battalion, 502nd, Lieutenant Colonel Robert G. Cole, who earned the Medal of Honor in Normandy, started out with the rest of his battalion to find Captain

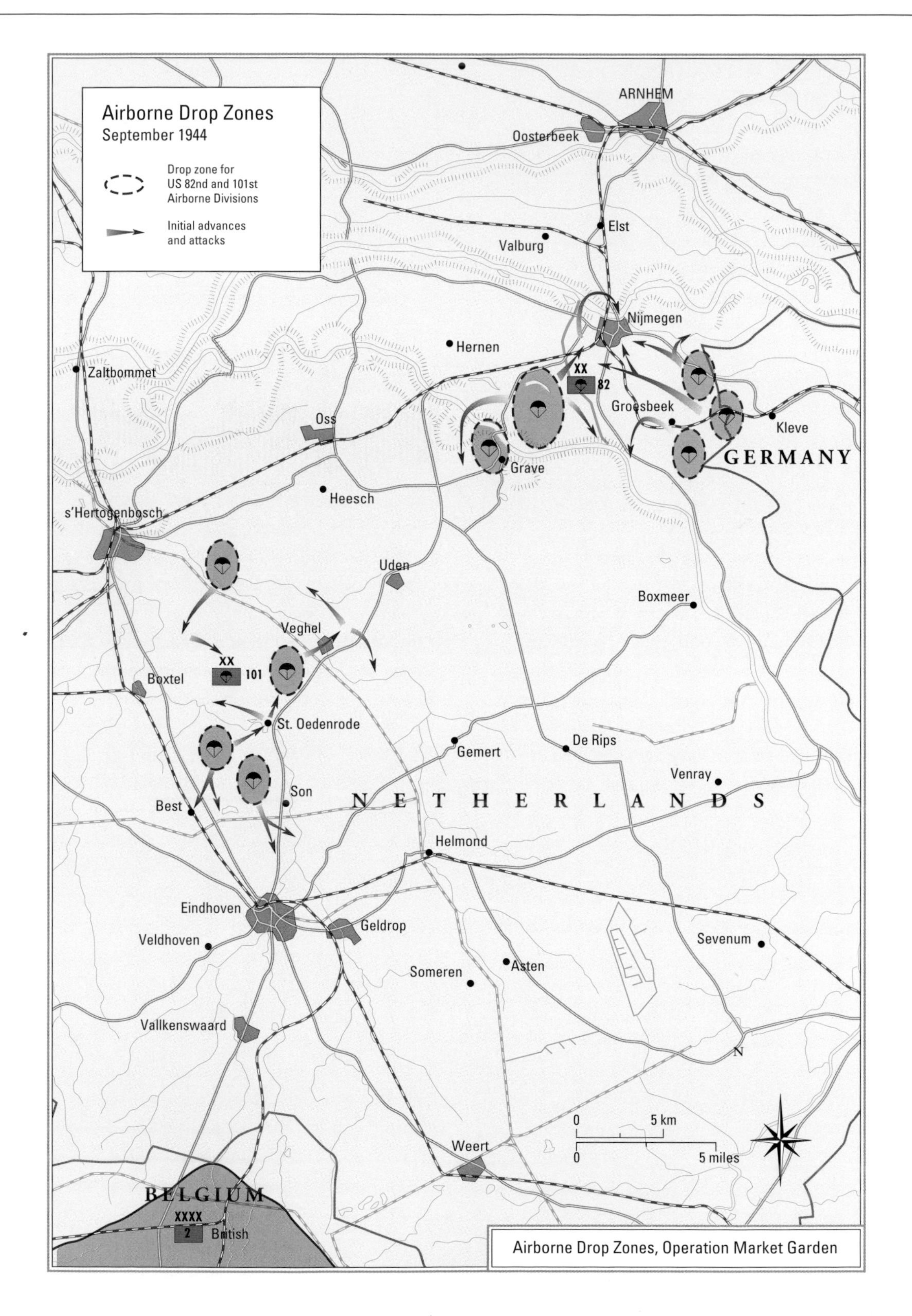

Airborne Drop Zones, Operation Market Garden

Jones and Company H at about 6 p.m. on the 17th, but the effort was cut short by darkness. The next morning, Cole spoke over his radio to a pilot flying nearby. The pilot asked for orange recognition panels to be placed on the ground near the battalion command post, and the officer decided to handle the chore himself. Cole raised his head slightly and shielded his eyes against the sun, looking overhead for the plane. A single shot rang out, and Cole fell dead from a sniper's bullet fired from a farmhouse 300 yards (275m) distant.

The capture of Best would ultimately require two more days and a significantly larger force, including British tanks and two more battalions of troops. Private First Class Joe E. Mann was posthumously awarded the Medal of Honor for heroism during the battle for Best. Like Cole, he was killed by a German sniper.

South of Son, General Taylor accompanied the 1st Battalion, 506th, in a move toward the Wilhelmina Canal road bridge. Just south of the town near the edge of the Zonsche Forest, German 88mm guns opened up on the paratroopers. More 88s zeroed in on the other two battalions of the 506th, led by Colonel Sink.

Paratrooper Don Burgett, a member of the 1st Battalion, recalled the vicious battle for Son. "We organized and we began to charge the guns," he said. "The only way we were going to survive was to knock out the 88s even though a lot of us were going to die trying to do it. As we were running toward them, they fired at us at point-blank range. We overran their positions. There were several 88s. They were sandbagged and dug in and used for antiaircraft. A trooper from D Company got in close enough and fired a bazooka and knocked out one of the guns."

Opposite: The Operation Market Garden drop zones of the 101st and 82nd Airborne Divisions were north of the town of Eindhoven and in the vicinity of Nijmegen respectively. The American paratroopers opened portions of a corridor toward the town of Arnhem on the Lower Rhine River.

Above: General Maxwell Taylor, commander of the 101st Airborne Division, salutes for a photographer as he poses at the door of a transport aircraft prior to Operation Market Garden.

Both groups of the 506th then moved toward the bridge. "We overran the 88s, took the German gunners prisoner, and someone said, 'Let's take the bridge,'" Burgett continued. "We started to run toward the bridge. We were within yards of the bridge when the Germans blew it up. It went off with quite a force... We hit the ground. I rolled over on my back because everything got real quiet, and I saw the debris in the air. I remember seeing this tiny straw that was turning slowly way up in the air and as it hit its maximum trajectory and it started to come down, it became larger and larger. About halfway down we realized the size of this thing. It was probably about two feet wide and forty feet long [0.6 by 12m]. There was no place to run. When it hit the ground, the ground shook like Jell-O."

With the Son Bridge in ruins, the capture of Eindhoven was impeded. However, XXX

Above: American paratroopers with bayonets fixed and one of them riding a bicycle escort German prisoners toward a rear area during Operation Market Garden. The American airborne troops remained in action for days after their jump into Holland.

Corps halted that evening at Valkenswaard, six miles (10km) away. Unexpectedly heavy German resistance had upset the timetable for Garden. The narrow road was elevated above the surrounding fields, and British tanks were silhouetted against the sun, perfect targets for German antitank weapons. Each time a machine-gun nest erupted, the narrow British column was required to halt and deploy infantry to remove the threat.

By the time XXX Corps got to Eindhoven the next day, the town was in the hands of the 101st. At nightfall on the 17th, the 101st was in control of Veghel, St. Oedenrode, and Son. Although the 502nd had encountered tough German troops around Best, the objective there was secondary. With a few more hours of hard fighting, the 101st would have its stretch of Hell's Highway completely open.

Almost from the beginning, jubilant Dutch civilians had welcomed the Allied paratroopers as liberators. Early on the morning of September 18, the 506th destroyed a pair of German 88s and pushed into Eindhoven. While throngs of citizens celebrated their apparent liberation in the streets, the paratroopers disarmed a handful of Germans. One American officer recalled, "The reception was terrific. The air seemed to reek with hate for the Germans...."

Finally, at 5 p.m. on the 18th, the leading elements of XXX Corps rumbled through Eindhoven virtually without stopping. At Son, Canadian engineers, who had been notified that the existing bridge had been destroyed, worked through the night to deploy a prefabricated

Bailey bridge. At 6:45 a.m. on the 19th, the tanks of XXX Corps rumbled across the Wilhelmina Canal, but they were 33 critical hours behind schedule.

Later on the morning of September 19, XXX Corps was across the Willems Canal and the Aa River at Veghel, moving into the zone of the 82nd Airborne. In the 101st sector, the primary job became holding the narrow corridor of hope open against repeated German counterattacks. While Allied armor was advancing northward, it was vital to keep the road open to facilitate the flow of troops and supplies.

The Germans, however, fought back viciously against 101st defensive positions around Eindhoven, Son, St. Oedenrode, and Veghel. General Taylor likened the actions to the bushwhacking style of Indian fighting in the Old American West. The Germans attacked repeatedly, cutting the vital road. The troopers of the 101st drove them back each time.

On the 22nd, the Germans mounted a counterattack against Veghel supported by heavy artillery and aircraft. The attack was not completely beaten back until two days later. "It was a very depressing atmosphere listening to the civilians moan, shriek, sing hymns and say their prayers," wrote Daniel Kenyon Webster of E Company, 506th PIR, remembering the steady concussions of artillery shells as they pelted the town.

Webster and Private Don Wiseman burrowed deeply into a foxhole. "Wiseman and I sat in our corners and cursed," Webster continued. "Every time we heard a shell come over, we closed our eyes and put our heads between our legs. Every time the shells went off, we looked up and grinned at each other."

On September 24, the Germans ravaged a British column on Hell's Highway at Koevering, northeast of Eindhoven. Burgett remembered, "Germans brought up some 40mm cannons and they had some self-propelled guns and they shot the British who were lined up on the side of the road and they were brewing tea in these five-gallon tins and the Germans just opened up on them. They killed over 300.

"When we got down to Koevering, the trucks were still burning," continued Burgett. "We went into the attack immediately. I remember we killed two Germans in a haystack. Then we made an attack west across the road to a farmhouse. The farmhouse was set on fire. We went into the German side and we drove them back."

When it became apparent that Market Garden was to be a strategic failure, the men of the 101st Airborne were able to say with pride that they

2¢ Weather FAIR — Daily Mirror — 2¢

Vol. 21. No. 74. R — NEW YORK, MONDAY, SEPTEMBER 18, 1944 — COMPLETE SPORTS

AIR ARMY REACHES RHINE IN HOLLAND

Huge Sky Force Routs Nazis

FLANK REICH DEFENSES

Story on Page 3

Right: An overly optimistic headline blares erroneous news of success in the aftermath of Operation Market Garden. Although some gains were made, the British 1st Airborne Division was nearly annihilated at Arnhem.

had done their part. Gains were made, and the division had killed many Germans and captured 3,511. Its own losses were 2,110 dead, wounded, and missing.

Island Fighting

General Taylor recognized that the 101st's hold on the highway corridor was threatened from both east and west and dependent on the movement of the British VIII and XII Corps coming up on the flanks to help in its defense. In response to German probing attacks, Taylor launched limited offensive actions of his own, keeping the enemy off balance and delaying a decisive blow against the vital roadway to the north.

Although most of the men of the 101st expected to be pulled out of the line at the end of September, the division was placed under the control of the British XII Corps on the 28th and transferred north to the front line in an area known as "the Island," a three-mile (5km) strip of land between the Lower Rhine and the Waal.

"I emptied the first clip (eight rounds) and, still standing in the middle of the road, put in a second clip and, still shooting from the hip, emptied that clip into the mass."

Due to the heavy casualties absorbed during Market Garden, the British were sorely pressed for troops, and both the 101st and 82nd Airborne Divisions found themselves in positions that resembled the static trench lines of World War I. They were regularly subjected to artillery duels between British and German guns. There were also sharp firefights with enemy troops.

On the night of October 5, a platoon of Company E, 506th PIR, supported by a detachment from Company F, mauled two companies of German SS troops attempting to infiltrate American lines in support of an attack by the 363rd Volksgrenadier Division. Captain Richard Winters, who had directed the successful attack at Brecourt Manor in Normandy and was now in charge of Company E, led his 35 men brilliantly, demonstrating bravery and coolness under fire.

Moving along a road adjacent to a dike near the banks of the Lower Rhine, Winters shot a German who was only three yards (2.75m) away, then opened up on a large mass of enemy troops. "The movements of the Germans seemed to be unreal to me," he reflected. "When they rose up, it seemed to be so slow, when they turned to look over their shoulders at me, it was in slow motion, when they started to raise their rifles to fire at me, it was in slow, slow motion. I emptied the first clip (eight rounds) and, still standing in the middle of the road, put in a second clip and, still shooting from the hip, emptied that clip into the mass."

Winters remembered that particular fight as the "highlight of all E Company actions for the entire war, even better than D-Day, because it demonstrated Easy's overall superiority in every phase of infantry tactics: patrol, defense, attack under a base of fire, withdrawal, and above all, superior marksmanship with rifles, machine gun, and mortar fire."

The 101st Airborne Division held its positions on the Island until late November, when it was withdrawn to Camp Mourmelon, outside the French village of Mourmelon-le-Grand. From the Market Garden drop until its last troopers were relieved, the 101st had spent 72 days in combat areas. In addition to its Market Garden losses, the defensive fighting at the Island cost the Screaming Eagles another 1,682 casualties.

Bridges and High Ground

While considering the role his 82nd Airborne Division was to play in Operation Market Garden, 37-year-old Brigadier General James

Above: Young Dutch civilians assist American airborne troopers in orienting themselves with a map during Operation Market Garden. Note that censors have obscured the paratroopers' shoulder patches identifying their division.

Gavin understood a few things clearly. His division would attempt to take each of its objectives in a single day. The 82nd would also be required to hold these objectives for at least 36 hours, since relief from XXX Corps could not realistically be expected until some time late on September 18.

Further, Gavin could easily see from maps that the terrain surrounding the towns and bridges that were critical to the prosecution of the offensive were dominated by a triangular ridgeline that ran from just southeast of Nijmegen past a resort hotel called the Berg en Dal through the towns of Wyler, Groesbeek, and Riethorst along the Maas River. Roughly eight miles (13km) long and 300 feet (90m) high, the ridge offered a clear view and fields of fire for a great distance. It terminated in the east along the Dutch–German frontier, disappearing into the deep, almost impenetrable, forest of the Reichswald.

Given the priority of the high ground, Gavin and General Browning, who served as deputy commander of the First Allied Airborne Army, initially agreed that all other objectives should be attained before the effort to secure the Nijmegen Bridge over the Waal. Later, Gavin concluded that he could spare a single battalion to take a stab at the bridge before the Germans reacted to the offensive in force.

Gavin ordered Colonel Roy E. Lundquist, commander of the 508th PIR, to send the single battalion against the span at Nijmegen while the remainder of the regiment secured about six miles (10km) of the ridgeline from Nijmegen south to Groesbeek. The 508th was also to assist in the capture of the bridges across the Maas–Waal Canal at Honinghutje and Hatert, cut the approaches from the north to delay the German response to the airdrop, and safeguard the perimeter of the glider landing zone south of Wyler.

Colonel William E. Eckman's 505th PIR was primarily tasked with capturing the town of Groesbeek and the ridgeline further south to the town of Kiekberg at Hill 77.2 and securing the second glider landing zone. Meanwhile, Colonel Reuben Tucker's 504th PIR was slated to capture the big bridge across the Maas River near the town of Grave, capture the bridges over the Maas–Waal Canal at Malden and Heumen, and prevent the Germans from shuttling troops between the Maas and the Maas–Waal Canal.

Encountering light resistance in and around the drop zones, the troopers of the 82nd Airborne moved out. The capture of the Grave bridge was eased unexpectedly when the 16 troopers of the 504th aboard a single C-47 were delayed a few seconds in jumping. When the green light was illuminated, Lieutenant John S. Thompson, commanding the stick, noticed the plane was above a cluster of buildings. He decided to hold off a moment and attempt to come down in a nearby field.

After Thompson's men hit the silk, they came to earth just 700 yards (640m) off the southern end of the bridge. With the rest of the 504th over a mile away, Thompson acted quickly. Dashing through sporadic rifle fire and crouching in drainage ditches, the troopers blasted a flak tower

Right: The embattled bridge over the Lower Rhine River at Arnhem is shown during Operation Market Garden. Elements of the British 1st Airborne Division reached the bridge and suffered mightily at the hands of superior German forces.

mounting a 20mm gun with a pair of bazooka rounds, cut wires to demolition charges, and took control of the southern end of the bridge.

On the other bank of the Maas, the remainder of Thompson's battalion assembled and moved toward the Grave Bridge, shrugging off the fire of a single flak gun near the water's edge. One of the principal objectives of Operation Market Garden was secured in only three hours. When patrols were sent into Grave, the Americans found that the Germans had pulled out. The townspeople were celebrating with a chorus of the popular tune "Tipperary."

Commanding a battalion of the 504th PIR, Major Willard E. Harrison sent single companies to seize bridges over the Maas–Waal Canal at Malden and Heumen. At Heumen, the Germans poured rifle and machine-gun fire from an island in the canal, but eight men crept forward to place covering fire on the island. Two officers, a radio operator, and a corporal rushed toward the bridge. One of the men was shot, but six more troopers rowed a small boat across the canal and joined the three who had survived the deadly run. When darkness fell, a reinforced patrol sprinted across a footbridge and overwhelmed the Germans on the island.

Leading the company at Heumen, Captain Thomas Helgeson had expected the Germans to blow the bridge sky high, but inexplicably it stood. Charges were spotted, and a demolition team cut the wires. Just as a squad of troopers reached the river at Malden, that bridge exploded in dust and debris. The bridge at Heumen later became the primary northward route of

Below: Paratroopers of the 101st Airborne Division inspect the wreckage of a crashed CG-4 Waco glider during Operation Market Garden. Glider troops played a significant role in the fighting in Holland.

Above: German trucks run a gauntlet of fire as they attempt to cross the bridge at Arnhem. The British 2nd Battalion, 1st Parachute Brigade, reached the span and fought doggedly before a handful of survivors surrendered to the enemy.

XXX Corps. Troopers of the 504th and 508th found the bridge over the Maas–Waal Canal at Hatert demolished. When more 508th men approached the last canal bridge at Honinghutje before daylight the next morning, the Germans detonated explosives that failed to destroy the span, but rendered it unusable.

On to Nijmegen

One battalion of the 508th PIR set up roadblocks on the highway from Mook to Nijmegen to contest any German move south, while a second set out to occupy the northern end of the long ridge from the outskirts of Nijmegen to the Berg en Dal resort, a distance of three and one-half miles (6km). Only light resistance was encountered in this effort, and the following day the battalion cut the Kleve–Nijmegen Highway with the occupation of the village of Beek at the base of the ridge.

Lieutenant Colonel Shields Warren, Jr., led the 1st Battalion, 508th, in the hopeful quick strike at the highway bridge across the formidably wide Waal at Nijmegen. An apparent misinterpretation of Gavin's order, which the general later remembered as instructing a battalion to advance on the big bridge "without delay after landing," led Colonel Lundquist to rely more directly on the original plan to secure other objectives prior to any move against the highway bridge across the Waal.

Lundquist, therefore, ordered Warren to organize defensive positions at De Ploeg, a suburb of Nijmegen, and establish communications with similar positions around the Berg en Dal. For Warren, pulling his troops together and reaching De Ploeg required more than three hours, and by the time the first assignment from Lundquist was completed it was 6:30 p.m. Dutch civilians reported to Lundquist that only 18 Germans were standing watch at the southern end of the highway bridge, and the battalion commander sent a reinforced patrol consisting of his intelligence section and a rifle company into Nijmegen to assess the situation. Due to a radio malfunction, the patrol was unable to send any information to Warren until the next day.

Gavin sensed an opportunity and prodded Lundquist with a terse order "to delay not a second longer and get the bridge as quickly as possible with Warren's battalion." Still, seven precious hours had slipped away before a concerted effort to seize the Nijmegen Bridge went forward. After a Dutch civilian offered to guide his battalion into the town to meet with resistance leaders who might have more information on German strength in the vicinity, Warren instead instructed Companies A and B to link up southeast of Nijmegen at 7 p.m. and follow the Dutchman to the bridge. Company A reached the designated point on time; however, Company B got lost along the way.

An hour later, when he could wait no longer, Warren left a guide for Company B and set out with Company A toward the highway bridge.

Below: American paratroopers of the 82nd Airborne Division offload from a British-manned DUKW amphibious vehicle that has just ferried them across the Waal River near the town of Nijmegen.

Advancing deliberately through the darkened streets of Nijmegen, the troopers of Company A cleared houses on the edge of town. Finding no Germans, they continued their stealthy approach until they reached the Keizer Karelplein, a traffic circle in the center of Nijmegen. At approximately 10 p.m., the staccato of automatic weapons halted their progress.

General Bittrich's insight was about to cost the Americans dearly. While the paratroopers took cover against the small-arms fire, they heard engines roaring forward, followed quickly by squeaking brakes and the sounds of men jumping from trucks. The leading elements of the 10th SS Panzer Division had arrived in Nijmegen. In that instant, the opportunity to capture the highway bridge against light opposition was snuffed out. Just a few hours earlier, the Germans in Nijmegen numbered a relative few troops of inferior combat efficiency. These newly arrived SS men were battle-hardened veterans.

Company A tried twice to take the southern end of the bridge, and twice they were thrown back by counterattacking Germans. With that, the effort to take the Nijmegen Bridge on September 17 petered out. Gavin arrived and observed that the paratroopers were hotly engaged, but getting nowhere. He ordered them to "withdraw from close proximity to the bridge and reorganize."

A small patrol led by Captain Jonathan Adams, Jr., received word from the Dutch resistance that the detonation equipment for the explosive charges wired to the bridge was located in the nearby post office. Shooting their way past the guards at the door, the Americans burst inside the building, destroyed what they believed to be the detonation equipment, and then found themselves cut off and unable to return to the traffic circle. With the help of resistance fighters, Adams and his men held off the Germans until they were rescued three days later.

The next morning at 7:45, Company G, 3rd Battalion, 508th, was called from atop Hill 64, about a mile from the southern end of the bridge. Renewing the effort to take the span, Captain Frank Novak led his men through some back streets on the edge of Nijmegen, somewhat shielded from the Germans' view. The troopers were greeted by smiling townspeople, who threw flowers and fruit to them. However, as the Americans got closer to the bridge, the adoring throng dissipated, a cloud of tension replacing it.

Shooting their way past the guards at the door, the Americans burst inside the building, destroyed the detonation equipment, and then found themselves cut off.

The Germans had worked through the night to strengthen their positions around the traffic circle and waited. When the Americans approached, they opened with rifles, machine guns, 20mm flak cannon, and 88mm artillery. Novak sent his men through the withering fire, and the troopers advanced to within a block of the traffic circle before they were stopped. Reinforcements could not be sent to Novak's aid without weakening the defenses along the critical ridgeline or jeopardizing the security of one of the glider-landing zones, where planes were expected at any time. At 2 p.m. Company G was pulled out of its hard-won position and returned to Hill 64.

While the Nijmegen highway bridge was firmly in German hands, at least for the time being, the gliders began to slide into their landing zones. The perimeters of the zones were thinly held, and German soldiers infiltrated from the Reichswald under cover of darkness, resulting in pitched battles. During one of these a company of the 508th PIR was surrounded for a while, and stiff resistance delayed the 505th in clearing the other of enemy troops.

The long bridge at Nijmegen was heavily defended by the Germans, and the 82nd Airborne Division fought savagely to capture it. An assault on both ends of the bridge was finally successful as paratroopers executed an amphibious crossing of the Waal River.

Colonel Lundquist sent a company of the 508th to sweep the northern landing zone, and the eight-mile (13-km) forced march from Nijmegen took its toll on the already exhausted troopers. Nevertheless, they mounted a downhill charge into the teeth of German small-arms fire and flak guns. When the battle reached a crescendo, the Germans finally broke and ran. Just as gliders began touching down, the paratroopers chased the last enemy soldiers from the area. They had killed 50 Germans and captured 150 more at the cost of 11 casualties. Bad weather, however, forced the postponement of the insertion of the 325th Glider Infantry Regiment set for the 19th.

American paratroopers along the corridor to Nijmegen consolidated defensive positions and held against German attacks here and there. Contradictory reports of the presence of enemy tanks in the Reichswald filtered through command posts. General Browning initially approved a plan to capture the bridge in a night assault on September 18, but then decided that holding the high ground in anticipation of the arrival of XXX Corps was the best tactic. Gavin canceled the plan.

Within hours of crossing the Wilhelmina Canal at Son, the vanguard of XXX Corps reached Nijmegen. A flicker of hope remained that the ground forces might reach Frost's men at Arnhem.

From Both Ends

On the afternoon of September 19, General Gavin conferred with General Sir Brian Horrocks, commander of XXX Corps, and described a plan that he believed offered the best opportunity to seize the highway bridge. "There's only one way to take this bridge," he had already briefed his staff. "We've got to get it simultaneously from both ends."

Gavin intended to send paratroopers across the Waal in small boats downstream from the highway bridge and a nearby railroad bridge that had been a secondary objective. Once on the northern bank of the river, these troopers would outflank the defenders of both bridges, forcing them to withdraw.

While the amphibious assault was underway, the defenders at the southern ends of both bridges were to be hit hard by combined elements of XXX Corps and the 82nd Airborne. The plan was rife with risk. However, while Gavin thought of his own men and the casualties they would likely absorb, he also considered the plight of the beleaguered 1st Airborne at Arnhem. It was imperative for XXX Corps to cross the Waal. At the same time, Gavin had been forced to divert troops from other sectors to Nijmegen, and prolonged fighting had reduced his strength along the ridgeline significantly. Two days into Market Garden, Company A, 505th PIR, was down to two officers and 42 men.

While the amphibious operation was being discussed, efforts to breach the German defenses at the bridges continued. On the afternoon of September 19, the 2nd Battalion, 505th PIR, under Lieutenant Colonel B.H. Vandervoort, supported by a British infantry company and a battalion of Guards Armoured Division tanks, attacked the southern end of the railroad bridge. Some American paratroopers hitched rides atop the British tanks for the run in, and the direct assault was underway at 3 p.m. Company D, 505th, commanded by Lieutenant Oliver B. Carr, began taking fire from the railroad marshaling yards about 1,000 yards (914m) from the southern end of the bridge.

Covered by supporting fire from the tanks and the artillery of the 82nd Airborne and Guards Armoured Divisions, Carr's men cut the distance to their objective in half, but came under a hail of fire from heavy-caliber guns between the bridge and the railroad station. A shell from a German 88mm gun slammed into the lead British tank and disabled it. Repeated efforts to renew the advance were fruitless.

At the same time, paratroopers, British infantry, and tanks hit the southern end of the highway bridge. When the attackers closed to within 300 yards (274m) of the traffic circle, they split left and right into two groups. Simultaneously, a German crossfire from the traffic circle and the streets that emptied into it began blazing away. On the left, Company F, 505th PIR, inched ahead, but its supporting tanks were stopped cold by a log barricade. On the right, the British troops, Company E, 505th, and the rest of the armor advanced within 100 yards (91m) of the traffic circle before an antitank gun destroyed the lead British tank and three more were crippled in rapid succession. The assault stalled, and further attempts during the long afternoon were also repulsed.

For the fourth time, the Allies had been denied the highway bridge over the Waal, and the Germans held firm at the railroad bridge as well. It seemed to some of the tired paratroopers that mere yards may as well have been miles. As twilight shrouded the scene, the firing dissipated.

On the night of the 19th, Gavin ordered Colonel Tucker to detach two companies to defend the bridges over the Maas and Maas–Waal Canal. The remainder of the 504th PIR received orders to make the hazardous amphibious crossing at Nijmegen. The Americans failed to

Below: British and American soldiers stack dynamite charges against the railing of the bridge at Nijmegen during Operation Market Garden. After the bridge was captured from the Germans, demolition charges had to be removed.

American paratroopers of the 82nd Airborne Division hitch a ride aboard an M4 Sherman medium tank of British XXX Corps. British armored forces crossed the Waal River at Nijmegen and waited for infantry support before proceeding toward Arnhem.

scrounge enough boats to make the assault, but the British offered a solution. Thirty-three canvas boats from the XXX Corps engineers could be brought up by midday on the 20th. Originally set for 1 p.m., the attack was postponed for two hours when the boats were delayed in rear echelon traffic.

While the area the amphibious assault would launch from along the southern bank of the Waal was cleared of Germans and the attack on the southern end of the highway bridge was renewed, strong German counterattacks from the Reichswald threatened the plans at Nijmegen. Although the 1st Battalion, 505th, gave ground around the villages of Riethorst and Mook, Major Talton W. Long committed two platoons of infantry, the only reserve he had, and tanks from the Coldstream Guards of XXX Corps rumbled up to bolster new defensive positions. When the Germans had finally been beaten back, Long's battalion counted 20 killed in action, 54 wounded, and seven men missing.

To the north, two platoons of the 508th PIR were forced out of the village of Wyler, and troopers were pushed back near the town of Beek toward the Berg en Dal. The Germans missed an opportunity to slip around the right flank of the defenders and reach the outskirts of Nijmegen unmolested. The 508th fought through the next day to regain the lost ground.

A River to Cross

As the hour of 3 p.m. on September 20, 1944 approached, Major Julian Cook and the troopers of the 3rd Battalion, 504th PIR, prepared for one of the epic assaults of World War II. The flimsy canvas and plywood boats that would carry them from the vicinity of a power plant on the southern bank across the 400-yard (365-m) breadth of the Waal River about a mile north of the railroad bridge were assembled. However, they reached the paratroopers only 20 minutes before the attack was to step off.

The boats were only 19 feet (6m) long, and when they arrived the men counted 26 of them rather than 33. To deliver all the troopers slated for the first wave to cross the Waal, these puny craft would be dangerously loaded beyond capacity. Three engineers rode in each boat, and were ordered to paddle back across the river for another load when the first men had reached the far side.

To support the crossing that was intended to outflank the Germans on the northern bank of the river and oblige them to withdraw from the bridges, a detail from another battalion of the 504th would join in the crossing while rocket-firing Hawker Typhoon fighter bombers would roar in to soften up the German positions and about 100 artillery pieces would fire a 15-minute preparatory barrage and lay a smokescreen to obscure the vision of the German gunners watching the paratroopers paddle across the choppy river like sitting ducks.

To effect the crossing in the face of heavy German small-arms and artillery fire, the paratroopers would also have to contend with the swift current of the Waal, running eight to 10 miles per hour (13–16km/h) in some locations. The surrounding terrain was flat and open, and though General Gavin had intended for the boats to load in a secluded area near the mouth of the Maas–Waal Canal, the current was so swift that it was necessary to load in the open with the barrels of German guns pointing at the men while observers among the tall steel girders of the railroad bridge watched their every move.

Seconds after the Allied artillery switched from high explosive to white phosphorous shells, the wind began to sweep the shroud of smoke away, and little cover was provided. Carrying the assault boats on their shoulders, the paratroopers stepped into the shallow water along the edge of the Waal. Some lost their footing in the current. Others were mired in the muddy bottom. Machine-gun bullets zipped into the water and

Above: British tanks of XXX Corps are shown along the Nijmegen Bridge after its capture. The tanks were within striking distance of Arnhem, but the final thrust came too late for the 1st Airborne Division fighting in the area.

tore the canvas sides of the boats while 20mm guns on and near the railroad bridge barked.

Several of the boats were shredded. One was hit by mortar fire and capsized a mere 20 yards (18m) from the northern bank. Private Joseph Jedlicka went straight to the bottom of the Waal in eight feet (2.5m) of water, but managed to maintain his wits, hold his breath and his Browning Automatic Rifle (BAR), and walk to the shoreline: The scene was reminiscent of Dante's *Inferno* with smoke, fire, blood, and death everywhere.

Lieutenant Colonel J.O.E. "Joe" Vandeleur, commander of the 3rd Battalion, Irish Guards, described what he saw unfolding. "It was a horrible, horrible sight," he later wrote. "Boats were literally blown out of the water. Huge geysers shot up as shells hit and small-arms fire from the northern bank made the river look like a seething cauldron. I remember almost trying to will the Americans to go faster."

Major Cook, a devout Catholic, was in the first wave, paddling and loudly reciting the "Hail Mary" amid the storm of enemy fire. Half the boats were lost, but the engineers turned the remaining 13 back for another load; 11 of them managed to run the gauntlet. The heroic men aboard these boats made six trips during the long afternoon, delivering the balance of the 3rd Battalion and then the 1st Battalion, 504th, to the northern bank.

Those who survived the harrowing crossing set to work in small groups, since unit cohesion was virtually nonexistent. Leaving more than 50 Germans dead along the riverbank, the first paratroopers sprinted across an open field to a roadbed lined with dikes about 800 yards (730m) from the Waal. In hand-to-hand combat they cleared out the Germans with bayonets and grenades.

Although they had become jumbled during the crossing, the paratroopers maintained the initiative, men following officers of different companies, but working as teams to silence machine-gun positions and scatter the defenders. When they came upon the German strongpoint at Fort Hof van Holland, the paratroopers had been ordered to bypass the spot, but instead seized an opportunity to take it. Sergeant Leroy Richmond of Company H swam underwater across a moat surrounding the fort and motioned to his comrades to follow across a causeway. They rushed forward to take out the machine guns and 20mm flak cannon that were firing at the Americans from the fort's towers.

While the attack pressed on, the Germans apparently never attempted to blow up either the railroad or the highway bridge. Men of Companies H and I reached the northern ends of both spans and played automatic weapons fire across them.

Finally, around 4:20 p.m., the German defenders at the traffic circle began to crack. Paratroopers of the 505th PIR and British tanks hammered their way through the streets and into the enemy perimeter to claim the southern end of the highway bridge. British tankers saw an American flag flying across the river and believed it was the signal to cross the highway bridge to the northern bank. The flag was actually at the railroad bridge, and the Americans on the other

Below: After a difficult fight with the Germans, paratroopers of the 82nd Airborne Division walk the streets of Nijmegen. Major Julian Cook led an amphibious assault that finally cracked the stubborn German defenses near the bridge over the Waal River.

side were still some distance from the highway bridge at the time. Nevertheless, four tanks started across the Waal, guns blazing as they went, and three of them reached the other side.

At 7:10 p.m., three privates of Companies H and I reached the northern end of the highway bridge to link up with the British tanks. The protracted fight was over.

Four tanks started across the Waal, guns blazing as they went, and three of them reached the other side.

At the railroad bridge, Germans streamed back toward the northern bank of the Waal and became trapped on the span as Allied troops sprayed them with rifle and machine-gun fire. A total of 267 Germans were killed on the railroad bridge, and dozens of prisoners were captured.

Cook's 3rd Battalion paid a high price for the success with 28 dead, 78 wounded, and one man missing. In the extended fight at the traffic circle, the 505th had lost about 200 men. During Market Garden, the 82nd Airborne suffered 1,432 casualties. Major Cook survived the ordeal and later received the Distinguished Service Cross. General Horrocks mused that the 3rd Battalion's combat transit of the Waal was "the most gallant attack ever carried out" in World War II.

Allied commanders were puzzled as to why the Germans had not blown the key bridges when it became apparent that their grip was slipping away. Courage and good fortune had, at long last, won the day.

Twilight Time

Colonel Reuben Tucker was justifiably proud of his command, which had finally kicked open the door to Arnhem. However, as some tanks of XXX Corps helped hold the lodgment on the northern bank of the Waal, the large armored column halted in and around Nijmegen. Running low on fuel and ammunition, the tankers were exhausted. Their infantry support, critical to the advance of the armor along the narrow, elevated road to Arnhem, had not come up yet, and daylight was ebbing away.

Tucker was dumbfounded. "We had killed ourselves crossing the Waal to grab the north end of the bridge. We just stood there seething, as the British settled in for the night, failing to take advantage of the situation. We couldn't understand it. It simply wasn't the way we did things in the American Army – especially if it had been our men hanging by their fingernails 11 miles [18km] away."

Frost's battalion lost its hold on the northern end of the Arnhem Bridge across the Lower Rhine on September 21 and was driven back into the town. The Germans controlled the span and used it to move tanks, artillery, and SS troops to block the advance of XXX Corps toward Arnhem. The first effort to reach the trapped British paras progressed four miles (6.5km), but could go no farther. An airdrop of the Polish 1st Independent Parachute Brigade was unable to establish a link with the bulk of the 1st Airborne ensconced at Oosterbeek and under constant pressure from German artillery and infantry probes.

By the afternoon of September 20, Frost's contingent in Arnhem had ceased to exist as a fighting force. On September 25, the remnants of the 1st Airborne Division began filtering back from the northern bank of the Lower Rhine. Although Market Garden had ended in disappointment, some gains were achieved. The northern flank of the Allied armies was extended 65 miles (105km) across two canals and the Maas and Waal rivers, while a considerable amount of Dutch territory had been freed from Nazi occupation.

Although the two U.S. airborne divisions that had participated in Operation Market Garden were to have been released as soon as possible after their missions were accomplished, the 82nd

Airborne, like the 101st, remained in the line for days. Its troopers successfully defended against attempts by the German II Parachute Corps to take the hills and ridges around Groesbeek, and elements of the division joined the 101st on the Island. While senior commanders argued for the release of the airborne divisions, particularly since additional operations were planned near the end of the year, the acute shortage of British manpower required that the Americans remain in the combat zone.

Finally, on November 11, a full 55 days after their Market Garden jump, the 82nd Airborne began pulling out of the line. In addition to its casualties in Market Garden, the division lost 1,912 men while defending the highway corridor, the high ground, and the Island.

As the paratroopers of the 82nd and 101st were trucked down the roads they had fought for nearly two months earlier, Dutch civilians often lined the streets in the towns and villages. Many of them shouted, "September 17!" To this day, they remember the heroism of all the Allied troops who made sacrifices for their freedom and for the bridges northward into Holland.

Below: After the fierce fight for Nijmegen and the long bridge across the Waal River, American paratroopers stand watch over wounded German prisoners. The heroic action at Nijmegen opened the last leg of the road to Arnhem for XXX Corps.

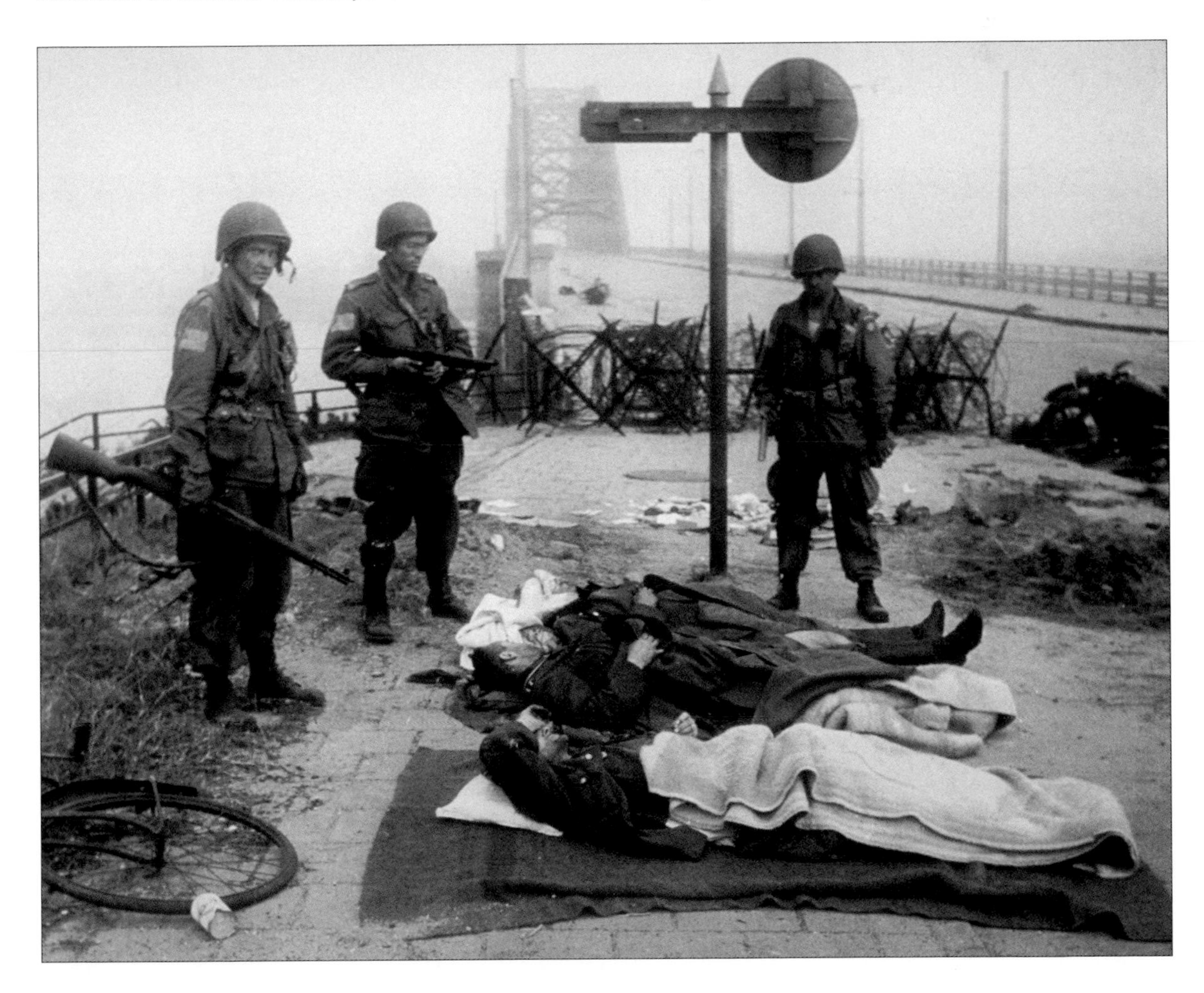

CHAPTER 6

THE BATTLE OF THE BULGE

Intelligence reports were discounted. The sounds of engines and troop movements were simply various units repositioning. The Germans were in no shape to mount an offensive in the dead of the coldest winter in Western Europe in 40 years—or so most Allied commanders believed.

At 5:30 a.m. on December 16, 1944, the roar of German artillery shattered the stillness of the Ardennes Forest, a usually quiet sector of the Allied lines near the borders shared by Germany, Belgium, Luxembourg, and France. Hitler had unleashed Operation Watch on the Rhine, his last desperate gamble in the West, to drive a wedge between the Allied 12th and 21st Army Groups. His armored spearheads were sweeping across the Meuse River, then rolling on to capture the great Belgian port of Antwerp.

With hundreds of tanks, 2,000 artillery pieces, and 275,000 troops, Hitler hoped to strike a decisive blow that would at least disrupt Allied supply lines and cripple the enemy's eastward push into Germany, possibly even compelling them to sue for peace. In the opening hours of the offensive, numerous American units were taken by surprise. Pockets of resistance held out, but the Germans advanced rapidly through the Ardennes, penetrating up to eight miles (13km) on the first day. The untested troops of the 106th Infantry Division were cut off in a rugged area called the Schnee Eifel; in about 48 hours, two entire regiments were forced to surrender.

Senior American commanders slowly became aware of the magnitude of the German offensive. At first they were bewildered, but then they took action to contain the breakthrough and stem the Nazi tide. At his headquarters in Versailles on the outskirts of Paris, Supreme Allied Commander General Dwight D. Eisenhower sorted through contradictory messages from the front.

The weather was atrocious, and Allied air power could not intervene for several days. On the ground, the only reserves available to Eisenhower were the battle-tested 82nd and 101st Airborne Divisions. He ordered them to get moving.

Opposite: After the lifting of the siege of Bastogne, trucks carry supplies through the town. The 101st Airborne Division and elements of other units made an epic stand there during the Battle of the Bulge.

The fighting in Holland had been hard, and the paratroopers of both divisions were resting, absorbing replacements, and coping with the toll that weeks of combat had taken on them mentally and physically. The German breakthrough had occurred more than 100 miles (160km) east of the 101st encampment at Mourmelon-le-Grand, France. The 82nd was billeted in old French Army facilities at Sissone and Suippes. Christmas was coming, and many of the men were hoping for leave, maybe even a trip home—or at least a pass for a couple of days in Paris.

General Matthew Ridgway, commander of the XVIII Airborne Corps, was in England observing the training of the 17th Airborne Division, which had arrived there in August. General Maxwell Taylor, commander of the 101st, was in Washington, D.C., for meetings. Colonel Robert Sink of the 506th PIR was preparing to go home for the holidays.

When General James M. Gavin, commander of the 82nd Airborne, received a telephone call from First Army on the evening of December 17, he was dressing for dinner. By 11:30 that night, he was racing in an open jeep with his aide, Captain Hugo Olsen, and Colonel Al Ireland, an 82nd Airborne staff officer, to the headquarters of General Courtney Hodges, commander of First Army, at Spa, Belgium, 125 miles (200km) away. The trio arrived at 9 a.m. on December 18.

Above: General Courtney Hodges commanded the First U.S. Army, which was hit hard during the opening hours of the Battle of the Bulge.

Left: A German Tiger II "King Tiger" heavy tank rolls along a muddy road past a column of dazed American prisoners. This photo was taken early in the Ardennes Offensive, which came to be known as the Battle of the Bulge.

With Ridgway and Taylor out of the combat area, Gavin was the temporary commander of the XVIII Airborne Corps. He had already issued orders to General Anthony McAuliffe, the artillery officer and acting commander of the 101st Airborne in Taylor's absence, to get the Screaming Eagles ready to deploy. According to the maps spread out at Hodges' headquarters, the Germans had slashed a great breach in the American lines; it appeared that control of the town of Bastogne, Belgium, where seven major roads intersected, would be critical to slowing the enemy's momentum.

Basic military training told the assembled officers that the best way to defeat a serious enemy penetration was to assault its flanks. Before counterattacks could be organized, though, the shoulders of the "bulge" had to be stabilized. South of Bastogne, the veteran 4th Infantry and 9th Armored Divisions were counted on to keep the situation in hand.

Hodges assigned the reinforcement of both Bastogne and the northern shoulder to the two airborne divisions. In the north, a logical focus for defense was the town of Werbomont: The steep banks of the narrow and shallow Amblève River might provide a firebreak against advancing German tanks, and a cluster of hills could offer strong defensive positions with interlocking fields of fire that dominated the approaches.

As word filtered back to the mess halls and barracks at Mourmelon-le-Grand, Sissone, and Suippes, paratroopers were recalled from leave, grumbled about moving out in foul winter weather, ate what would be their last hot meals for days, and gathered weapons, ammunition, and other gear—but no parachutes. This time they rode into action aboard two and one-half ton and open-topped 10-ton trucks.

The historical records of the commands involved are somewhat at odds regarding the eventual deployment of the 82nd Airborne to Werbomont and the 101st to Bastogne. However, when Gavin arrived at First Army headquarters, it was obvious that the major concern involved the armored spearhead of the German Sixth Panzer Army commanded by General Josef "Sepp" Dietrich. Elements of the 1st SS Panzer Division commanded by the ruthless 29-year-old Lieutenant Colonel Joachim Peiper were thrusting toward Werbomont.

"At that time the situation appeared rather vague," Gavin recalled. "The first reports of enemy contact at Stavelot were

Left: A paratrooper of the 101st Airborne Division stands amid the ruins of Bastogne, where his outfit participated in the epic stand that defied German attempts to capture the vital town.

just coming in. It was reported that an enemy force at Stavelot had driven our troops across the [Amblève] river...The situation south and west of Stavelot was unknown except that the enemy had evidently overrun our front positions. There appeared to be a large force of U.S. troops centered at St. Vith."

General Hodges ordered the 82nd, already on the road to Bastogne and leading the drive of the two airborne divisions into Belgium, to head toward Werbomont, where McAuliffe also originally intended to report to Gavin. However, McAuliffe subsequently decided to divert to Bastogne and the headquarters of General Troy Middleton, commanding the battered VIII Corps, to gain a clearer assessment of the situation. Shortly after McAuliffe arrived at Middleton's headquarters, the VIII Corps commander contacted General Omar Bradley, commanding the 12th Army Group, for approval to bring the 101st to Bastogne instead.

Meanwhile, Gavin headed for Werbomont and made a personal reconnaissance of the ground the 82nd Airborne was to defend. Elements of the 30th Infantry Division, commanded by General Leland Hobbs, had moved into the area around Malmedy and Stavelot on December 17; by the following day, they were in position to screen the deployment of the 82nd Airborne. As Ridgway was arriving on the scene and establishing his corps headquarters near the command post of the 82nd, Gavin drove back to Bastogne and conferred with McAuliffe and Middleton, returning to Werbomont around 8 p.m. on the 18th, just as the first troopers of the 82nd were climbing out of their trucks.

Above: General Anthony McAuliffe assumed temporary command of the 101st Airborne Division and led capably during the critical siege of Bastogne during the Battle of the Bulge.

Order from Chaos

The tactical mission of the XVIII Airborne Corps was to block the advance of Peiper's armored spearhead in the area of the Amblève River through the towns of Manhay and Houffalize along a line to La Roche near the banks of the Ourthe River. Thus, the corps' right flank terminated 20 miles (32km) north of Bastogne. The most vulnerable areas were identified as the Amblève crossing areas where the 119th Infantry Regiment was defending, the Salm River crossings, particularly at Trois-Ponts, the confluence of the Amblève and the Salm, where Company C, 51st Engineer Combat Battalion, was writing its own incredible story of bravery in the face of overwhelming odds, and the rough country north of the Ourthe River, where some evidence of German movement was trickling into headquarters. Another daunting task for Ridgway was responsibility for covering a 20-mile (32-km) gap that had opened between the V and VII Corps.

To accomplish its mission, the XVIII Airborne Corps was handed tactical control of the 119th

Above: Shrouded in thick fog on December 20, 1944, troopers of the 2nd Battalion, 325th Glider Infantry Regiment, 82nd Airborne Division move to positions along the north shoulder of the "Bulge."

Infantry Regiment and the 740th Tank Battalion from the 30th Infantry Division, along with the 3rd Armored Division. On the morning of December 19, the 504th and 505th PIR moved out of their assembly area to advance as far as possible toward the trouble spots, relieve the 119th Infantry, and establish a bridgehead across shallow Lienne Creek.

By midafternoon, the concentrated 82nd Airborne had the 508th PIR on the road in support of its other two regiments marching between La Gleize and Trois-Ponts. When the 82nd deployments were completed on December 20, a defensive cordon had been established around Werbomont.

On the same day, a concerted effort to surround and cut off Peiper's spearhead was undertaken. The 1st Battalion, 119th Infantry, and Combat Command B, 740th Tank Battalion, attacked the Germans around the towns of Stoumont and La Gleize, while Task Force Lovelady, named for its commander Lieutenant Colonel William B. Lovelady, severed Peiper's line of supply, communication, and most important, retreat, at the village of Stavelot.

To tighten the noose around the Germans' neck, the 82nd Airborne attacked a small German bridgehead across the Amblève River at Cheneux. Patrols made contact with the 119th Infantry and discovered that the single company of the 51st

Engineers had held up Peiper's column at Trois-Ponts, destroying or damaging the bridges there and detonating at least one of them as enemy tanks were beginning to rumble across. Southwest of Trois-Ponts, the troopers made contact with a reconnaissance party of the 7th Armored Division.

Meatgrinder at Cheneux

Colonel Reuben Tucker, commander of the 504th PIR, sent two companies of his 1st Battalion toward Cheneux, where the troopers quickly ran into enemy machine-gun fire. A night attack supported by a pair of tank destroyers ran into strong defenses manned by the 2nd SS Panzergrenadier Regiment. Cresting a small hill that offered little or no cover, the troopers advanced across 400 yards (365m) of open ground in four echelons spaced 50 yards (45m) apart. They gained a slight lodgment on the edge of town, but at terrible cost. Two attacks were thrown back as the first two waves were decimated by heavy fire from automatic weapons and flak guns, their barrels depressed for use against infantry.

The third attack gained control of a few houses on the edge of Cheneux as the tank destroyers blasted some of the flak gun positions. With that, the troopers rushed forward, engaging in hand-to-hand fighting with some of the gun crews. Knives rose and fell. Fists flew. Although seriously wounded, Private First Class Daniel Del Grippo shot down the crew of one German self-propelled gun, while Staff Sergeant William Walsh destroyed a German flak gun that had caught his platoon with withering fire on its flank. Walsh was seriously wounded and ordered another soldier to arm the grenade that he then threw at the enemy.

The Germans broke and ran.

For six hours, Lieutenant Colonel Julian Cook's 3rd Battalion, 504th, worked its way northward in rough terrain, flanking the enemy positions in the town. By the time it was in position to attack, however, many Germans had escaped. Those SS troops that stood their ground were annihilated.

Tucker lost 225 dead and wounded in the brutal fighting. Every officer in Company B was killed or wounded, and only 18 men were unhurt. Company C could muster only 38 men and three officers, but the Germans had been thwarted at Cheneux. Peiper's only bridgehead south of the Amblève was eliminated.

While Tucker and the 504th hit Cheneux, the 505th, under Colonel William Ekman, linked up with the embattled engineers at Trois-Ponts and consolidated the hold on the town, destroying or seriously damaging every bridge across the Amblève in the vicinity. The 505th held an 8,000-yard (7,315-m) line from Trois-Ponts south to Grand-Halleux, and on December 21 the Germans tried to force a river crossing once again, hitting Company E in its small bridgehead on the east side of the Amblève.

Just before noon, a company of German infantry supported by self-propelled guns came down the road from the village of Wanne. As patchy fog lifted, the column advanced in front of an ambush set up along the roadside. A single eight-man bazooka team knocked out the armored vehicles, but all of the troopers were either killed or captured. The guns of the 456th Parachute Field Artillery Battalion scattered the infantry, but other German formations supported by tanks were seen milling about in the neighboring forest.

The troopers rushed forward, engaging in hand-to-hand fighting with some of the gun crews. Knives rose and fell. Fists flew.

Lieutenant Colonel Benjamin H. Vandervoort, commanding the 2nd Battalion, 505th PIR, sent Company F across the river on a heavily damaged bridge to occupy high ground to the right of Company E. A towed 57mm anti-tank gun went into action against several German tanks, but its shells could not penetrate their thick armor. Lieutenant Jake Wurtich was killed while servicing the gun. The tanks were unable to maneuver efficiently in the mud and snow, and the battle devolved into isolated combat between infantrymen. That afternoon, the paratroopers withdrew from the high ground on the east bank of the river. Two platoons of Germans followed to the other side and were thrown back.

South of Trois-Ponts, the 3rd Battalion, 505th, occupied a few houses at La Nouville on the Salm, where one bridge still stood. At dusk on the 21st, an armored column of the 1st SS Panzer Division attacked a platoon manning a forward roadblock. The paratroopers blew the bridge in the Germans' faces and called artillery fire down on the enemy, forcing them to turn away. Four German tanks remained close to the river, but withdrew during the night, and attempts by German infantry to cross the river under cover of darkness were repulsed. The Germans exerted some pressure on the 505th in the vicinity of Trois-Ponts on the 22nd. Two companies of infantry tried to seize the bridge at Grand-Halleux, but the span was destroyed while enemy troops were actually crossing. On December 23, when it was apparent that the 505th would not yield, the 1st SS Panzer Division ceased its efforts to reach Peiper's encircled spearhead.

Meanwhile, on the afternoon of December 22, Peiper received permission to break out

Below: Paratroopers of the 505th Parachute Infantry Regiment, 82nd Airborne Division, take cover along a railroad embankment during movement on the north shoulder of the German penetration that occurred during the Ardennes Offensive.

of the trap. Leaving a rear guard to destroy abandoned tanks and armored vehicles, he led approximately 800 men back toward the lines of the 1st SS Panzer Division. By 1 a.m. on the 24th, his command moved single file through heavy woods, skirted La Gleize to the south, crossed the Amblève River, and hid in the hills north of Trois-Ponts during daylight hours. That night, Peiper's fugitives crossed the Salm and fought briefly but savagely with patrols of the 505th PIR before reaching the 1st SS Panzer Division lines south of Stavelot on Christmas Day.

Above: General Matthew Ridgway (left), commander of the XVIII Airborne Corps, and General James M. Gavin, commander of the 82nd Airborne Division, confer amid the snowy Belgian landscape.

Embattled Crossroads

On the western edge of the 82nd Airborne deployment, concern centered around the crossroads at Baraque de Fraiture, near its junction with the 3rd Armored Division. Since the afternoon of December 19, the crossroads had been defended by troops, armored vehicles, and three 105mm howitzers under the command of Major Arthur C. Parker. General Gavin realized the tactical importance of the intersection (which later bore the name Parker's Crossroads); he ordered the 2nd Battalion, 325th Glider Regiment, under Colonel Charles Billingslea, to the town of Fraiture on a ridgeline about three-quarters of a mile (1km) from the crossroads. Company F was detailed to strengthen the crossroads defenses.

Fuel shortages delayed the Germans in their attempt to take the crossroads, but when it came on the 23rd the fight was furious. The 2nd Battalion, 4th Panzergrenadier Regiment, attacked Fraiture before daylight, but the glidermen held firm. However, time was running out at the crossroads. By 4 p.m., the entire 4th Panzergrenadier Regiment was in position to overwhelm the defenders. After a 20-minute artillery bombardment, two panzer companies led the assault.

As the German attack gained momentum, General Gavin ventured forward to assess the situation. "It was clearly evident that the attack at the crossroads was an all-out affair of great magnitude," he later reported. "As it developed, it was the attack of a regiment of the 2nd SS Panzer Division supported by attached armor, attacking with the mission of driving up the main highway to Werbomont."

Within two hours, the Germans had taken the crossroads, capturing the three howitzers along with halftracks and scores of prisoners. Heeding Gavin's order to "hold at all costs," Billingslea waited until the last moment to authorize the withdrawal of Company F. Only 44 of its original 116 men escaped.

The loss of the Baraque de Fraiture crossroads threatened the flanks of both the 82nd Airborne and 3rd Armored Divisions. Four miles (6km) up the road was another intersection at Manhay. From there, the route to Trois-Ponts and Hotton lay open, and allowing the Germans to reach the

The 509th PIB at the Bulge

The veteran 509th Parachute Infantry Battalion relocated from southern France northward to the area around Villers-Cotterêts in early December 1944. Following a brief attachment to the 101st Airborne Division, the battalion moved on to Manhay to join elements of the 3rd Armored Division. While the 101st was invested at Bastogne, the 509th PIB fought with distinction at the towns of Soy and Hotton.

Near the small village of Sadzot, the troopers of the 509th defended against the last effort of the Sixth Panzer Army to penetrate the American defenses between the Salm and Ourthe rivers. From December 22 to 30, they engaged the 1st and 2nd Battalions of the 25th SS Panzergrenadier Regiment. Charged with holding open a supply corridor through the towns of Erezée, Grandmenil, and Manhay, they held their ground. The toughest fighting occurred on December 28 when at least two companies of panzergrenadiers advanced through a 1,000-yard (914m) gap between two neighboring battalions of the 289th Infantry Regiment. The Germans managed to reach Sadzot and entered the town from the south. Alerted to the enemy's presence, the American troops in the town maintained firm control of its northern side, alerting the 509th to the opportunity to envelop the enemy from the east and west. As the paratroopers moved forward, the engagement devolved into sharp clashes between squads and platoons. Amid the confusion, German crews dropped mortar rounds on their own troops. The Germans inside Sadzot were cut off, and by the morning of the 29th the gap between the regiments of the 289th Infantry was closed.

To the Americans who fought at Sadzot, the engagement became known as the "Sad Sack Affair," in reference to a popular comic strip.

Later attached to the 7th Armored Division, the 509th PIB advanced through Belgium and cleared the rugged forest north of St. Vith. By January 29, 1945, its strength had been reduced to seven officers and 43 men. On March 1, the 509th was disbanded. Its personnel were absorbed by the 82nd and 13th Airborne Divisions. From North Africa to Italy, southern France, and the Battle of the Bulge, the battalion had amassed an outstanding combat record.

rear areas of both divisions would spell disaster. Gavin, Ridgway, and General Maurice Rose, commanding the 3rd Armored Division, patched together defenses at Manhay even as the fight at Baraque de Fraiture was taking place.

Roughly 3,000 yards (2,740m) north of the Baraque de Fraiture crossroads, Major Olin Brewster established a defensive line with tanks and infantry, including Company C, 509th PIR. Brewster effectively blocked the road to Manhay, frustrating the movement of the 2nd SS Panzer Division, while other American forces, some retreating from the embattled town of St. Vith, took up defensive positions to deny the Germans vital roadways and cost the enemy precious time in its westward push. After a spirited defense, Manhay fell to the Germans on December 24.

Three days later, the 517th PIR, with the assistance of a battalion of the 7th Armored Division, retook the tactically vital crossroads on December 27. By then, the skies had begun to clear, and Allied tactical air support weighed in. Fighter bombers interdicted German troop movements and armored columns, making movement during daylight hours a perilous proposition. Fuel and supply shortages were also beginning to take their toll on the impetus of Operation Watch on the Rhine.

Tough Stand at St. Vith

As the great German bulge had expanded, the town of St. Vith became the easternmost organized point of American resistance in its center. Elements of several units had concentrated there, including the shattered 106th Infantry Division, the 9th Armored, 28th Infantry, 14th Cavalry Group, and the 7th Armored Division, commanded by General Robert Hasbrouck.

By December 20, it was apparent that the Americans in St. Vith were surrounded. The XVIII Airborne Corps occupied a long defensive line to the northeast and was engaged that day with no fewer than three German corps: the 1st SS Panzer, LVIII Panzer, and the LXVI. There were doubts that anything of consequence could be immediately done offensively to assist the defenders of St. Vith. By December 22, heavy German attacks were pressing the salient to the breaking point, and the issue became whether the battered American forces being pushed away from the town should attempt to stand and fight or withdraw to the XVIII Airborne Corps line.

Amid the confusion of the German offensive, General Eisenhower temporarily reorganized his command structure, giving Field Marshal Bernard Montgomery, commander of 21st Army Group, control of all forces north of the bulge while General Omar Bradley, 12th Army Group Commander, retained control south of the breakthrough. The decision regarding St. Vith belonged to Montgomery, who ordered a tactical withdrawal on the afternoon of December 22. Ridgway was enraged and still advocated an

Below: Paratroopers of the 505th Parachute Infantry Regiment rest near the town of St. Vith, Belgium. The tires of a Jeep parked nearby have been outfitted with chains to assist in negotiating icy roadways.

Above: General Bernard Law Montgomery, commander of 21st Army Group, stands between General J. Lawton Collins (left), commander of VII Corps, and General Matthew Ridgway, commander of the XVIII Airborne Corps, during a conference.

attack toward St. Vith. Montgomery, however, refused and then urged that Ridgway order Gavin to pull the 82nd Airborne back to better corps defensive positions with shorter lines.

Amid a firestorm of tension among senior Allied commanders, Montgomery imposed his decisions but offered, "They can come back with all honor. They can come back to the more secure positions. They put up a wonderful show."

When Ridgway was compelled to order the withdrawal of the St. Vith defenders on December 23, he had moved small groups of 82nd Airborne troopers to guard bridges at the towns of Vielsalm and Salmchâteau for the retreating troops to cross. The division had also rushed reinforcements from the north, where troopers had been locked in tough fighting with the 1st SS Panzer Division at Cheneux and Trois-Ponts, to the south to shore up the open flank at Fraiture.

German tanks were west of the Salm; if they moved hastily, they could possibly roll up this vulnerable flank, pinning the 82nd Airborne Division against the river and destroying it. Another option for the Germans was to drive along the west bank of the river and attack the bridgeheads in Vielsalm and Salmchâteau. While the bulk of the 9th SS Panzer Division was tardy in launching the chosen attack against the bridgeheads and then turning on the southern flank of the 82nd Airborne, its covering force, the 19th SS Panzergrenadier Regiment, had thrown patrols across the river at Vielsalm early on December 24. When the presence of the 9th SS Panzer Division was discovered, it added to the rationale for withdrawing the 82nd Airborne from its vulnerable positions.

General Gavin knew that he faced elements of three or more enemy divisions and that a large German force, the survivors of Peiper's retreating command, was active in his rear. The

A paratrooper of the 82nd Airborne Division sets out across a bleak landscape toward the area to his front. Another trooper is visible at right, his head just above the cover of a dug-in position.

division occupied strong positions, dug in behind minefields and thick hedgehogs of barbed wire, and the troopers were prepared to fight, possibly in more than one direction, on Christmas Day. However, the decision to pull back held sway. The majority of the 82nd was to be withdrawn under cover of darkness on Christmas Eve, and the movement began around 9 p.m.

As word of the withdrawal filtered through the ranks, the troopers of the 82nd Airborne were incredulous. They had fought, bled, and died to advance against the Germans and were reluctant to give up the ground they had paid such a high price to gain. Nevertheless, they began their withdrawal to the area near their original assembly points around Werbomont. The defenders of St. Vith had held out for six crucial days, contributing substantially to the ability of the XVIII Airborne Corps to organize its coordinated defensive effort, and their withdrawal continued as well.

Gavin wrote in his diary that Ridgway had previously expressed complete confidence in the ability of the 82nd to continue the battle and, in fact, to mount a renewed attack. Now, the first tactical withdrawal in the history of the division was taking place. "Rather than withdraw, if the troopers had had their way, they would have much preferred to attack," Gavin added. "Besides, they knew they had beaten the Germans in every tactical engagement so far, and they did not see why they should not resume the offensive."

The 82nd Airborne came in contact with the enemy only twice during the retirement. When Peiper's men and elements of the 505th PIR, retreating in different directions, stumbled into one another and a brisk firefight developed, Colonel Ekman received permission to disengage and continue his pivoting movement away

Below: Paratroopers of the 101st Airborne Division march into Bastogne after traveling about 100 miles (160km) by truck through the night from their quarters in rear areas.

The 551st PIB Takes Rochelinval

Arriving at Werbomont on December 21, 1944, the 551st Parachute Infantry Battalion was attached to the 30th Infantry Division along the north shoulder of the German penetration that developed into the Battle of the Bulge. Within a week, the battalion was reassigned to the 82nd Airborne Division near the 508th PIR at Basse Bordeaux.

On the night of December 28, the 551st conducted a raid on the village of Noirefontaine, which was occupied by elements of the German 62nd Volksgrenadier Division. Fighting across Belgium, the battalion engaged the same enemy unit on several occasions, including an assault with fixed bayonets on January 4, 1945, in which 64 enemy soldiers were killed and a series of German machine-gun positions silenced. Although its original fighting strength of 643 troopers had been reduced to 250, the 551st was ordered on the morning of January 7 to take the town of Rochelinval, eliminating a German bridgehead across the Salm River. A blanket of snow 12 inches (30cm) deep impeded the progress of the attack across a half-mile (0.8km) of open ground. The troopers charged down a slope and into murderous enemy machine-gun and rifle fire, but succeeded in capturing the town. Lieutenant Colonel Wood Joerg, the battalion commander, was killed in the assault.

When the 551st PIB was disbanded on January 27, 1945, combat losses had reached a staggering 85 percent. Only 14 officers and 96 troopers remained to be absorbed into the 82nd Airborne Division. On February 23, 2001, half a century after its heroic sacrifice in the Battle of the Bulge, the battalion was awarded a Presidential Unit Citation.

from the river at Trois-Ponts and execute the withdrawal.

The second incident occurred as the covering force of the 508th PIR, under Lieutenant Colonel Thomas Shanley, settled into its new positions around 4:15 a.m. on Christmas Day. One platoon each from Companies A and B had moved ahead toward the Vielsalm Bridge. Around midnight, these men heard the sounds of construction work around the span that had been partially demolished by American engineers. A short time later, a fusillade of artillery and mortar shells began falling around them. A barrage of smoke shells followed.

Within minutes, the silhouettes of enemy soldiers were emerging through the thick smoke. These were German troops of the 1st Battalion, 19th Regiment, and they came on at a run, yelling and screeching. The troopers from Company B opened with .30-caliber (7.62mm) machine guns and stopped the enemy cold. Closer to the riverbank, Company A was pressed harder. Some German soldiers reached the American lines and fought hand to hand with the troopers, while others circled behind them to cut off their line of escape to the west.

For a while, the chances for the platoon looked bleak. However, 1st Lieutenant George D. Lamm led a determined fight to break through the German barrier. Although the 508th headquarters had believed Lamm's platoon was completely destroyed, the troopers made it back to friendly lines. The historian of the 508th PIR called the action of Lamm's platoon "one of the best pieces of fighting in the 508th's history."

For the next few days, the 19th Regiment shadowed the 508th. On the night of the 25th, two German battalions hit the left flank of the new 508th line, only to be repulsed after a tough, three-hour battle. On the night of December 27,

Above: On January 11, 1945, after the crisis of the Battle of the Bulge has passed, a corporal of the 463rd Parachute Field Artillery Battalion, 327th Glider Infantry Regiment, 101st Airborne Division, pauses to examine his feet for frostbite.

the Germans struck the right flank of the 508th, driving Company G out of its bivouac in the towns of Erria and Villettes. A pair of American artillery battalions opened up on the exposed Germans, pinning them down in Erria. On the morning of the 28th, Lieutenant Colonel Louis G. Mendez led his 3rd Battalion, 508th, in a fast-moving counterattack, rolling through Erria and regaining the lost ground. Coupled with the previous day's artillery barrage, the attack of the 3rd Battalion inflicted at least 100 dead and an unknown number of wounded on the enemy. The German report on the action at Erria said bluntly that the 1st Battalion, 19th Regiment was "cut to pieces."

While the withdrawal of the 82nd Airborne Division was concluding, the momentum of the German offensive was blowing itself out. General Gavin noted in his after-action report that the attacks of the 19th Regiment were the last enemy offensive efforts of the Battle of the Bulge. He also praised the stamina and fighting prowess of the 82nd Airborne Division.

"In all the operations in which we have participated in our two years of combat, and they have been many of multitudinous types," Gavin wrote, "I have never seen a better executed operation than the withdrawal on Christmas Eve. The troops willingly and promptly carried into execution all the withdrawal plans, although they openly and frankly criticized it and failed to understand the necessity for it. But everybody pitched in and the withdrawal went smoothly."

On December 31, Gavin added a diary entry that resonated with pride. "Our Army has a hell of a lot to learn, but at present these airborne troopers of this division are making monkeys out of the Germans opposing them. They are better trained and far superior combat soldiers...."

First Army Forward

As 1944 gave way to the new year, even Adolf Hitler was coming to grips with the fact that his Ardennes offensive was doomed to failure. The Führer admitted on January 3, 1945, that his grand scheme was "no longer promising of success."

On the same day, the Allies launched an offensive of their own to regain lost ground and punish the retiring enemy, further eroding the combat effectiveness of the German Army. Although some senior Allied commanders had advocated an earlier jump-off to the counteroffensive, Field Marshal Montgomery chose to delay until he was confident that the Germans had exhausted their own offensive capability. While General George S. Patton, Jr.'s Third Army pushed in the south, General Hodges' First Army began its own eastward thrust. The main attack was to be made by the VII Corps, under General J. Lawton Collins; the role of the XVIII Airborne Corps was to maintain a coordinated advance with Collins' command by pushing its own right flank forward.

The 82nd Airborne, its strength augmented with the attachment of the 517th PIR, was ordered forward to a line along the Salm River. On the first day of its advance, the troopers overran the remnants of the 62nd Volksgrenadier Division and the 9th SS Panzer Division, capturing 2,500 prisoners, including five battalion commanders. Moving through thick forest and deep snow, the advance became rapid. The 505th PIR encountered little resistance, covering four miles (6km) in three days and clearing the eastern edge of the forest above the valley of the Salm.

The Allied advance was deliberate and accomplished along phase lines so that units remained roughly abreast of one another over the extended front. After such swift movement, the order to halt was somewhat disconcerting; however, the 82nd Airborne Division had recovered all the territory it had relinquished during the Christmas Eve retreat two weeks earlier.

"Our Army has a hell of a lot to learn, but at present these airborne troopers of this division are making monkeys out of the Germans opposing them."

On January 8, Lieutenant Colonel Vandervoort, commanding the 2nd Battalion, 505th PIR, was grievously wounded by a shell fragment that penetrated his left eye. A veteran commander since the Sicily invasion, Vandervoort survived.

General Gavin continually exposed himself to enemy fire, and his aide, Captain Olsen, was wounded in the left leg when an artillery round exploded near them. In quick succession, another shellburst wounded the young officer in the right leg and blew off the leg of a second soldier just a few yards distant. Gavin wrote, "I was very lucky. The boy between Olsen and myself had his leg severed just above the knee.

I put a tourniquet on him, and to our surprise we saved his life. Olsen gave him the morphine. His leg flew across the road, and for a moment Olsen thought it was his."

Operating close to the boundary with VII Corps, the 517th PIR faced stiff resistance from the terrain, the weather, and the enemy before pivoting quickly on January 7 to hit the German flank. The next day, the troopers of the 517th swept the last German troops from the west bank of the Salm and sent patrols that penetrated two miles (3km) across the stream.

On January 9, the 517th consolidated a small bridgehead across the Salm, and the lodgment became a focal point for the later reorientation of the offensive toward St. Vith. That same day, the 82nd Airborne Division was withdrawn from the front line to rear areas at Chevron and Pepinster. Three weeks of welcome rest awaited the weary troopers, but their war was not yet over. Casualties during the Battle of the Bulge had topped 2,000.

Battling Bastards

The 101st Airborne Division, its commander marooned thousands of miles away in Washington, D.C., was on the road toward Belgium within hours of its deployment orders, but just where it was headed remained a mystery to the troopers aboard the bouncing trucks that carried them 107 miles (172km) through an uncomfortable mixture of rain and snow. Around 8 p.m. on December 18, the head of the division's column reached the village of Herbomont, where roads slanted away, northeastward toward Houffalize and Werbomont and southeastward to Bastogne.

Colonel Thomas L. Sherburne, Jr., who had stepped in as artillery commander while McAuliffe

Left: Paratroopers from the 2nd Battalion, 517th Parachute Infantry Regiment, attached to the 7th Armored Division, prepare for an attack on German positions in the St. Vith area, January 1945.

led the division, watched MPs direct traffic, all of it airborne, in the same direction toward Houffalize. Then, as the last truck carrying the 82nd Airborne moved on, the MPs waved Sherburne toward Bastogne. As the 101st rolled on toward its rendezvous with destiny, the roads became choked with clusters of retreating soldiers, some hurrying toward the rear on foot and others in speeding jeeps or trucks. Most of these were the retreating remnants of the shattered 110th Infantry Regiment, 106th Division, which had been devastated on the Schnee Eifel.

McAuliffe and much of his staff had already passed along the road to Bastogne, well aware that the situation was grave. Lieutenant Colonel Harry Kinnard, the 101st operations officer, leaned toward McAuliffe and remarked wryly, "Sir, unless those people are having a premature case of the jitters, I'd say the Germans must be barreling this way fast." The acting commander responded, "We'll soon find out."

McAuliffe chose an assembly area four miles (6km) west of Bastogne at Mande-St. Etienne, and by midnight the trucks carrying the 501st PIR, under Lieutenant Colonel Julian Ewell, were unloading. At 9 a.m. the next morning, the 502nd PIR, under Lieutenant Colonel Steve A. Chappuis, Colonel Sink's 506th PIR, and Colonel Joseph Harper's 327th Glider Infantry Regiment with an attached battalion of the 401st Glider Infantry Regiment, were under McAuliffe's direct control. During the coming hours, several other units joined in the defense of Bastogne. Among these were the 705th Tank Destroyer Battalion, the 755th Armored Field Artillery Battalion, and the 969th Field Artillery Battalion.

As the 101st began arriving in Bastogne, Combat Command B (CCB), 10th Armored Division, commanded by Colonel William L. Roberts, was already deploying in three combat teams named for their commanders. Team Desobry (Major William R. Desobry) was at Noville, northeast of Bastogne, while Team

Below: On January 6, 1945, troopers of the 325th Glider Infantry Regiment, 82nd Airborne Division, man a .30-caliber Browning machine gun near Odrimont, Belgium. The 82nd Airborne strengthened the Allied lines on the north shoulder of the "Bulge."

Above: Following in the path of an M4 Sherman medium tank, whose treads have packed the snow and made footing more secure, paratroopers of the 82nd Airborne Division trudge forward during the Battle of the Bulge.

O'Hara (Lieutenant Colonel James O'Hara) was blocking the road from Wiltz, Luxembourg, to the southeast. Due east was Team Cherry (Lieutenant Colonel Henry T. Cherry), moving toward the town of Longvilly, where a combat team of the 9th Armored Division was manning a roadblock.

While General Middleton relocated his VIII Corps headquarters 18 miles (29km) southwest to the village of Neufchâteau, McAuliffe was left to arrange the rest of Bastogne's defenses as three German divisions—Panzer Lehr, the 26th Volksgrenadier, and 2nd Panzer—pressed hurriedly toward the crossroads town. McAuliffe sent the 506th PIR two and one-half miles (4km) north to Foy and the 501st east to Longvilly to support Team Cherry. Each of these units was ordered to delay the German advance on Bastogne as long as possible.

During its thrust directly at the medieval market town, Panzer Lehr had reached the village of Niederwampach, just six miles (10km) from Bastogne, but lost precious time when its commander, General Fritz Bayerlein, acted on information provided by Belgian civilians. Detouring on a supposed shortcut that proved to be an unpaved road toward the town of Mageret, his leading tanks became mired in mud. It took four hours to travel three miles (5km).

Once in Mageret, Bayerlein was informed that at least 50 American tanks with supporting infantry had passed through the town hours earlier – and that a major general commanded the formation. The Belgian informant had actually seen a portion of Team Cherry, a much smaller force than the division Bayerlein thought was on the march, moving toward Longvilly. Bayerlein became concerned that he faced a strong

Some of them wearing winter camouflage, troopers of the 82nd Airborne Division drag sleds loaded with ammunition toward a scene of expected fighting near Herresbach, Germany. This photo was taken in January 1945.

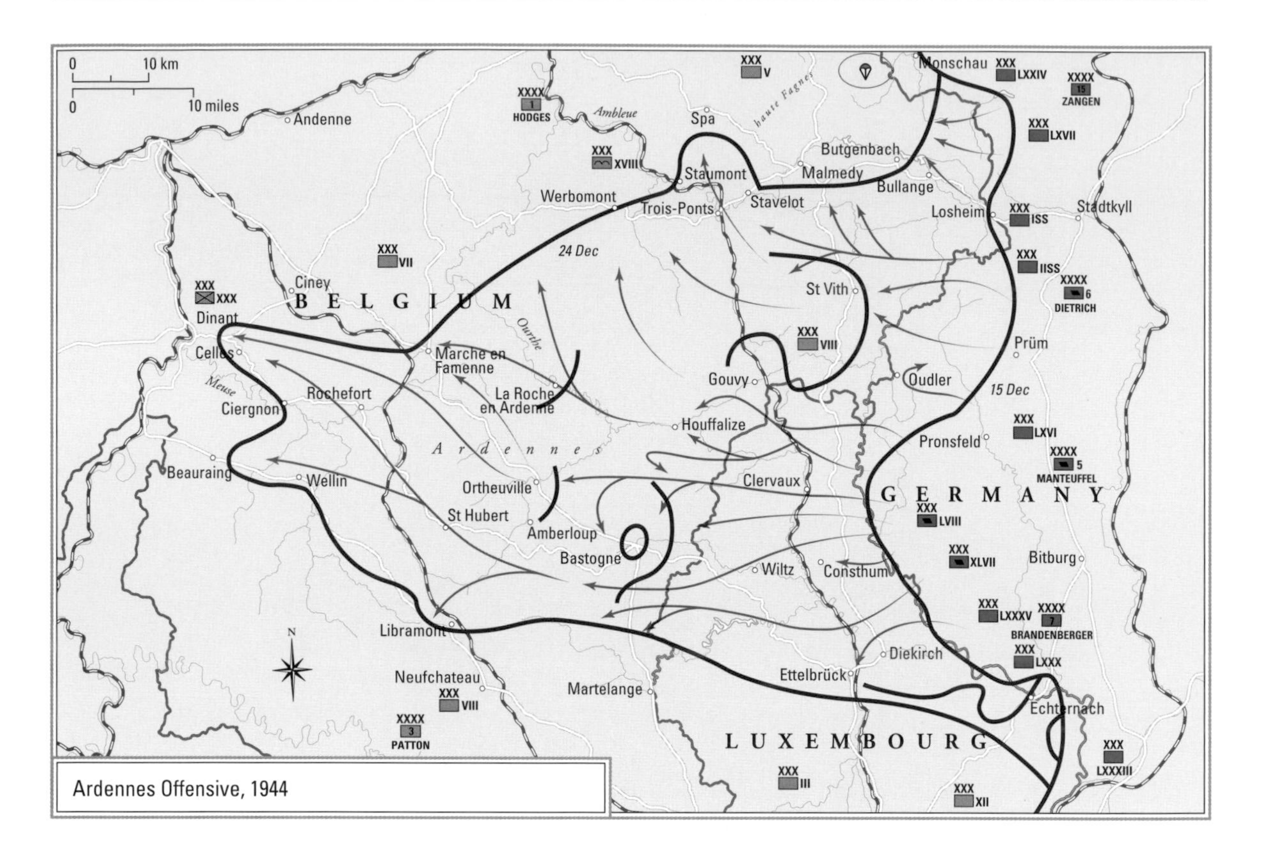

Ardennes Offensive, 1944

Above: The German Ardennes Offensive of December 1944, created a sizable salient in the American lines, and the subsequent fight to stem the enemy thrust toward the port of Antwerp, Belgium, became known as the Battle of the Bulge.

American armored force; he elected not to throw the weight of Panzer Lehr against Bastogne on the night of December 18, squandering a golden opportunity to capture the town. At 5 a.m. on the 19th, Panzer Lehr and two battalions of the 26th Volksgrenadier Division were back on the road and headed straight for Bastogne.

General McAuliffe had ordered Ewell to start toward Longvilly at 6 a.m., and about 2,000 yards (1,830m) outside Bastogne his paratroopers encountered a few howitzers of the 9th Armored Division. The artillerymen turned their guns to support the 501st. Moving warily ahead, Ewell sent his 1st Battalion down the road as a screening force. Within minutes, the battalion reported contact with Germans near the village of Neffe, less than 3,000 yards (2,740m) from the town limits of Bastogne.

The 501st PIR joined in a fight around Neffe that had begun a day earlier as combat engineers and Team Cherry of CCB, 10th Armored, delayed the enemy. Ewell ordered his 1st Battalion to stand fast and brought up the 2nd and 3rd Battalions. Soon, his 2,200 troopers were heavily engaged, seizing high ground at Hill 510 and the town of Bizory on the flanks of the 1st Battalion position. Ewell then called on the 101st divisional artillery, unlimbered in Bastogne, and the 9th Armored gunners to plaster the German advance.

Heavy fog obscured the battlefield, and German officers were unsure of the strength of the enemy force blocking the road. The deadly, well-timed artillery clinched the decision for Bayerlein. Panzer Lehr recoiled and spent the

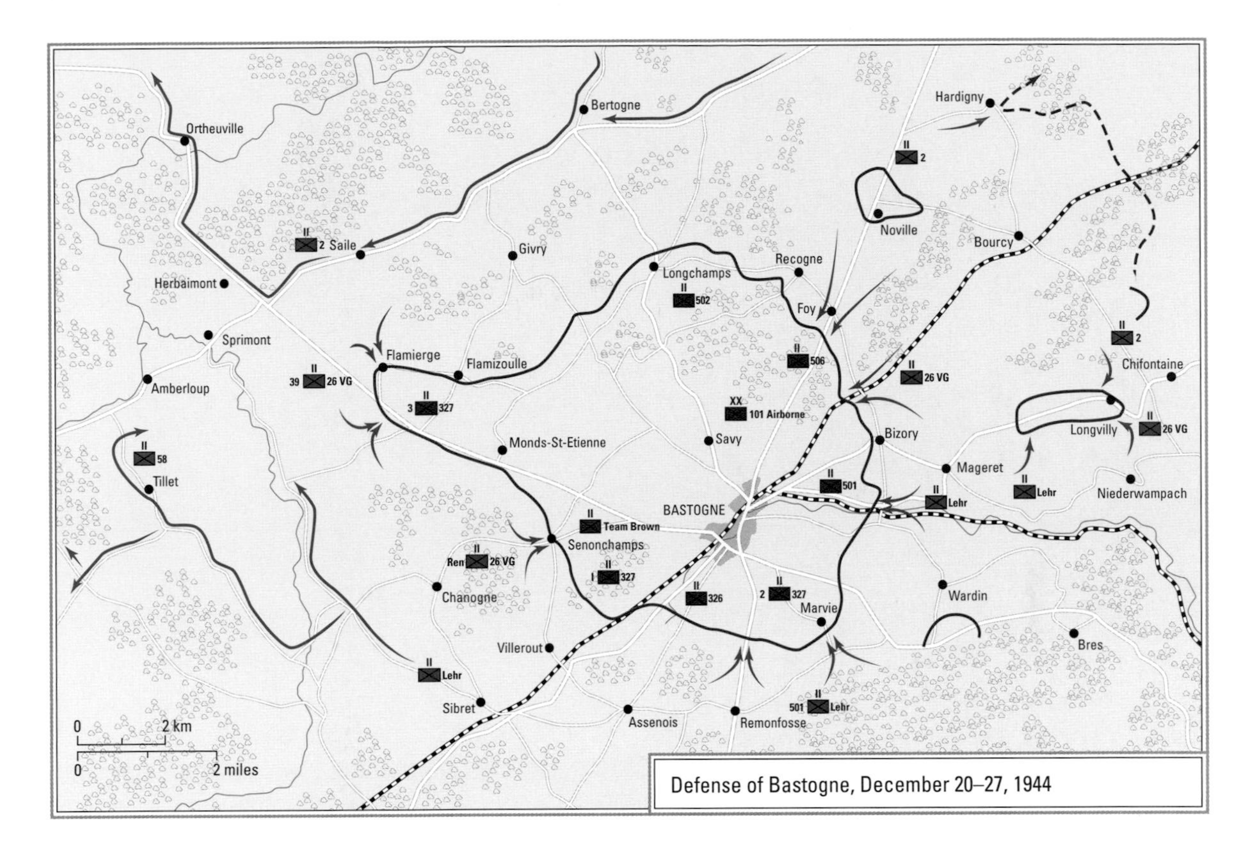

Above: The Belgian crossroads town of Bastogne became a focal point of resistance to the Germans. The 101st Airborne Division and elements of several other units maintained control of the town despite repeated German attempts to capture it.

balance of the day in probing attacks east of Bastogne, looking for a weak spot in the stout American defenses.

While Panzer Lehr's attack fizzled, the 2nd Panzer Division made for Bastogne from the northeast, hitting two of Team Desobry's roadblocks before first light. The young major instructed his men to abandon these forward positions, and they fell back to Noville as German tanks rumbled after them. Heavy fog lifted around 10 a.m., and the men of Team Desobry were shocked to see at least 30 German tanks—medium Panthers with high-velocity 75mm guns and dreaded Tigers mounting 88mm cannon—spread before them.

Fourteen tanks of the 3rd Panzer Regiment were silhouetted against the bleak morning sky as they crossed a ridgeline. Desobry's tank destroyers hit 10 of these in succession, brewing them up with 90mm rounds. Still, the pressure was mounting, and Desobry radioed Colonel Roberts for permission to pull back. Roberts informed the major that reinforcements were en route, but added that Desobry could use his own judgment. The major decided to stay put.

Lieutenant Colonel James LaPrade hurried the troopers of the 1st Battalion, 506th PIR, toward the raging battle, dashing through the heavy German artillery fire that greeted them. A platoon of the 705th Tank Destroyer Battalion pulled up. The paratroopers and Desobry's armored infantry totaled about 1,000 men, and the two commanders organized a counterattack that met immediately with heavy small-arms fire and gained little ground.

Above: The corpse of a German soldier, his stiffened arm upraised in death, lies unburied in the snow during the Battle of the Bulge.

Two companies of paratroopers worked their way in fits and starts to the base of a hill, prepared to rush the crest, and ran headlong into an attack by the 2nd Panzer Division. As the Americans jumped off, a flurry of enemy troops backed by 16 tanks was coming toward them. The opposing forces fought one another to a standstill in the late afternoon as the enemy tanks hesitated, wary of American bazooka teams and tank destroyers that rolled up south of Noville to destroy five German armored vehicles at a distance of 1,500 yards (1,370m).

The paratrooper companies withdrew to the town as darkness fell. Throughout the night of December 19, the Germans lobbed 20 to 30 artillery shells into Noville at half-hour intervals. One round struck the defenders' command post killing LaPrade and seriously wounding Desobry. Eight Sherman tanks remained active, patrolling the perimeter against enemy armor and panzergrenadiers who occasionally probed in the darkness looking for weak spots.

As dawn broke on the 20th, Panzer Lehr and the 26th Volksgrenadier Division renewed their attacks with the support of the 2nd Panzer Division artillery. An early attack was broken up, but not before a pair of German tanks burst into the streets of Noville, only to be disabled by a bazooka round and a well-placed shot from a Sherman's 75mm gun. As the day wore on, the Noville defenders were ordered to pull back to the town of Foy, about two miles (3km) to the southwest.

By noon the 2nd and 3rd Battalions, 506th PIR, had established a defensive base at Foy and subsequently linked up with the 501st to the east. The 3rd Battalion, 502nd PIR, held the Germans back as they attempted to cut the road from Noville to Foy. A harrowing withdrawal ensued. A pair of halftracks collided, and a tank driver was wounded. When no other tankers could be found, a paratrooper took the controls of the wounded man's Sherman and led the column. By 5 p.m., the last Americans were inside the lines at Foy.

Both sides suffered heavy casualties in the fight at Noville, the 1st Battalion, 506th PIR, losing 13 officers and 199 troopers killed, wounded, or taken prisoner. One battalion of the 3rd Panzer Regiment was chewed to pieces. Sometime after the battle an American soldier surveyed the grisly scene and remarked, "We found all manner of horrors. Stuff like a galosh with a foot still in it, a headless paratrooper, a blackened tree stump which turned out to be a cremated Kraut sitting in a foxhole, a paratrooper's helmet full of brains and meltwater, a severed arm with a wristwatch on it – all that sort of mincing machine warfare."

The 2nd Panzer Division had lost two valuable days and an estimated 31 tanks and armored vehicles trying to take Bastogne, which was not its primary objective. The job of taking the town was left to Panzer Lehr and the 26th Volksgrenadier Divisions when 2nd Panzer was ordered on toward the crucial bridges across the River Meuse.

Southwest of Bastogne, Team O'Hara was ensconced around the town of Marvie on the southern flank of the 501st PIR. Remnants of the 35th Engineer Combat Battalion had also dug in, and McAuliffe detailed the 2nd Battalion, 327th Glider Infantry, to bolster the defenses. As the engineers began to vacate their foxholes for the relieving glider troops, a German column was spotted heading toward Marvie. In a sharp hour-long clash, the defenders threw back a rifle company and four tanks of Panzer Lehr's 901st Regiment in disarray. All four German armored vehicles were knocked out.

The defenders braced for another attack, which never materialized due to the focus of Panzer Lehr on Ewell's 1st Battalion positions. Preceded by an artillery barrage, German infantry and tanks moved toward the road from Neffe to Bastogne. Three of the armored vehicles were disabled, and the accompanying infantry was mowed down by machine-gun fire. After dark, another thrust was cut to pieces as panzergrenadiers became tangled in the wire fences along the perimeter of a farmer's field. Firing in the dark, the paratroopers heard the cries of wounded enemy soldiers, but were unable to fully grasp what had happened until the carnage was revealed at first light.

Surrounded

Despite the spirited defensive efforts of December 20, German forces were on the two roads leading

Below: American combat engineers return from a night patrol during the Battle of the Bulge. Engineers fought heroic delaying actions and slowed the momentum of the German advance.

south from Bastogne. Other enemy units were ranging west along the Bastogne–St. Hubert highway. When the 2nd SS Panzer Division rolled into the town of Ortheuville that night, cutting the Marche road, the Americans were encircled, defending a perimeter only five miles (8km) in diameter at its widest points.

With the primary German focus on reaching the Meuse bridges, the network of paved roads stretching from Bastogne in all directions would have proven quite useful; however, as the panzer columns were denied quick possession of the town the Nazi tide swept around and beyond the obstacle. For more than two days after the ring around Bastogne closed, the heavy combat of the previous desperate hours ebbed.

German artillery continued to make life miserable and deadly in Bastogne, and occasional probing attacks were repulsed. Infiltrators were eliminated. By December 21, the 77th and 78th Regiments of the 26th Volksgrenadier Division had located a gap between the 506th and 501st PIR defensive lines. When these interlopers were discovered, two companies of the 506th attacked while the 501st stood firm to prevent movement on its left flank. As more and more Germans were encountered, the 1st Battalion, 506th, which had fought hard at Noville, came up to assist. Three hours of fighting finally eliminated the enemy incursion with 50 Germans dead and 85 captured.

A threat to the American 105mm artillery positions west of Bastogne at Senonchamps was stopped as the Germans tried at least three times to breach the lines. Sherman tanks and bazooka teams got the drop on German armor, destroying 18 enemy tanks.

Below: Manning his position outside the encircled town of Bastogne, a German soldiers peers from behind a PaK 36 antitank gun. The 101st Airborne Division led a spirited defense that held Bastogne against numerous German attacks.

Above: Paratroopers of the 101st Airborne Division spend Christmas Eve in the encircled Belgian town of Bastogne. The paratroopers and other American forces denied the Germans the road network in the town, delaying their westward advance.

As the Germans consolidated their positions around the town and counted their losses, Colonel Roberts continued to scoop up stragglers and soldiers from units that had lost cohesion and lumped them into an ad hoc force called Team SNAFU (Situation Normal All Fouled Up). This served as a pool for replacements or from which special task groups were formed and dispatched to hot spots.

After several days of fighting, the defenders of Bastogne were running low on supplies of all kinds. Artillery rounds were being fired sparingly. Reserves of rifle ammunition were growing thin. Rations were dwindling—with one exception. An abandoned Red Cross supply dump yielded a large cache of donut flour, and the cooks made pancakes by the thousands. A large number of 101st Airborne medical personnel had been taken prisoner in early action, and the few medics and townspeople that tended the wounded scrounged for blankets, medicine, and bandages.

Nuts!

Amid the deteriorating situation in Bastogne, Sergeant Oswald Butler of the 2nd Battalion, 327th Glider Infantry, spotted four German soldiers walking up the road toward a farmhouse on the southern edge of the American perimeter. At a nearby platoon command post, two German officers were blindfolded. They were then marched to the company command post while their accompanying enlisted men were held back.

Major Alvin Jones took possession of a message the Germans had brought, and rumors swirled that the enemy had had enough and was asking for surrender terms. On the contrary, Jones carried an ultimatum to Lieutenant Colonel Ned Moore, the 101st Airborne chief of staff, at division headquarters. As Moore read the typewritten message, General McAuliffe asked impatiently, "What does it say?"

Signed simply "The German Commander," the demand read in part, "To the U.S.A. commander of the encircled town of Bastogne: The fortune of war is changing. This time the U.S.A. forces in and near Bastogne have been encircled by strong German armored units. There is only one possibility to save the encircled troops from total annihilation: that is the honorable surrender of the encircled town."

McAuliffe took the message in hand and exclaimed, "Aw nuts!" He stalked out of the room, dropping the two typewritten pages to the floor.

A few minutes later, the acting commander of the 101st was reminded that the German envoys were still waiting for a response. "Well, I don't know what to tell them," he remarked. Lieutenant Colonel Kinnard perked up and said, "That first crack you made would be hard to beat, general."

McAuliffe asked, "What was that?" Kinnard responded, "You said 'Nuts!'"

Snapping his fingers, McAuliffe declared, "That's it!" A piece of paper was quickly fed into the nearest typewriter, and the appropriate response was tapped out:

"To the German Commander: Nuts! The American Commander"

McAuliffe turned and handed the reply to Lieutenant Colonel Joseph Harper, commander of the 327th Glider Infantry, saying, "Will you see that it's delivered?" Harper beamed, "I'll deliver it myself."

Harper returned to the Germans and escorted them back to their lines. When the officers, a major and a captain, read the response and claimed that they did not understand its meaning, Harper shouted, "If you don't understand what 'Nuts!' means, in plain English it is the same as 'Go to Hell!' And I will tell you something else – if you continue to attack we will kill every goddamn German that tries to break into this city."

Word of McAuliffe's terse response to the German surrender demand began to circulate among the weary troops. Morale soared. More good news arrived. General Patton was coming through with his pledge during a meeting of senior commanders at Verdun at the height of the crisis. The Third Army had pivoted northward, and its spearhead, the veteran 4th Armored Division, was making all haste to relieve the embattled garrison.

Right: Bundled up in cold weather gear, this private of the 101st Airborne Division is typical of those paratroopers who fought the Germans to a standstill at the besieged town of Bastogne during the Battle of the Bulge.

Above: Troopers from A Company, the 507th Parachute Infantry Regiment, 17th Airborne Division, advance along a snow covered road near La Roche-en-Ardennes, January 1945.

Daybreak

December 23, 1944, dawned crystal clear and bitterly cold. Buoyed by their commander's stouthearted leadership, the defenders of Bastogne welcomed the sight of fighter bombers streaming toward German targets, their silver wings glinting in the sun. Then, 241 Troop Carrier Command planes headed for Bastogne, some of them managing to airdrop much-needed supplies. On Christmas Eve, 160 more planes flew in with sustenance. Two days later, nearly 300 aircraft made supply runs.

When the airdrop on the 23rd had been completed, the escorting fighter bombers, 82 Republic P-47 Thunderbolts, peeled away to hit exposed German targets with fragmentation and general-purpose bombs and canisters of napalm. They made repeated firing passes, with eight .50-caliber (12.7mm) machine guns shredding anything in their path.

The tenacious Germans renewed their attacks that day as 2nd Panzer moved on. The 26th Volksgrenadier and Panzer Lehr Divisions attacked at Senonchamps to the west and the villages of Marvie in the southeast and Flamierge in the northwest. At dusk, the 327th Glider Infantry and Team O'Hara braced as tanks of Panzer Lehr rumbled out of a wooded area 1,000 yards (914m) from the paper-thin American line and headed for Hill 500, where a single platoon under Lieutenant Stanley Morrison was positioned.

Overwhelmed, Morrison and his men fought to the last. Colonel Harper checked in by phone, and the gallant lieutenant reported, "Now they are all around me. I see tanks just outside my window. We are continuing to fight them back, but it looks like they have us." Responding to a follow-up call from the colonel, Morrison said grimly, "We're still holding on."

As the Germans swept over Hill 500, the line went dead.

The glidermen fought like lions, but the Germans managed to reach the outskirts of Marvie, where a wild brawl developed between the panzergrenadiers and German armored vehicles and the tanks and guns of Team O'Hara. One German halftrack blazed like a funeral pyre after a Sherman tank put a 75mm shell into it. Streaks of flame backlit the German infantry, and the Americans shot them down in heaps. West of Marvie, the Germans got within 50 yards (45m) of the 327th foxholes. Intrepid bazooka teams rushed from cover to fire at German tanks, which trundled out of harm's way.

Colonel Kinnard skillfully moved units toward trouble spots like pieces on a chessboard. He shifted troopers from Ewell's 501st PIR and elements of Team Cherry to parry each German thrust. As the clock struck midnight during the height of the melee with Team O'Hara, one German tank was blocked by a burned-out American halftrack sitting across a road. When the tank commander started to back away, several Shermans blasted the enemy vehicle. The remaining panzergrenadiers melted into the darkness.

Below: Infantrymen of the 4th Armored Division approach the outskirts of Bastogne on December 26, 1944, raising the siege of the town that held out against the Germans during the Battle of the Bulge.

Earlier in the evening, Colonel Kinnard had dashed off a report that was preserved in the XVIII Airborne Corps combat journal. "In regard to our situation it is getting pretty sticky around here," he wrote. "They [4th Armored] must keep coming. The enemy has attacked all along the south and some tanks are through and running around in our area. Request you inform 4th Armored Division of our situation and ask them to put on all possible pressure."

On Christmas Eve, Luftwaffe bombers pounded the rubble that was Bastogne. One bomb struck a makeshift hospital, the walls caving in on more than 30 wounded men. Though death and destruction reigned, some of the soldiers took up the hymn "Silent Night," penned, perhaps ironically, by the Austrian Franz Gruber and originally written in German. An uneasy calm then settled in before the storm of Christmas Day.

Last Lunge

Lieutenant Colonel Chappuis had taken command of the 502nd PIR in September, while the 101st was locked in battle in Holland. On Christmas, his command occupied positions around the towns of Champs and Rolle northwest of Bastogne. After Christmas Eve Mass and the best dinner he had eaten in weeks, prepared by Belgian civilians, Chappuis and his staff were awakened at 2:30 a.m. by German artillery.

Enemy infantry reached the streets of Champs and fought hand to hand in the darkness with the paratroopers. The sounds of gunfire carried across the landscape. By morning, another powerful German punch was being thrown at Champs, where the bone-tired men of the 327th Glider Infantry clung doggedly to their line. Eighteen German Panzerkampfwagen IV tanks and a host of panzergrenadiers roared down the slope of a nearby hill. The tanks rolled across the

Above: General Maxwell Taylor, commander of the 101st Airborne Division, meets General Anthony McAuliffe, the division's ranking artillery officer who led the 101st while Taylor was in the U.S. during the Battle of the Bulge.

American foxholes, and the glidermen hunkered down until they passed. Then, they rose up and emptied their rifles into the German infantry.

The enemy tanks kept going and reached the command post of the 3rd Battalion, 327th, forcing the battalion commander, Lieutenant Colonel Ray C. Allen, to race toward a copse of trees as tank shells burst and machine-gun bullets kicked up snow. Several of the German tanks turned northward, threatening to take the 502nd from the rear.

A superb tactician, Chappuis was waiting for this exact moment. He turned two companies of paratroopers and the tank destroyers he had available to the south along a treeline. As the German column rushed toward Champs to cut off the 502nd, the tank destroyers and troopers slashed into its exposed flank. Three German tanks were brewed up immediately by 76mm shells, and bazooka rounds accounted for two more. The lone German tank that ventured on into Champs was demolished by a torrent of antitank rounds.

While the Germans rushing toward Champs came to grief, the rest of the Panzerkampfwagen IVs were systematically eliminated as they went straight for Bastogne. Of the 18 tanks that originally attacked, 17 were left smoking ruins. One was captured. For his brilliant conduct of the crucial defensive battle, Chappuis was later awarded the Distinguished Service Cross. For now, though, a Christmas dinner of hard crackers and canned sardines was reward enough.

Blessed Relief

For four days, the 4th Armored Division had been in a running fight northward as the commander of its leading element, Lieutenant Colonel Creighton Abrams of the 37th Tank Battalion, realized time was running out for the brave men in Bastogne.

On the day after Christmas, Abrams stood on a hillside with Lieutenant Colonel George L. Jacques of the 53rd Armored Infantry Battalion. Below them lay the villages of Sibret and Assenois. There were plenty of Germans in Sibret, where their original plan of attack was to take them. They believed reinforcements would be needed to batter their way through that town and devised a daring alternative—a headlong dash through Assenois.

Abrams' request for permission to deviate from the original plan went all the way to General Patton. When asked if he would approve the change, Patton bellowed, "I sure as hell will!" Abrams rushed back to his command and shouted, "We're going in now! Let her roll!"

Blasting their way through Assenois as infantrymen dismounted from the tanks and shot German gun crews where they stood, the Shermans of the 37th Tank Battalion rocketed toward Bastogne. By 5 p.m., Lieutenant Charles Boggess, in one of the leading Shermans, noticed soldiers diving into foxholes a few hundred yards ahead. He stood up in his turret and shouted, "Come here! This is the 4th Armored!"

Warily, their guns trained on the young tanker, a few men began to approach. One of them, his finger on the trigger of his M1 carbine, finally relaxed and shouted back, "Second Lieutenant Duane J. Webster, 326th Engineer Battalion, 101st Airborne Division."

The epic siege of Bastogne was over.

Screaming Eagle Honor

General McAuliffe made his way to an observation post on a hilltop and greeted Captain William Dwight, the commander of Lieutenant Boggess' unit. "Gee! I am mighty glad to see you," McAuliffe smiled. As the two officers shook hands, relief rolled toward the shattered crossroads town that had cost the 101st Airborne Division 1,641 killed, wounded, and captured—quite a price to pay for a defensive battle that has gone down in history as one of the most heroic struggles of modern warfare.

Of the 18 German tanks that originally attacked, 17 were left smoking ruins.

Hitler's great offensive in the West was eventually defeated, and then the end of Nazi Germany was only a matter of time. The 101st Airborne Division, the Battling Bastards of Bastogne, fought the Germans for three more weeks, first continuing to repel attacks on the town and then working in tandem with the Third Army to reduce the bulge. Retaking ground east of Bastogne, the 101st captured the town of Recogne, cleared the Bois des Corbeaux of Germans, and occupied Foy by mid-January 1945. The 506th PIR pushed the Germans out of Noville for good on January 15 and followed up hours later with the liberation of Rachamps. A joint effort of the 502nd PIR and the 327th Glider Infantry liberated Bourcy on January 17.

The next day, the 101st Airborne Division was finally relieved, moving to Alsace and assuming defensive positions in the Seventh Army lines until late February.

CHAPTER 7

OPERATION VARSITY AND BEYOND

In the autumn of 1944, even before the misadventure of Operation Market Garden, Allied eyes were on the Rhine. In early September, General Bradley had contemplated an airborne operation to facilitate the crossing of 12th Army Group.

Throughout the first three months of 1945, Allied troops advanced toward the Rhine, reducing the "bulge" that had resulted from the ill-fated German Ardennes Offensive, an effort that ultimately cost the Wehrmacht irreplaceable men and resources, hastening the end of the war. By the end of February, the west bank of the Rhine was within reach. The 21st Army Group was massing in the north, and the successful clearing of the Saar-Palatinate had breached the Siegfried Line and brought Allied forces forward to the great river from Holland to the Swiss border. Despite the Market Garden setback the previous September, airborne operations were considered a viable component of concerted efforts to breach the natural obstacle all along the broad Allied front.

Opposite: In preparation for the construction of a temporary bridge near Dorsten, Germany, paratroopers of the 17th Airborne Division work on the approach by laying bricks and stones. This photo was taken on March 29, 1945.

However, the electrifying capture of the intact Ludendorff railroad bridge at Remagen on March 7–8, 1945, by the U.S. 9th Armored Division, and the subsequent expansion of a bridgehead east of the Rhine, eliminated the need for airborne support in the First Army sector. On March 22, General Patton managed to breach the Rhine at Oppenheim, south of Mainz, and no airborne participation had been required.

Patton took great pleasure in beating Field Marshal Montgomery across the Rhine. In fact, elements of the Third Army crossed only hours before Montgomery unleashed his effort in the north, a ground-amphibious operation codenamed Plunder complemented by a spectacular single-day airborne deployment labeled Operation Varsity.

Astonishing Airborne Armada

Overwhelming Allied force was poised to strike deep into Germany in March 1945. A total strength of 85 divisions, 23 armored and five of them airborne, were positioned to carry the fight to final victory. In the north, Montgomery's 21st Army Group was tasked with crossing the Rhine, establishing a secure bridgehead north of the Ruhr, the industrial heart of Germany, and with the Ninth U.S. Army covering its right flank, preparing for further operations to isolate and reduce the vital region.

Montgomery originally set the date for Operations Plunder and Varsity for March 15, issuing his final orders on March 9, the same day that the last German forces withdrew from the west bank of the Rhine. The initial date was pushed back several days due to a supreme headquarters directive that further outlined planned objectives. The ground operation was launched on March 23 as elements of the British Second Army began crossing the Rhine at 9 p.m. The Ninth Army, commanded by General William H. Simpson, began its own amphibious crossing south of the town of Wesel at 2 a.m. on March 24.

Although the planners at General Lewis Brereton's First Allied Airborne Army headquarters had worked on Operation Varsity for several months, the tactical outline was not finalized until early March. Originally envisioned with three airborne divisions participating, the number of troops had to be scaled back by roughly one-third when it was discovered that existing ground facilities and transport aircraft were not capable of supporting such a large effort.

The operation was then assigned to the British 6th and American 17th Airborne Divisions of

Below: The Ludendorff railroad bridge crossing the Rhine at Remagen is viewed from a cliff high above the waterway, the last great natural barrier to Allied forces on the German frontier.

Above: During training exercises prior to Operation Varsity, the airborne crossing of the Rhine, paratroopers of the 513th Parachute Infantry Regiment, 17th Airborne Division, plummet from C-46 Commando transport aircraft.

General Ridgway's XVIII Airborne Corps. The 6th had participated in Operation Overlord in Normandy, while the 17th had fought as ground troops for five weeks, from January 3 to February 10, in the Ardennes.

During the counterstroke to reduce the bulge created during Hitler's failed offensive, the 17th Airborne fought its way through Belgium, forcing enemy troops across the Ourthe River, relieving the 11th Armored Division at Houffalize, and taking Espeler and Wattermal by the end of January. Turning southward toward Luxembourg, the division liberated the towns of Eschweiler and Clervaux and secured the west bank of the Our River. Prior to being relieved by the 6th Armored Division, troopers of the 17th Airborne had established a limited bridgehead across the Our near the town of Dasburg in Germany.

Its reduction in manpower notwithstanding, Operation Varsity remained a tremendous undertaking. The last offensive airborne operation of the war in Europe and the largest single-day airlift of the war, Varsity included 21,680 paratroopers and glidermen, 1,696 transport and 1,348 glider aircraft, and a covering air contingent of 3,000 fighter planes. While more than 1.25 million ground troops were poised to cross the Rhine, the air armada was taking wing. Eventually, the sky train stretched for miles, from horizon to horizon.

Montgomery had offered limited direction to the airborne planners, asking simply that they attack in support of the Second Army and conduct independent operations to reduce enemy strongpoints, disrupt communications,

Douglas C-47 transport planes disgorge paratroopers of the 82nd Airborne Division during a demonstration jump in the vicinity of the Ardennes Forest on March 14, 1945. Any parachute jump was hazardous, and demonstrations always carried an element of risk.

and impede troop movements for up to 10 days. Well before that time, the airborne and ground elements of Operation Plunder were to have linked up. The 6th Airborne was to join Second Army, and the 17th was to become a component of Ninth Army as soon as practicable and join the eastward advance on the ground.

Once the Diersfordter Wald was cleared of Germans, the paratroopers were to link up with the Second Army to the west and push southward toward Wesel.

General Miles Dempsey, commander of the Second Army, was more specific in terms of Varsity's objectives. He identified the Diersfordter Wald, high ground that sloped gently to about 100 feet (30m) above the level of the Rhine from three to five miles (5–8km) east of the riverbank. If the airborne troops could secure this area, the Germans would be deprived of artillery positions and observation posts that threatened the establishment of a secure bridgehead. Implementing a lesson learned during Market Garden, the airborne troops were to be inserted as close to the objective as possible, eliminating a long march such as the British 1st Airborne Division had experienced, contributing to the disaster at Arnhem.

Once the Diersfordter Wald was cleared of Germans, the paratroopers were to link up with the Second Army to the west and push southward toward Wesel, where important rail lines and roads intersected. The airborne troops were to block the roads north from Wesel and further form a junction with the Ninth Army. Early plans for a night airdrop were set aside in favor of the accuracy of a daylight operation. Again, practical experience influenced the decision to go in daylight despite the concerns about enemy fighter aircraft and intense flak that might take their toll on the transport planes.

The IX Troop Carrier Command, under General Williams, again shouldered responsibility for delivering the airborne contingent. The Royal Air Force 38 and 46 Groups were attached to the command along with the American troop carrier groups. Their aircraft would take off from fields in England and on the European continent, where engineers had worked to expand runways and other facilities to accommodate large numbers of transport planes and an influx of troops.

In the midst of the preparations for Operation Varsity, the U.S. War Department issued a reorganization of the standard airborne division, and the 17th conformed by disbanding one glider regiment and transferring its troop strength to other formations. Divisional glider artillery was augmented from two batteries to three; however, the valuable third battery was not due to reach the 17th Division until the middle of March, about 10 days before Operation Varsity launched.

The antitank bazooka had received mixed reviews at best, and innovative weapons development debuted during Operation Varsity in the form of the 57mm and 75mm recoilless rifles. These weapons were designed for field use, and about 100 of them were sent to Europe for distribution to the airborne divisions in theater. The light weapons—the 57mm at 45 pounds (20kg) and the 75mm at 114 pounds (52kg)—were designed to pack a powerful punch with much less difficulty than the deployment of the 75mm pack howitzer or standard artillery pieces. The guns were easier to handle since their recoil was absorbed internally. The 57mm weapon could even be fired from a trooper's shoulder.

On the morning of Operation Plunder/Varsity, Field Marshal Montgomery was obliged to entertain Prime Minister Winston Churchill and Field Marshal Sir Alan Brook, Chief of the Imperial General Staff. Although their presence was an annoyance to Montgomery, he endeavored to keep the high-level visitors close at hand to avoid their interference with the operation or any unfortunate incident that might endanger their lives. General Eisenhower was a spectator from a separate location, as was General Gavin of the 82nd Airborne Division, who had not previously witnessed such a large-scale airborne deployment in which he was not a participant. Gavin called the show "an awesome spectacle." In addition, General Ridgway and General Brereton were in position on the west bank of the Rhine.

Dawn's Early Light

Although planners believed that the distance from the amphibious landing zones on the east bank of the Rhine to the anticipated positions of the airborne troops was acceptable, another reason for the airlift to occur during daylight hours was to give the ground assault a head start, compressing the timeframe for a linkup. The first planes in the Operation Varsity airlift were those of the 61st, 315th, and 316th Troop Carrier Groups, which began clawing their way into the air at 7:09 a.m. on March 24 bearing troopers of the 6th Airborne from Wethersfield, Chipping Ongar, and Boreham.

The Americans got into the air at 7:25 a.m., as pathfinders leading the veteran 507th PIR lifted off from Chartres, one of 12 airfields located north and south of Paris that were designated for Operation Varsity.

Below: The ground and amphibious phase of Operation Plunder was covered by a thick smokescreen generated to conceal troop movements from enemy positions across the Rhine. In this photo, smoke laid by American units billows toward the banks of the great river.

Above: Prior to Operation Varsity, pilots and crewmen of a troop carrier unit of the Allied First Airborne Army synchronize their watches during a briefing on the airdrop of American and British airborne troops on the east bank of the Rhine.

Just before 10 a.m., the first American planes reached the vicinity of their designated drop zones. A thick, drifting haze, much of it caused by the smokescreen laid to cloak the amphibious assault across the Rhine, obscured the ground below the transports. The pilots missed their drop zone northwest of Wesel, and the first paratroopers descended in a widely dispersed area one and three-quarter miles (3km) northwest, close to the town of Diersfordt.

Two groups of 1st Battalion, 507th troopers, one under Colonel Edson Raff, the regimental commander, and the other under Major Paul Smith, commanding the 1st Battalion, swung into action. Raff's men eliminated machine-gun nests and engaged in sharp firefights with German infantry, taking time to also disable a battery of five 150mm guns and scoop up the enemy artillerymen as prisoners. When they secured their objective of high ground in the nearby woods, Raff and company had captured 300 Germans, and nearly 100 enemy soldiers were dead or wounded in their wake. Meanwhile, Major Smith's men silenced several antiaircraft batteries, and the remaining battalions of the 507th hit their drop zones accurately.

The 3rd Battalion, 507th, headed for Diersfordt and an ancient castle that dominated the town. When the paratroopers stepped toward the village, they were confronted with a pair of German tanks rolling out of the castle and down the road with heavy forest on either side. An accurate antitank grenade shocked the crew of the lead tank, and these Germans promptly surrendered. In the first successful use of the 57mm recoilless rifle in combat, other troopers set the second tank ablaze with a direct hit.

While two companies of paratroopers kept the Germans pinned down below windows and behind doors, Company G stormed the castle, working room to room. Two hours later, around 3 p.m., the structure was secured and 300 prisoners were taken. Private George Peters of Company G had already sacrificed his life in the landing zone, singlehandedly silencing a German machine gun and scattering enemy soldiers that were firing on his fellow troopers before he was killed. Peters received a posthumous Medal of Honor.

As night closed in, the 507th PIR was firmly established with substantial artillery support along the edge of the forest near Diersfordt, and paratroopers had linked up with the British 1st Commando Brigade in Wesel.

Antiaircraft Alert

The last three American paratrooper serials carried the 513th PIR, commanded by Colonel James W. Coutts. By the time the transports carrying the 513th arrived over their drop zones, German antiaircraft gunners were shaking off the effects of pre-Varsity bombing and were ready to respond. Thick fog still shrouded the landscape below. The three battalions of the 513th were dropped over a mile (1.6km) from their assigned zones, one of them coming down in the 6th Airborne sector near the village of Hamminkeln.

When Company E attacked a fortified building in Wesel, Private First Class Stuart Stryker ran forward and was cut down by enemy machine-gun fire 25 yards (23m) from the German position. Stryker's rush created a diversion that allowed other troops to assault the building, capturing 200 Germans and freeing three American airmen who had been held prisoner. Stryker received a posthumous Medal of Honor.

The troopers of the 513th PIR were subjected to enemy small-arms fire during their descent and while still in their parachute harnesses. Nevertheless, they organized and fought off the Germans, battling southward toward their assigned objectives and accounting for two batteries of 88mm guns, a self-propelled gun, and a pair of enemy tanks along the way. While one battalion secured the landing zone perimeter, the other two swept the wooded area north of

Below: Paratroopers of the 513th Parachute Infantry Regiment, 17th Airborne Division secure positions on the east bank of the Rhine River and search a group of German prisoners during the opening hours of Operation Varsity. This photo was probably taken near the town of Hamminkeln.

Diersfordt and took up a line along the Issel River at the eastern edge of the operational zone.

Within half an hour of landing on their assigned drop zone southwest of Hamminkeln, the troopers of the 466th Parachute Field Artillery Battalion were in action against the Germans despite the fact that they had encountered devastating enemy rifle and machine-gun fire as they came down. One battery had lost all its officers killed or wounded, but the troopers also captured 10 enemy 76mm guns by noon.

Glider operations fared better in terms of reaching their assigned landing zones; however, a number of the aircraft were riddled with bullets and shells in the air and after landing. Nevertheless, the action of the 194th Glider Infantry is indicative of the adroit offensive effort of March 24. Within two hours of landing, the troopers of the 194th cleared the Issel River and Issel Canal of enemy troops, and a pair of glider field artillery battalions was in action. By the end of the day, the 194th had destroyed or taken 37 enemy artillery pieces, 10 20mm antiaircraft guns, two flakwagens, and 10 tanks, and had captured 1,150 prisoners.

The glider pilots of the 435th Group took up their rifles and fought as an infantry company,

Below: Glidermen of the U.S. 17th Airborne Division walk toward their gliders during the predawn hours of March 24, 1945. Operation Varsity, the airborne crossing of the Rhine, involved two full airborne divisions including parachute and glider troops.

holding a crossroads northeast of Wesel against an enemy counterattack. With the assistance of two antiaircraft batteries, the pilots waited for the enemy to advance dangerously close before unleashing a devastating single volley that broke the back of the advance and left 50 Germans dead and a tank destroyed.

Above: A paratrooper of the 17th Airborne Division carries an injured comrade toward an aid station near the town of Wesel during Operation Varsity. A parachute packet has draped across a utility line at the edge of a nearby field.

The Value of Varsity

As the American and British airborne units seized their objectives, linked up with ground forces, and night fell on March 24, the contribution of Operation Varsity to the successful crossing of the Rhine was already being evaluated against its cost in men and materiel. Much had been achieved with the elimination of German positions in the Diersfordter Wald, and the enemy had suffered serious casualties. The airborne troops had all been delivered by 12:30 p.m. with more than 100 artillery pieces and nearly 700 vehicles.

Operation Varsity was an impressive logistical achievement, and there was universal agreement that the airborne phase of Operation Plunder had aided the ground advance. However, in a single day, the 17th Airborne Division had lost 159 men killed, 522 wounded, and 840 men missing in action, while the airmen of the IX Troop Carrier Command had suffered 194 dead and wounded and another 163 missing. The British 6th Airborne had suffered 2,400 casualties.

More than 50 gliders and at least 44 transport aircraft were destroyed, and a substantial number—332—were damaged. One of the most disturbing aspects of the airdrop had been the performance of the Curtiss C-46 Commando transport aircraft. Substantially larger than the C-47, the Commando was fast and had exit doors on both sides of its fuselage, but lacked self-sealing gasoline tanks. When the integrity of the C-46's fuel tanks was compromised, leaking high-octane aviation fuel gushed along the wings and collected at the wing roots and fuselage.

Left: Paratroopers of the 17th Airborne Division climb aboard a C-46 Commando transport plane prior to takeoff during Operation Varsity on March 24, 1945. The C-46 proved vulnerable to ground fire during the airdrop, with a propensity to catch fire if its fuel tanks were hit.

A single spark might cause a catastrophic explosion. During Operation Varsity, 19 of the 72 participating C-46s were shot down, and 38 others were damaged.

Subsequently, General Ridgway issued orders that the C-46 was not to be used in future airborne operations. In fairness, it must be noted that the C-46 presented a large, slow-flying target at low altitude in daylight. Given those circumstances, the losses incurred were not due to the lack of self-sealing fuel tanks, but were the inevitable result of a command decision to deploy them in the first place.

Although some contemporary observers and historians have concluded that an airborne operation was not necessary to support Montgomery's crossing of the Rhine, Operation Varsity was still successful. Nonetheless, lingering detractors are firm in their assertions that ground troops should have been able to capture the objectives assigned to the airborne troops within a reasonable period of time and with perhaps fewer casualties. The depth of the bridgehead established by the 30th Infantry Division at Wesel was not substantially enlarged by airborne troops, and the speed of bridge construction was not appreciably enhanced.

Ground Integration

During the night of March 24, the troopers of the 17th Airborne Division repulsed sporadic German counterattacks. The next day, they subdued pockets of diminishing resistance. In the afternoon, the division crossed the Issel River and advanced to the nearby autobahn. By the morning of March 26, the division was attacking with artillery and tank support, advancing six miles (10km) east of Wesel in two hours, capturing a bridge across the Lippe River at Krudenberg, and linking up with the Ninth Army.

On the morning of March 27, General Miley, commander of the 17th Airborne Division, ordered a broad advance toward Dorsten with the words: "This is a pursuit." Around midnight, the British 6th Guards Armoured Brigade passed through the 17th Division as Field Marshal Montgomery's spearheads plunged deeper into Germany against crumbling resistance. The troopers of the 17th Division hopped aboard the British Churchill tanks, rode into Dorsten 14 miles (23km) east of Wesel, and advanced another 17 miles (27km). The stark reality of the German collapse and its massive scope is well illustrated by the casualty figures of the 17th Airborne Division. During two days of action on March 24–26, the division lost 231 troopers killed and 670 wounded. In the next five days, losses amounted to only 74 killed and 102 wounded, including 40 who had been listed as missing.

With the end of the war only weeks away, the 17th Airborne Division continued its rapid movement, capturing Haltern on March 29 and the city of Münster on April 2. During the fighting to reduce the pocket of German resistance in the Ruhr, the 17th relieved the 79th Infantry Division, crossing the Rhine–Herne Canal on April 6 and establishing a bridgehead to be used as a springboard for the attack on the city of Essen, the center of Krupp steel production, which fell on April 10.

By the end of the month, the 17th Airborne Division had ended active operations against the enemy and assumed military government duties in northern Germany. Relieved by British troops in mid-June, the division was deactivated and its personnel reassigned to the 82nd and 13th Airborne Divisions, the latter preparing for possible deployment to the Pacific.

Below: Weapons at the ready, paratroopers of the 17th Airborne Division move warily forward near the town of Wesel during Operation Varsity. Although some units sustained significant casualties, the airdrop was considered a tactical success.

Days of Decision

For the troopers of the 82nd Airborne Division, destined to end the war fighting as ground troops, their brief respite ended on January 28, 1945, with the launch of offensive operations against the Siegfried Line, or West Wall, that guarded the German border in a region known as the Eifel. After four days of trudging through deep snow to staging areas opposite the enemy fortifications at Losheim, the paratroopers were alongside the GIs of the 1st Infantry Division.

Several odd occurrences took place in the confused fighting. On January 29, a company of the 508th PIR captured 80 prisoners in the town of Holzheim. Most of the company moved on, leaving four men to guard the prisoners. Some time later, a German patrol stealthily moved back into the town and freed the prisoners. First Sergeant Leonard Funk, Jr., returned to Holzheim and was surprised to be confronted by German soldiers demanding his surrender. Funk pretended to acquiesce, but quickly swung his submachine gun from his shoulder and opened fire. The four former guards grabbed German weapons and joined in. Within seconds, 21 Germans were dead and the remainder surrendered once again.

On another occasion, a platoon of paratroopers advanced down a road previously cleared by German plows that left three-foot (1m) snow banks on either side. Three tanks rumbled along between the marching troopers, and suddenly a company of German soldiers emerged from the darkness coming toward them. The Americans opened fire, and the Germans were trapped between the high walls of snow. Nearly 200 enemy soldiers were slain, and only a few survived to be taken prisoner.

Left: Troopers of the 17th Airborne Division march past a blazing building en route to the German city of Munster. After parachuting across the Rhine River during Operation Varsity, these troops fought as infantry.

The 13th Airborne Division

Activated at Camp Mackall, North Carolina, on August 13, 1943, the 13th Airborne Division deployed to the European Theater on January 25, 1945. Based in France, the division trained vigorously for a combat assignment that never came, although one component, the 517th PIR, was absorbed on March 1, after participating in combat operations in Italy, southern France, and the Ardennes.

In the spring of 1945, as enemy resistance ebbed in southern Germany, General Dwight D. Eisenhower, the Supreme Allied Commander, offered the 13th Airborne Division, then assigned to the First Allied Airborne Army, to General Jacob L. Devers, commander of the 6th Army Group, for a possible airborne assault 30 miles (48km) south of the city of Stuttgart. Its objective was to seize an airfield and cut off the escape route of retreating German troops; however, the rapid progress of the French First Army and the 10th Armored and 44th Infantry Divisions, which bypassed Stuttgart, rendered the airborne operation unnecessary.

Below: The 13th Airborne Division was identified by the stylized unicorn on its shoulder patch.

After the end of World War II in Europe, the 13th Airborne Division returned to the United States, arriving in New York City on August 23, 1945, two weeks after the atomic bombs were dropped on Hiroshima and Nagasaki. In anticipation of deployment to the Pacific, the 13th had received several formations from the deactivated 17th Airborne Division, but the surrender of Japan ended any prospects for combat deployment.

The 13th Airborne Division was deactivated at Fort Bragg, North Carolina, on February 25, 1946, and its personnel transferred to the 82nd Airborne Division.

On February 1, the 82nd Airborne and 1st Infantry divisions made their initial assaults against the West Wall fortifications. Some pillboxes and bunkers were unoccupied; others were hotly contested. The harsh winter weather conditions further slowed progress, and by February 4 the American penetration was a mere one mile (1.6km) along a five-mile (5km) front. Unimpressive at first glance, this was nevertheless enough to have effectively breached the fortifications in the area—some of the most concentrated works of the Siegfried Line—allowing the Americans to exert control over numerous villages inside Germany.

The limited offensive in this sector of the Eifel was halted on February 6, and the XVIII Airborne Corps was relieved. The 82nd Airborne Division was moved northward toward the Roer River and the seven dams that held back millions of gallons of water from the Roer and its tributaries. Previous attempts to secure the dams had failed, and the bloody action in the Hürtgen Forest the previous fall had resulted in horrendous casualties.

The 82nd Airborne participated in the effort to secure the dams, prevent the enemy from intentionally flooding the Roer Valley, which could cause a significant delay in the advance into Germany itself, and encircle any retreating enemy troops. On February 7, a regiment of paratroopers advanced south from the town of Schmidt, hoping to trap retiring German troops before they could move along the road to the northeast. However, elements of the 311th Infantry Regiment advancing directly on the town were impeded by difficult terrain and were unable to close the jaws of the trap. Within 24 hours, the 82nd moved on to the banks of the Roer. While preparations were being made to cross the turbulent stream, the division was pulled out of the line on February 17 and returned to the familiar Sissonne-Suippes area in France for another rest.

Although American forces did take control of the Hürtgen area in February, the Germans damaged the Schwammenauel Dam sufficiently to flood the surrounding Roer basin, delaying Operation Grenade, a Ninth Army thrust across the Roer and into farmland approaching the west bank of the Rhine.

The strategic situation began to gel as winter turned to spring in 1945, and General Eisenhower conceded the Nazi capital of Berlin to the Soviet Red Army. Although the decision was unpopular in many quarters of the Allied military establishment, Eisenhower reasoned that the casualties sustained in an attempt to beat the Soviets to Berlin and capture the city against fanatical Nazi resistance would be too high a

Below: Crouching with the sounds of nearby gunfire, American soldiers press forward through a small town in the Hürtgen area where the 82nd Airborne Division participated in the effort to secure the dams that controlled the waters of the Roer River.

price to pay, particularly given the prevailing political atmosphere and the fact that some portion of Berlin would be vacated to Soviet occupation after the war anyway.

One operational casualty of Eisenhower's decision was the planning for a preemptive airborne operation to secure Berlin ahead of the Soviets. The 82nd Airborne Division was to parachute two regiments south of Tempelhof airfield in the south-central section of the capital city while its third regiment seized the airfield outright. During the latter part of February, General Gavin contemplated the plan that was envisioned with two American airborne divisions and a British airborne brigade taking part.

"It was a sobering prospect," Gavin remembered, "especially to the veterans with four combat jumps." The commanding general and the troopers of the 82nd Airborne were spared this stern test.

Watch on the Rhine

Back in the line in early April, the 82nd Airborne was assigned a sector of the Allied line at Weiden near the city of Cologne. Patrolling the west bank of the great river, the division was not ordered to engage in sustained combat but allowed to patrol aggressively. Colonel Reuben Tucker, the veteran commander of the 504th PIR, conducted nightly forays across the Rhine to collect prisoners.

Perhaps the most aggressive regimental commander in the 82nd, Tucker proposed the capture of a town on the east bank of the Rhine in order to facilitate future raiding operations. On April 5, Tucker's troopers occupied the town of Hitdorf, provoking an immediate response from the enemy, including the elite German 3rd Parachute Regiment. A pitched battle raged through the town, and the Americans were steadily forced back toward the riverbank, finally clinging to just a few houses at the water's edge.

The 504th PIR made good its escape to the safety of the west bank with the loss of six men killed. They estimated that they had inflicted 150 casualties on the Germans.

Meanwhile, General Ridgway and the XVIII Airborne Corps, which at any given time included several infantry and armored formations up to division size, had participated in the reduction of the Ruhr Pocket. German soldiers and Nazi Party and political officials had surrendered in droves, including former Chancellor of Germany Franz von Papen, arrested by troopers of the 194th Glider Infantry Regiment at his estate near Hirschberg on April 10. When resistance ended in the Ruhr, nearly 320,000 German troops, including 25 general officers, had given up the fight.

A month after Operation Plunder/Varsity had put the 21st Army Group across the Rhine, Field Marshal Montgomery had slowed the pace of his advance into Germany to a ponderous phase-line offensive. General Eisenhower had initially emphasized the attack in the north, but as the Red Army steadily moved westward he reenergized the Allied advance into Germany on a broad front, assigning Ridgway the task of crossing the Elbe River and meeting the Soviets as far east as possible, preventing the incursion of Red Army forces into Denmark in the process.

Across the Elbe

At 1 a.m., on April 30, hours after British Commandos crossed the Elbe virtually unopposed at nearby Lauenberg, the single available battalion of the 505th PIR traversed the waterway and cleared German soldiers from foxholes along the opposite bank. Under sporadic artillery fire, engineers began throwing a bridge across the Elbe. Ridgway now had the British 6th Airborne Division, another regiment of the 82nd,

Opposite: After the reduction of the Ruhr pocket, hundreds of German prisoners have been herded into a holding area. During the last days of World War II, enemy soldiers surrendered to American and British forces in large numbers.

and four battalions of the 8th Infantry Division to exploit the crossing. Within two days the advance had progressed six miles (10km).

A combat command of the 7th Armored Division was attached to the 82nd, which rapidly moved eastward to Ludwigslust and southeast to secure the right flank of the 21st Army Group. General Gavin rolled into Ludwigslust, famed for its palace, which had once been home to the Mecklenburg princes. On May 2, General Kurt von Tippelskirch surrendered the German 21st Army, approximately 140,000 men, to Gavin, signing the surrender document inside the ornate palace.

All the while, the troopers of the 82nd Airborne were on the lookout for the advancing Soviets. On May 3, a patrol made contact with the Red Army 25 miles (40km) east of the Elbe. General Gavin officially met with the Soviets on May 5. Three days later, World War II was over.

The 82nd Airborne Division subsequently moved to Berlin for occupation duty until December 1945. The following month the division returned to the United States and led a huge victory parade in New York City on January

Below: American and Red Army troops toast their meeting along the Elbe River in Germany in May 1945, while a Soviet soldier in the center of the photo sings and plays an accordion. The linkup at the Elbe split Nazi Germany in two.

12, 1946. The division was not disbanded after the war and was assigned a permanent base at Fort Bragg, North Carolina.

During World War II, Presidential Unit Citations were awarded to the 551st PIR, attached to the 82nd Airborne Division during the Battle of the Bulge, for action in Belgium, the 505th PIR for action at Ste. Mere-Eglise on D-Day, and the 1st Battalion, 504th PIR, for Operation Market Garden.

The 82nd Division spent 422 days in combat and sustained nearly 9,000 casualties—1,951 killed and 6,560 wounded.

Screaming Eagles Ascendant

The darlings of the press following their epic stand at Bastogne, the paratroopers of the 101st Airborne Division were dog tired after weeks of combat in the Battle of the Bulge, and their subsequent duty in Alsace, primarily around the villages of Drulingen and Pfaffenhoffen, involved aggressive patrolling and a raid by three companies of troopers across the Moder River.

On February 25, 1945, the Screaming Eagles were ordered to assemble and board railway boxcars for the journey to Mourmelon, France, where veterans and replacements alike participated in training and exercises that seemed to have no end. On March 15, the 101st Airborne received the Presidential Unit Citation for its gallantry at Bastogne, the first time a unit of division size had received such a prestigious award. Another Presidential Unit Citation was awarded to the division for action during D-Day and the Normandy Campaign.

On March 31, the 101st Airborne Division was ordered to the Ruhr as the last vestiges of enemy resistance were extinguished and thousands of prisoners were taken. The paratroopers conducted raids and patrols and participated in the military government of the area around the cities of Rheydt and München Gladbach on the west bank of the Rhine.

To the Eagle's Nest

Near the end of April, the 101st Airborne was reassigned to the Seventh Army, under General Alexander M. Patch, which, along with the French First Army, comprised the 6th Army Group, commanded by General Jacob L. Devers. The division moved south into Bavaria and advanced at a rapid pace against wilting German resistance. Provisions were plentiful as the paratroopers swept through otherwise pastoral alpine villages of southern Germany.

The 82nd Division spent 422 days in combat and sustained nearly 9,000 casualties—1,951 killed and 6,560 wounded.

The drive through Bavaria was initially a joyride compared to the hard fighting the 101st had endured during the previous 11 months. Then, the division reached Landsberg on April 29. On the outskirts of the town lay a labor camp that served as an overflow facility for the notorious concentration camp at Dachau. General Taylor was taken aback by the cruel carnage that his troopers witnessed as they liberated the emaciated inmates. Taylor decreed that every citizen of Landsberg between the ages of 14 and 80 was to be brought to the camp to see the atrocities that the Nazi regime had perpetrated just a short distance from their previously tranquil homes and businesses.

By May 3, orders came down that the 101st was again going into action. Extra ammunition and rations were ordered up the line as the troopers reached the towering, snow-covered peaks of the Alps. Quickly another round of directives sent them aboard trucks to Salzburg, Austria, renowned as the birthplace of composer Wolfgang Amadeus Mozart and a center of musical culture. However, a fight failed to

Above: Emaciated inmates of the Nazi concentration camp at Dachau cheer their liberation during the last days of World War II in Europe. As troopers of the 101st Airborne Division rolled through Bavaria, they came upon scenes of indescribable horror.

materialize at Salzburg as a delegation of citizens and German Army officers surrendered on May 4.

With three of his divisions temporarily out of a job, General Patch authorized General Wade Haislip of XV Corps to veer to the southwest toward the town of Berchtesgaden. Elements of the XXI Corps, under General Frank Milburn, including the French 2nd Armored and the 101st Airborne Divisions, made the turn as well.

The prize at Berchtesgaden was Adolf Hitler's alpine retreat—the Eagle's Nest, or Berghof. The race was on as the Cottonbalers of the 7th Regiment, 3rd Infantry Division, approached the picturesque Bavarian town from the rear while the French tankers and Screaming Eagles rushed down from the northwest hoping to claim the prestigious prize.

Initially, the paratroopers were confused by the quickening pace. They soon discovered the reason. Colonel Robert F. Sink, commanding the 506th PIR, badly wanted the Berghof, but he was aware that the war was coming to an end and also wanted to avoid unnecessary casualties. Sink led the 506th through the villages of Rosenheim and Chiemsee as springtime snow and sleet pelted the troopers and few German soldiers appeared to offer resistance. At Siegsdorf, the vanguard of the 506th made a right turn and sped up the highway amid spectacular mountain vistas—directly toward the Eagle's Nest.

Dashing along the highway, the 506th encountered the French ahead of them, but stymied by a blown bridge. Diehard SS troops were firing at the stalled Allied columns, and although his fighting blood was up, Colonel Sink declined to order an attack at such a late stage in the war. His executive officer, Lieutenant Colonel Robert Strayer, set off on a scouting mission and found a dirt road that was not on any maps.

Colonel Sink detailed his 2nd Battalion to follow the new route and instructed its commander, Major Richard Winters, to secure a famous local inn for his headquarters. "Reserve the Berchtesgaden Hof for the regimental HQ," he grinned. Sink then turned to bring up bridging

The 555th Parachute Infantry Battalion

The all-Black 555th Parachute Infantry Battalion was authorized in December 1942, originally as a single company, on the recommendation of the War Department's Advisory Committee on Negro Troop Policies. On February 25, 1943, the original company of the "Triple Nickel" was formed, and the unit was activated at Fort Benning, Georgia, on December 30. It was soon expanded to battalion strength.

Eventually, the 555th was stationed at Pendleton Field, Oregon, while a detachment was based at Chico, California. Although the unit never deployed overseas during World War II, its primary focus was designated as Operation Firefly, guarding against an ingenious enemy onslaught.

During the war, the Japanese sent thousands of balloon bombs across the Pacific Ocean; however, only about 300 were confirmed to have reached the United States. These aerial devices carried incendiary bombs, and the hope was that they would cause rampant wildfires in the U.S. Pacific Northwest. The troopers of the 555th fought 28 fires during the summer and fall of 1945, but none of these could be directly attributed to the Japanese weapons. Fifteen of these fires were accessed by parachute jumps.

Above: Troopers of the all-Black 555th Parachute Infantry Battalion board an aircraft during training exercises. The 555th fought wildfires in the Pacific Northwest.

In late 1945, the 555th returned to Camp Mackall, North Carolina, a previous training location. The unit was subsequently attached to the 82nd Airborne Division at Fort Bragg, North Carolina, and then deactivated in December 1947, its personnel transferred to the 3rd Battalion, 505th Parachute Infantry Regiment.

During its service in World War II, the 555th lost only one man, who died during a jump on August 6, 1945.

equipment (which the French were not equipped with) to cross the Saalach River, only to learn that the Cottonbalers of the 7th Regiment were in the best position to take the Eagle's Nest and that General John W. "Iron Mike" O'Daniel, commander of the 3rd Infantry Division, was not letting any other troops pass through.

The Cottonbalers moved into Berchtesgaden early on May 2, accepting the surrender of 2,000 German soldiers; four hours later, only after General O'Daniel was sure that his infantrymen were in possession of the Eagle's Nest, were any other units allowed further access across bridges and up the available mountain roads. Occupation zones were worked out after a flap was settled with the French over a ceremonial flag raising.

Soon enough, however, Colonel Sink appeared at the command post of Colonel John Heintges, commander of the 7th Regiment. The officers were old friends and exchanged pleasant greetings. They enjoyed lunch and a few drinks in Heintges' quarters. Then Sink sat down with his friend and said, "Well Johnny, I'm up here to relieve you. My regiment is on the way up here."

Heintges was quite surprised, responding, "I just talked to division a little while ago, and they told me I'd be up here for five or six days!"

Sink concluded, "Oh yes, but those plans were all changed, and you're going back to Salzburg."

Below: High in the Bavarian Alps, soldiers from the 101st Airborne Division enter a German village along its main street. The 101st participated in the race to Hitler's Eagle's Nest as the war in Europe came to a close.

Right: Paratroopers of the 101st Airborne Division examine silver and other items taken from Hitler's Eagle's Nest as the paratroopers occupied the Nazi leader's former Alpine retreat. The 101st remained at the Eagle's Nest for several weeks.

The 7th Regiment spent one more night at Berchtesgaden.

As Sink later prepared to move the 506th PIR to the south, he received a message from supreme headquarters. It read, "Effective immediately all troops will stand fast on present positions. German Army Group G in this sector has surrendered. No firing on Germans unless fired upon. Notify French units in vicinity. Full details, to be broadcast, will be issued by SHAEF."

The order meant that the Screaming Eagles would remain in Berchtesgaden for several more weeks, enjoying the spoils of war, liquor and fine foods in copious amounts, and collecting souvenirs—among them many of the personal effects of Hitler and other top Nazis. The Führer's photo albums, stationery, personal china, and silverware, were discovered, along with the stolen art collection of Luftwaffe Reichsmarschall Hermann Göring and his luxury Mercedes automobile.

During this period, several prominent Nazi officers and political leaders were captured. Troopers of the 506th PIR captured Field Marshal Albert Kesselring, who had fought a skillful battle during the arduous campaign in Italy. The 502nd arrested Julius Streicher, the odious Jew-baiter and editor of the virulently anti-Semitic newspaper *Der Stürmer*; Obergruppenführer Karl Oberg, former head of the notorious SS in occupied France; and Colonel General Heinz Guderian, the father of Blitzkrieg warfare tactics and an architect of the German invasion of Poland in 1939.

Postscript

On August 1, 1945, the 42nd Infantry Division relieved the 101st, and the paratroopers began their journey to Auxerre, France, expecting a renewed round of training for deployment to the Pacific. On the 25th, the 501st PIR was detached from the division and headed back to the United States for deactivation at Fort Benning, Georgia.

The dropping of two atomic bombs ended the war in the Pacific prior to any deployment orders, and the division was deactivated on November 30, 1945. During the course of the war, the 101st Airborne Division served 214 days in combat and suffered 11,212 casualties, including 2,043 killed in action, 7,976 wounded, and 1,193 missing.

CHAPTER 8

AIRBORNE OPERATIONS IN THE PACIFIC

The vast expanse of the Pacific, a lingering shortage of transport aircraft, jungle terrain, and the Allied prioritization of the defeat of Nazi Germany contributed to the rather limited scope of airborne operations in the Pacific during World War II.

The commitment of airborne assets to the European Theater and their employment in combat dwarfed the airborne effort on the other side of the world. Nevertheless, the U.S. Army airborne units engaged against the Japanese in the Pacific demonstrated precision, skill, and daring during the relentless march toward the enemy's home islands. Senior American military planners in the Pacific realized, as their European Theater counterparts did, that airborne forces were capable of supporting amphibious and other ground operations with the seizure of bridges, crossroads, high ground, airfields, and other objectives and subsequently contributing to offensive efforts as infantry.

One of the earliest airborne units organized in the U.S. Army, the 503rd PIR trained in the United States and the Panama Canal Zone prior to deployment to the Pacific. During General Douglas MacArthur's effort to push the Japanese out of northern New Guinea and eliminate the enemy threat to Australia, the 503rd trained for eight months at Australian bases prior to its first combat mission.

Opposite: A trooper of the 503rd Parachute Infantry Regiment drags his parachute to a central location on the island of Noemfoor. The regiment's 1st and 3rd Battalions dropped on the island off the coast of New Guinea in July 1944.

Airborne in New Guinea

In the face of a severe shortage of adequate shipping and landing craft, General George Kenney, commander of the Fifth Air Force, conceived a plan to support operations against the Japanese base at Lae, New Guinea. While the Australian 9th Infantry Division landed on the northeastern coastline of the large island, the 503rd PIR would parachute into Nadzab, seize and clear an abandoned jungle airstrip, and join the battle against the Japanese at Lae. Resupply would be accomplished from the air.

On September 5, 1943, three columns of transport planes—a total of 79 aircraft—swept in at 600 feet (180m), and the paratroopers descended on target. Packets of supplies weighing 300 pounds (136kg) each were dropped from the air, and the troopers secured their position against virtually no opposition. The 841st Airborne Engineer Battalion improved the landing site, and Australian reinforcements flew in on September 6. Within three days, the 503rd PIR was on the move, and the defenders of Lae were caught in a vise between two attacking forces. The objective fell on September 16, and General MacArthur praised the operation for its rapid success.

Airborne in Burma

The cooperative effort to disrupt Japanese expansion from Burma into neighboring India and eventually drive the enemy from the region developed largely into a series of long-range penetration missions under the leadership of British Brigadier Orde Wingate. Wingate envisioned the introduction of Commonwealth combat troops, known as the Chindits, behind enemy lines to disrupt communications, inflict casualties, and generally wreak havoc. These troops would be supplied by air.

American support for Chindit operations was delivered through a commitment of air transport and supply under the auspices of the 1st Air Commando Group. Led by intrepid Lieutenant Colonel Philip Cochran, American planes and pilots delivered supplies and reinforcements to the Chindits during Operation Thursday in the spring of 1944. The gliders of the 319th Troop Carrier Squadron flew from bases in India and brought tons of supplies into landing zones hacked from the jungle. Under the command of General Frank Merrill, the American 5307th Provisional Unit, better known as "Merrill's

Below: Paratroopers of the 503rd Parachute Infantry Regiment train for a planned jump during the Allied offensive on the island of New Guinea in the Pacific.

Right: Paratroopers of Company C, 1st Marine Parachute Battalion, prepare for a training exercise aboard a Douglas C-47 transport aircraft. This photo was taken on the Pacific island of New Caledonia on January 15, 1943. Within a year, the Marine airborne program was discontinued and the units were disbanded.

Marauders," also fought the Japanese in southern Burma with the support of air resupply missions flown by Troop Carrier Command and the 1st Air Commando Group pilots.

Among the most active American airborne units in the China-Burma-India Theater (CBI) was the 900th Airborne Engineer Aviation Company. Under the command of Captain Patrick R. Casey, the 900th reached its base in India in August 1943, and constructed the first operational airstrip behind Japanese lines at Shingbwiyang, Burma, in December. Through the course of the war in the CBI, the 900th Airborne Engineers made more glider landings than any other Allied unit. During a nine-week period in the spring of 1944, the battling engineers, the 1st Air Commando Group, and the Chindits completed a total of 14 glider-borne landing operations.

Battle at Noemfoor

A combined amphibious and airborne attack to clear the Japanese from the island of Noemfoor off the coast of New Guinea took place in early July 1944. The 1st and 3rd Battalions, 503rd PIR, were dropped on the island on July 2. Buffeted by high winds, the troopers were scattered around their focal point, the island's airstrip. Many of them came slamming to the ground amid wrecked enemy aircraft, in supply dumps, and on top of parked vehicles. Japanese fire failed to inflict any casualties, but 128 paratroopers sustained injuries, 59 of them serious bone fractures. To avoid the risk of further airdrop-related casualties, the 2nd Battalion, 503rd, was delivered by amphibious landing craft the following day.

The paratroopers then participated in securing Noemfoor, at times engaging in spirited firefights. Using the jungle for concealment, a Japanese force ambushed a platoon of 503rd on July 23, and 22-year-old Sergeant Ray E. Eubanks earned a posthumous Medal of Honor while leading his squad to assist the beleaguered platoon. Eubanks was wounded, and his rifle was smashed by enemy fire. He continued forward, using his rifle as a club, and killed four enemy soldiers before he was mortally wounded.

Return to the Philippines

Aircraft flying from fields on Noemfoor assisted in the subsequent return of General MacArthur and American troops to the Philippines. The 503rd PIR reached the island of Leyte with

Paratroopers of the 503rd Parachute Infantry Regiment come to earth at Kamiri Airstrip on the island of Noemfoor on July 3, 1944. High winds scattered the troopers and contributed to a significant number of jump-related injuries.

an amphibious landing on secured beaches in the fall of 1944. By December, the 503rd had moved by landing craft to the island of Mindoro. Original plans for an airdrop on Mindoro were scrapped, and Japanese resistance on the island was sometimes fierce as the troopers secured landing strips for air operations in support of further American landings at Lingayen Gulf on Luzon. Intense Japanese airstrikes and naval bombardment caused some casualties. A company of 503rd troopers fought a sharp battle with at least a company of Japanese soldiers to gain control of a radar station in Mindoro.

Capturing Corregidor

During the darkest period of the war in the Pacific, the Japanese had captured thousands of American prisoners in the Philippines in the spring of 1942, and taken control of the islands. At the mouth of Manila Bay, the tiny spit of land called Corregidor had come to symbolize the plight and the gallantry of the American defenders who ultimately surrendered.

Three years later, on February 16, 1945, the 503rd PIR descended upon Corregidor determined to retake the island. At 8:30 a.m., C-47s of the 317th Troop Carrier Command flew in at only 500 feet (150m) to release the paratroopers in reduced sticks of only six men due to the limited size of the drop zone. Led by Colonel George M. Jones, the troopers landed hard among Corregidor's jagged rocks and ragged vegetation. Some of them were blown across the drop zone by strong winds and hung from cliffs above the water's edge. The 24th Infantry Regiment, 34th Division, landed on the beach at Corregidor, and a reinforcing parachute drop occurred around 12:30 p.m. on the 16th.

As darkness descended on Corregidor, the 503rd held the heights on the island, and a third parachute drop originally set for early on the 17th was canceled. The remaining paratroopers came ashore in landing craft. For the next 10 days, the paratroopers and infantrymen fought off Japanese suicide charges and rooted diehard defenders from caves and bunkers. When Corregidor fell on February 27, only 20 enemy troops were left alive to be taken prisoner.

After briefly returning to Mindoro, the 503rd PIR, an independent airborne unit throughout World War II, was ordered to the Philippine island of Negros in support of the 40th Infantry Division. Plans for yet another parachute operation were considered and then dropped. The troopers reached Negros by landing craft and fought the Japanese in the mountainous interior of the island for the next five months. With the end of the war in August 1945, a total of 7,500 Japanese troops surrendered on Negros. The 503rd Parachute Infantry Regiment was deactivated at Camp Anza, California, in December of that year.

Angels in the Pacific

In February 1943, General Joseph M. Swing was given command of the 11th Airborne Division. He led the 11th Airborne from Camp Mackall, North Carolina, to New Guinea, and into combat in the Philippines. The division came ashore aboard landing craft at Leyte on November 18, 1944. Fighting as infantry, the paratroopers pushed inland and supported the 7th Infantry Division in its drive toward the town of Ormoc. In early December, elements of the 11th Airborne fought Japanese paratroopers at San Pablo airstrip, and the enemy force was annihilated during five days of combat. By the end of the month, Japanese resistance on Leyte was crushed after the troopers had engaged in heavy fighting at Rock Hill and Hacksaw Hill.

In January 1945, the 187th and 188th Glider Infantry Regiments rode in landing craft to the beaches of Luzon at Nasugbu, initiating a second prong of the American drive toward the Philippine capital of Manila, 60 miles (97km) to the north. The division's first combat jump was completed on February 3 at Tagaytay Ridge by the 511th PIR, commanded by Colonel Orin D. "Hard Rock" Haugen. The paratroopers crossed the Parañaque River and reached the outskirts of Manila two days later. After a fierce battle, the city was liberated on March 3, 1945.

Two weeks earlier, on February 13, Private First Class Manuel Perez of Company A, 511th PIR, had earned the Medal of Honor during fighting at Fort William McKinley in Manila. Serving as the company's lead scout, Perez singlehandedly attacked the last of a dozen enemy pillboxes. He killed 18 enemy soldiers, some of them in hand-to-hand combat, before being mortally wounded. He died a month later.

Liberating Los Baños

On February 23, the 11th Airborne Division executed one of the most successful tactical raids of World War II. When the paratroopers came ashore on Luzon, one of their objectives was the liberation of 2,147 internees—1,575 of them Americans—suffering in captivity at the prison of Los Baños, 40 miles (65km) behind enemy lines.

While his troopers fought south of Manila, General Swing and the staff of the 11th Airborne devised a risky but ingenious plan to combine airborne and amphibious thrusts toward the prison camp. In company with Filipino guerrillas, a flying column of truck-borne glidermen would dash for the gates of the prison while other forces kept the many Japanese

Airborne Marines

The U.S. Marine Corps authorized both paratroop and glider formations during World War II. The initial unit was the 1st Marine Parachute Battalion, which began training in October 1940. The 2nd and 3rd Battalions followed, and training was conducted at camps in New Jersey, North Carolina, and California. Several Marine airborne units participated in amphibious landings and ground operations in the Pacific, and on April 1, 1943, the 1st Marine Parachute Regiment was activated on the island of Vella Lavella in the Solomons. A day later, the 4th Marine Parachute Battalion was activated in the United States; however, it was disbanded 10 months later in January 1944.

Plans to deploy the Pacific-based Marine parachute battalions in airborne jumps were considered, particularly during the battle for the island of Bougainville, but these were canceled amid concerns over potential casualties. None of the battalions made a combat jump during World War II. Early in 1944, the three operational parachute battalions were ordered to return to the United States and disbanded along with the Marine Raider battalions.

The formation of Marine glider units began in the summer of 1941, and the first gliders were delivered by the end of the year. Training was undertaken at Parris Island, South Carolina, while the Glider Detachment was formed at Cherry Point, North Carolina, only to be replaced by Glider Group 71 in March 1942. In the fall of that year, Glider Group 71, consisting of Headquarters and Service Group 71 and Marine Glider Squadron 711, reached its permanent base at Eagle Mountain Lake, Texas.

While the training of both Marine parachute and glider formations was taking place, senior Marine officers concluded that the use of gliders in the Pacific was too hazardous to both men and machines. The Marine glider program was terminated on June 24, 1943.

Left: Officers from Task Force Gypsy, 511th Parachute Infantry Regiment, 11th Airborne Division, plan their next move, Luzon, June 26, 1945.

troops in the area busy. The prisoners would be loaded aboard 54 amphibious vehicles (amtracs) and evacuated.

Company B, 1st Battalion, boarded 10 C-47s and parachuted near the camp to engage the Japanese and join the remainder of the battalion and the Filipino guerrillas in providing a rear guard for the evacuation while a reinforced infantry battalion blocked the road toward the camp to prevent a Japanese counterattack.

General Swing watched the progress of the raid from a Piper Cub artillery liaison aircraft, and it proceeded rapidly. One Army officer remembered, "The results were spectacular. Internees poured out and into the loading area. Troops started clearing the barracks ... and carried out to the loading area over 130 people who were too weak or too sick to walk."

By 1 p.m. on February 23, six hours after the C-47s carrying Company B had become airborne, the raid on Los Baños was over. Every prisoner was evacuated safely. The paratroopers and Filipino troops lost four men killed and six wounded. The Los Baños Raid is considered one of the most successful tactical operations of World War II and is studied in military classrooms to this day. In 1979, airborne historian Major Gerard Devlin wrote, "Because of the highly accurate intelligence information, a perfect plan, and a faultless performance by the attacking troops, the Los Baños mission is still considered to be the finest example of a small-scale operation ever executed by American airborne troops. There is no doubt that it will remain a masterpiece of planning and execution and the blueprint for any future daring prisoner-rescue operation."

Last Day in Luzon

During the spring of 1945, the 11th Airborne continued the fight on Luzon, rooting the Japanese out of a ring of strong defensive positions at Lake Taal and Laguna de Bay. By May 1, the division had participated in clearing the enemy from all of Batangas Province, and the fighting in southern Luzon had ended. The final engagement of the 11th Airborne took place on June 23 as a detachment parachuted onto Camalaniugan Airfield south of Aparri in support of a ground advance by the 37th Infantry Division. The detachment fought through enemy defenses and made contact with the infantrymen three days later.

In August, the 11th Airborne was withdrawn for training; at the end of the month, the division was airlifted to Japan to begin four years of occupation duty.

INDEX

Page numbers in **bold** indicate a photograph or illustration

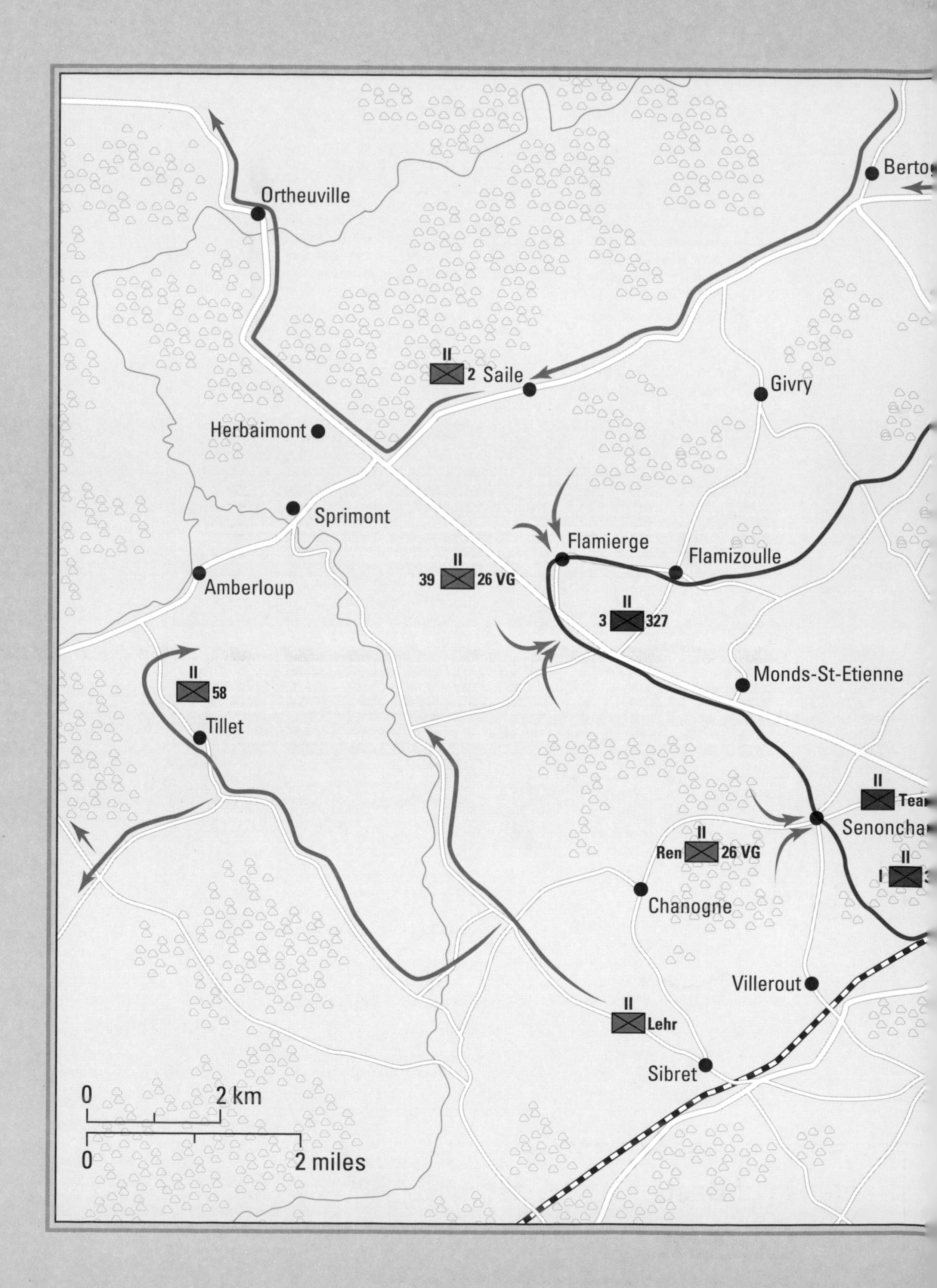

Ortheuville
Saile
II
2
Herbaimont
Sprimont
Amberloup
Flamierge
Flamizoulle
Givry
39
26 VG
3
327
Monds-St-Etienne
58
Tillet
Ren
Chanogne
Senonchan
Villerout
Lehr
Sibret
0
2 km
0
2 miles